Possessing the Gates
of the Enemy

Ellies

Possessing the Gates of the Enemy

A Training Manual for Militant Intercession

Third Edition, Revised with Study Guide

Cindy Jacobs

Foreword by C. Peter Wagner

Chosen

a division of Baker Publishing Group
Grand Rapids, Michigan

Published by Chosen Books
A division of Baker Publishing Group
P.O. Box 6287, Grand Rapids, MI 49516-6287
www.chosenbooks.com

Printed in the United States of America

Library of Congress Cataloging-in-Publication Data
Jacobs, Cindy, 1951–
    Possessing the gates of the enemy : a training manual for militant intercession / Cindy Jacobs ; foreword by C. Peter Wagner.—3rd ed., rev. with study guide.
        p.   cm.
    Includes index.
    ISBN 978-0-8007-9463-7 (pbk.)
    1. Intercessory prayer—Christianity. I. Title.
BV215.J33 2009
248.3'2—dc22   2009002778

Unless otherwise indicated, Scripture is taken from the New King James Version. Copyright © 1982 by Thomas Nelson, Inc. Used by permission. All rights reserved.

Scripture marked AMP is taken from the Amplified® Bible, Copyright © 1954, 1958, 1962, 1964, 1965, 1987 by The Lockman Foundation. Used by permission.

Scripture marked NIV is taken from the HOLY BIBLE, NEW INTERNATIONAL VERSION®. NIV®. Copyright © 1973, 1978, 1984 by International Bible Society. Used by permission of Zondervan. All rights reserved.

Scripture marked TLB is taken from *The Living Bible*, copyright © 1971. Used by permission of Tyndale House Publishers, Inc., Wheaton, Illinois 60189. All rights reserved.

Scripture marked KJV is taken from the King James Version of the Bible.

15   8 7 6

Dedicated to
my loving husband, Mike
my daughter, Mary
my son, Daniel

Contents

Foreword

The book you hold in your hands now qualifies as a classic. What is a classic? The dictionary says it is a literary work of the first rank, especially one of demonstrably enduring quality. *Possessing the Gates of the Enemy* fits that description.

Over the years I have built quite a library on prayer and spiritual warfare. None of the other books approaches the content of *Possessing the Gates of the Enemy*.

Not many people are equipped to write a book like this. There may still be some segments of the Body of Christ that are not quite ready for it, but my hope is that they soon will be. This is not the milk of the Word, it is meat; and a certain amount of Christian maturity is necessary for it to be adequately digested. But God has been doing remarkable things across the lines of different ecclesiastical traditions these days, and that has been producing new and fresh maturity in the area of prayer.

Indeed, we now find ourselves well into the greatest worldwide prayer movement in history. It began around 1970 and has steadily been gaining influence, strength and momentum. Since then, prayer ministries, prayer leaders, prayer for cities and nations, prayer conferences, local church prayer programs and books on prayer have been multiplying. There is a growing quantity of prayer across regional and denominational lines that amazes many. The latest addition has been Cindy Jacobs's powerful Reformation Prayer Network.

All this is why I am excited that *Possessing the Gates of the Enemy* is now available in a revised and updated form. We need to get back to the basics, and the basics of strategic-level intercession are right here.

Seven characteristics blend together to establish this book in the category of a classic.

It is personal. Cindy Jacobs is an outstanding woman, wife, mother, teacher, learner, preacher and intercessor. My wife, Doris, and I consider it an honor to count her as one of our closest personal friends. As you read this book, you will get to know Cindy as an unpretentious person who shares both laughter and tears, victory and defeat, all in the context of transparency and integrity.

It is biblical. While this is not an expanded sermon series or Bible study, Cindy takes great pains throughout the book to relate whatever she teaches to Scripture. She is focused on testing all that she says and does against the Word of God.

It is informed. Few Christian leaders have moved as extensively both nationally and internationally as has Cindy Jacobs. She has accumulated profound firsthand knowledge of what is going on in today's world and how prophetic prayer can advance the Kingdom of God. You will see that reflected on page after page.

It is compassionate. Cindy is not afraid to step out of the box and address cutting-edge issues that may pull some readers out of their comfort zones. Still, she is able to do this in a gentle way that avoids any haughtiness or self-righteousness. She allows you to disagree with her and still be friends!

It is analytical. This is not to disparage them in any way, but many intercessors are so right-brained that they find it almost impossible to analyze or explain what they are doing. Cindy Jacobs, however, is one of those rare individuals who balances intuition with understanding in such a way that she clarifies to others what God is doing to and through her.

It is practical. This is a manual based on much hands-on field experience. It is the kind of guidebook that will tell you not only what needs to be done, but what steps you can take to make that happen.

It is motivational. You may be one who has considered prayer boring. If so, when you read this book, you will catch the fire of how powerful and exciting prayer can really be. You will end up praying as you have never prayed before, and you will love it!

I think this will happen to you because it happened to Doris and me. Through Cindy Jacobs we have become open to allowing God to do new things through us that we did not know were possible.

Possessing the Gates of the Enemy is a book I know will excite and uplift you. Watch and see. You will soon be recommending it to your friends!

C. Peter Wagner, chancellor
Wagner Leadership Institute

Acknowledgments

This book was made possible through the love, prayers and support of many special friends. First of all, I want to thank the Lord for helping me to do something I thought was impossible for me—writing this book!

The Lord used some very special human vessels to teach me how to write *Possessing the Gates of the Enemy*. Peter Wagner has been my mentor. I really do not think this book would have been written without his wisdom and advice. Doris Wagner, my good friend, has always been there to offer practical advice as well as being my friend on the battlefield.

Of course, my husband, Mike, has been a great encouragement to me. When I felt I couldn't make it through with this assignment he would sit down and pray and talk with me and offer great wisdom. We have often teased about other writers who thank their families in their acknowledgments for the meals missed. (Mike, are you reading this?)

Also, Mary and Daniel, my children, are to be commended for loving their mom through the writing of this book. They have been some of my best prayer partners and have often encouraged me not to give up.

My mom, Eleanor Lindsey, has faithfully typed the manuscript and spent hours reading and editing. Thank you, Mom! You went above and beyond the call of duty. Also, thanks to Thomas Lindsey for his proofreading.

Becky Wagner deserves a special thanks for her administrative help. Her gentleness in her task as my administrative assistant is indeed Christlike.

I cannot adequately express my gratitude to the prayer partners of Generals International who have fasted, prayed and loved me as I poured out my needs in our prayer letter for this book. Also, thanks to the church groups who set aside time to pray each week that I would meet the publishing deadline.

Jane Campbell, editor of Chosen Books, has given a listening ear to me when I reached times of enormous frustration. Writing a book without any training has created a huge learning curve for me. She patiently answered my many questions.

Thank you to Ann McMath for God's editing abilities through you. You are a joy.

I would like to thank and acknowledge my friend Jane Rumph for the excellent job she did in writing the study guide for this new edition. Your prayers are important to me and my family.

John Jemison, thanks so much for helping me look up references and check on facts.

Introduction

Possessing the Gates of the Enemy might seem to some to be an unusual title for a book on intercession. It comes from Genesis 22:17–18: "That in blessing I will bless thee, and in multiplying I will multiply thy seed as the stars of the heaven, and as the sand which is upon the sea shore; and thy seed shall possess the gate of his enemies; And in thy seed shall all the nations of the earth be blessed; because thou hast obeyed my voice" (KJV).

This powerful promise was given to Abraham for his seed. We, the Church, are Abraham's spiritual seed and so this promise to possess the gates of the enemy pertains to us today. The gates of hell will not prevail against a praying Church.

Today's praying Church is rising up in militant force to possess the promised land of our nations. *Possessing the Gates of the Enemy* is a training manual for God's prayer army. This manual is needed because a tremendous spirit of prayer is being poured out—worldwide. Intercessory prayer groups are springing up across the nations. Generals International, formerly known as Generals of Intercession, the ministry God has given to my husband and me, is rather like a networking center for new strategies pertaining to intercession. We are receiving reports of intercessors doing things like going to the banking centers of the world to pray. Some go regularly to their state capitols. Others have gone by dogsled as far north as they could go. Groups have gathered at Wall Street to pray for America's economy.

We currently have a prayer movement across the earth called The Global Reformation Prayer Network—geared at seeing each part of society brought into a biblical worldview. These include what has become known as the Seven Mountains of Influence: Religion, Family, Education, Government, Business, Art, Entertainment and Media.

Why the need for a new edition of *Possessing the Gates of the Enemy*? I have found that many of the truths we as prayer leaders taught in the late '80s and '90s are totally unknown to a new generation. Even if they know these truths in part, there are wide gaps that need to be re-taught. It behooves all of us as leaders of intercessory prayer to begin with the basics and not just assume that the next generation of intercessors knows all we have learned through the years.

This movement of intercession is powerful and exciting! As with any new move of God, there is much need for teaching. Study of past revivals of prayer shows me we need to guard this present visitation from error and deception.

Years ago, as I prepared to write this book, I went to bookstores in many places looking for research material of a practical nature. Many of them had a large section on prayer but little, if any, on intercession. The books I did find on intercession had a sad lack of practical guidelines. Today, there are many good books on the subject, many of them by my good friends like Peter Wagner, Dutch Sheets and Chuck Pierce. However, we are all feeling a need to go back once again and teach subjects such as spiritual warfare that God gave us years ago.

Originally I had thought simply to write a book warning of the "flaky" or out-of-balance practices that were cropping up in intercessory groups. However, Peter Wagner sat me down one day in his study in Altadena, California, and challenged me to broaden my scope to include intercession as a whole. From this discussion came the vision to write *Possessing the Gates of the Enemy* in its present form.

Who will benefit from reading this book? *Possessing the Gates of the Enemy* is written with a broad brush to include beginning intercessors as well as those who are mature leaders. Pastors and ministry leaders will reap much by studying the practical sections written for them.

One of my greatest frustrations as a young intercessor was that I had no one to talk to on a practical level about intercession. I was not really sure if I was praying "on target" or if I was out in left field. *Possessing the Gates of the Enemy* begins with chapters for those with this same frustration, and I have attempted to share my heart with those who are interested in the call to intercede. I have tried to remember the numerous questions that spilled out of me when seasoned prayer warriors would take time to listen. Since I cannot speak to each of you personally, I have tried to talk to you as if we were sitting down across a table and you were asking me the many questions you have about intercession.

Since this book has been written from my life experiences, you will see a transition from chapter to chapter as I grew and the gifting matured. To tell you the truth, it was a very (and that's an understatement) stretching experience to try to analyze the process the Lord took me through from intercessor to prayer leader. As Peter Wagner says, it is usually not the nature of intercessors to analyze what God is doing in their lives; they are too busy just praying. In the original writing of this book I would sit at my typewriter day after day and pray, "Lord, show me Your ways in the life of an intercessor. What are the traps the enemy lays for people as they intercede? What can I share that will save them heartache?" For this new and updated edition, I asked the Lord to amplify what He gave me at that time.

For the chapters on the language and the manifestations of intercession, I spoke with numerous intercessors to see what they understood to be the definitions of terms they use such as *binding* and *loosing* and *travail*. In addition, many called me with sad stories of gross error and problems with intercessory groups.

In the chapter on corporate intercession you will find many practical insights gleaned from some of God's generals who lead intercession. Many prayer groups are weak or ineffective because they lack strong leadership. I also included guidelines for pastors and ministry leaders. Many of these individuals are strong intercessors themselves and are on the cutting edge of this prayer movement. I have a special heart for the pastors of the nations and hope this section will save them some grief in working with their prayer leaders. In addition, prayer leaders will find guidelines to give out to their prayer groups that will bring order and peace to the meetings.

The interest in prophetic intercession is on the upswing. The chapter on this tells how to prophesy in prayer, and includes material for those who already prophesy in intercession.

Intercessory praise is a pertinent topic among prayer groups today. Many are realizing the need to war in the heavenlies through praise and worship. I have tried to include contemporary examples as well as those from the great hymns of the Church.

As I reflect back over the years since I wrote *Possessing the Gates of the Enemy*, I am amazed at what has happened to the prayer movement. God has used this book in its own way to start prayer groups all over the world. It always touches me to hear the stories of intercessors who say, "We started our prayer group from reading your book." How humbling and gratifying! It often causes me to reflect on what I was going through when I wrote the book. The devil seemed to be sitting on my shoulder the whole time, whispering comments like, *No one will ever read this book. Who do you think you are, writing a book no one will want to read?*

For those who are picking up this book for the first time: These principles really work! They are tried and tested. I pray that you will be encouraged as you read its pages. Time and again intercessors have said to me, "I didn't know there was anyone else like me. I just thought I was weird." My friend, you are not alone. There are thousands of intercessors like you all over the world.

I started writing the original manuscript of *Possessing the Gates of the Enemy* in 1989, and the book was first released in 1991. Of course, the Lord has increased my understanding of intercessory prayer since that time. For that reason, this updated version contains new stories and revelations concerning healing nations, prophetic intercession, and legislating in the heavens.

God is never static! His Kingdom is ever-increasing, as is knowledge of Him in the earth and we, as people who pray, need to stay current and fresh in our understanding.

You might feel the call to be a "general of intercession," such as I wrote about in this book. If that is so, I want to encourage you in your calling and destiny. However, even if you are just beginning to learn to pray, this book is a manual to launch you into one of the most exciting adventures of the Christian life—intercessory prayer!

It is my hope and prayer that you will learn so much from what you read in these pages that you will shake our world for the Lord Jesus Christ.

Yours in heavenly combat,
Cindy Jacobs

1

The Call to Intercede

A beginning of a new decade—thoughts tumbled out one after another as I tried to fall asleep in a hotel room in Bradenton, Florida. My husband, Mike, and I had just flown in from our home in Texas to meet with other prayer leaders and to partake in a prayer session we called "Ninety Hours of Prayer for the Nineties." We all had a sense of God's moving and felt that a tremendous outpouring of the Spirit was imminent. As I began to relax, I mulled over the events of the '80s. God has been so gracious. Five of those years had been spent bringing prayer leaders together from different nations—a networking that had come to be known as "Generals of Intercession." Mike and I had learned a lot on the battlefield about tearing down the strongholds of the enemy and looked forward to what God's new assignments would bring.

At two A.M. I awakened with a start. The indicators were familiar: I felt a sense of danger and agitation. Deep within I began to pray, *God, what is wrong? Is someone in trouble?* Almost instantly I saw a mental picture or vision of good friends, David and Cheryl Barton. They were driving their van from the Dallas area where they lived to our meeting, with their three children curled up asleep in the back. All of a sudden, in the vision, the van's right front wheel rolled off, and the van careened wildly into a horrible accident.

I knew immediately that they were in serious danger and that God wanted me to pray that the wheel bearings would hold until we could see the Bartons and warn them. David was doing a mighty work for God with his book *America: To Pray or Not to Pray?* and he was coming under spiritual attack. The hours dragged on as I cried out to God to keep that wheel in place and protect them. All through the night I sensed a tremendous battle taking place in the heavenlies.

The next day I hounded the registration desk until finally a call came into the room. They had arrived. I ran to their room and pounced on them. "Are you all right? Has anything happened to the van?" Between hugs they said that everything was just fine. After I told them about my night of prayer, Cheryl mentioned that she had heard a funny sound in the van the night before, but David had not noticed it. I urged them strongly to check the right wheel bearings. David and Cheryl know me well enough to know that I would not say this lightly; so before David took the van on the road again, he and Mike drove it to a garage.

When they finally returned to the hotel they were grinning from ear to ear. Mike had a little bag in his hand. "The trophies of intercession," he said. It held the bearings from the right front wheel.

As we heard their story we marveled at God's mercy and care for the Barton family. The mechanic took off the left wheel bearings first and exclaimed, "I don't see how you could have driven this without having it seize up on you." After checking the right wheel he was really amazed: "This one is worse than the other!" He said that there was no way they should have been able to drive without having the wheels come off. He went on to explain that the spindle, which should have been totally ruined, was not damaged.

David grinned and told us, "We couldn't let an opportunity to share about the Lord pass by, and so I said, 'Do you know why we came in to have our wheels checked?'" For the next half hour the men witnessed to an astonished mechanic and I thanked God in my heart for waking me to pray.

Perhaps you have had an experience in which you, too, felt impressed to pray for a certain urgent need. Or perhaps you have heard stories from other intercessors and have questions: How do you know when someone needs your prayers? How do you pray? Do our prayers really battle the devil? Can we thwart plans of destruction?

It takes courage and perseverance to be the kind of intercessor who will make a difference. It is not always easy. But if you have an interest in putting what God will show you into action, and if you are a prayer warrior, a prayer leader, a minister or "simply" a Christian who prays, you can recognize the call of God to intercede and wage a holy war against the enemy.

Before we get into the ABCs of militant intercession, let me tell you briefly about the three phases or depths God led me through, which I hope will help you understand what God might be doing in your life. It was all quite a new experience for me. In fact, when the Lord first touched me to pray I had no idea what was going on. I only knew that something unusual was happening to me. Prior to that time I had been a rather "normal" Christian, mom and schoolteacher. I knew that I had a call of God on my life but had no idea what it was or how it would be fulfilled.

As the weeks progressed, I began to awaken during the night on a regular basis. The pattern was always the same: I would wake up suddenly, be wide awake and wonder why. After this happened to me for a week or so, I finally figured out that I must be waking up for a reason. It occurred to me that perhaps I should ask God about it. In answer to my questioning, God began to show me the beginning of a marvelous adventure of serving the King of kings as an intercessor. The Lord made it clear to me that I was to pray during these wide-awake times. Sometimes it would be at three o'clock on the nose for a week or so (God's alarm clock is incredible), and then it would be at two o'clock for a few days. As I began to seek His guidance, names would come to me and specific thoughts about what to pray.

I remember thinking, *Well, there's no one around who will think I'm crazy. The rest of the family is asleep, and it is just me and God.* So I would pray those thoughts that came to me.

I prayed in this fashion for a while without mentioning it to anyone. I wasn't sure but that they *would* think I was crazy.

One cold night, I felt led to pray for a minister from my church named Todd whom I knew only casually. I pulled the covers over my head and began whispering quietly the thoughts that came. "Lord, Todd needs healing, and he feels lonely and afraid. I pray that You will comfort him, heal him and let him know that he is not alone." Then I attached an addendum: "God, I really would like some confirmation from You that these prayers I am praying are making any kind of difference." This cry came from my heart because suddenly, on that cold winter night, I felt rather foolish. I noticed that the clock said 3:10 A.M.

My answer came quickly. The next night at our Wednesday night service Todd stopped me before I went out the door and asked if he could speak with me. He said, "Cindy, not many people know this, but I have cancer. Last night I was awake in extreme pain. I felt so lonely and cried out to God, 'God, doesn't anyone care?'" Todd said that God spoke to him at that moment and said, *Cindy Jacobs is awake and is praying for you*. The clock read 3:10. Needless to say, I was—to use a word a friend has coined—"awesomized." All the time I had spent praying those outlandish things for people around the world had made a difference! I found out later that Todd had been healed of cancer.

I was greatly encouraged by that experience, so much so that when God impressed me around four o'clock one morning to pray that an older man in our church would not get hurt at work, I prayed with great conviction. God seemed to have spoken so clearly that I actually went to Buster in person and told him that God was going to protect him from harm on the job.

The following week Buster was working high on the nosecone of a Boeing 767. He took a step, lost his balance and found himself falling some twelve feet, crashing down face first on the cement floor. He lay there for a few moments, stunned by the fall, then cautiously began to check himself out as his co-workers came running. To everyone's amazement, he was a little sore but fine otherwise. God's protection was a great testimony to his co-workers.

The next Sunday morning, Buster took me by the shoulders and told me his incredible story of God's mercy. Buster's deliverance from injury did a lot for him. But it did a lot deep inside me as well. I realized something: Intercessory prayer really works!

Waking up in the middle of the night was not the only unusual thing that started happening to me in phase one of my training in intercession. One day I was in a healing service, and a mother brought her critically ill little son in for prayer. As I watched the pastor lay his hands on the child, tears began gushing down my face. I realized my heart was breaking for the child as though he were my own. After a few minutes I put my head down on my knees and tried to be as inconspicuous as possible. Mike was trying to comfort me. Neither of us understood exactly what was happening.

All at once, as quickly as the weeping came, it left! I took a handful of Kleenex, wiped my eyes, blew my nose and looked around to see if anyone had noticed my outburst. It had gone seemingly unnoticed. Then I realized that deep inside I had a sense of peace and wonderment. I knew that God had done something for that child. I was sure that he would be fine. I later read that Charles Spurgeon called tears "liquid prayers."

Other remarkable occurrences happened that were new to me. One day during a prayer meeting in our home, a group of us was praying about a job for Mike. He had been laid off from his job with an airline, and we desperately needed for him to find another one. Out of nowhere I began to laugh—loud! The more I laughed, the more I wanted to stop. Laughing seemed so irreverent—and besides that, some of the others were staring at me. It was much later that I found the Scripture that says:

> When the LORD brought back the captivity of Zion, we were like those who dream. Then our mouth was filled with laughter, and our tongue with singing. Then they said among the nations, "The LORD has done great things for them."
>
> Psalm 126:1–2

I am convinced that Mike's job was given in the heavenlies at that moment even though it was two months before we actually possessed in the natural what had happened that day in the Spirit.

Why was all this happening to me? It seemed that the Lord had taken me up on some rash prayers that I had prayed before any of these prayer experiences began. God began to remind me that, prior to these unusual experiences, I had said, "God, use me in the way You see fit. I will do anything You want me to do; go anywhere, anyhow." As I searched the Scriptures for direction, one in particular leapt out at me: "I sought for a man among them who would . . . stand in the gap before Me on behalf of the land" (Ezekiel 22:30). I could see then that God had chosen me to be an intercessor.

For several years, I prayed in the manner in which the Holy Spirit directed me. I did not know why I was praying as I was, but was comforted by the fact that it was bringing results for the Kingdom.

As my confidence grew that I could be used of the Lord to stand in the gap, it seemed that people began to tell others about the remarkable answers to prayer such as what happened to Buster and Todd. Churches asked me to speak on intercession, and I dug into the Word to find out how to teach others to intercede. I felt joyful that my ministry was growing and many doors were opening, when God spoke to me one day and said, *Cindy, I want you to lay your ministry down and learn to intercede.* Well, I thought that I had done that already, but all of a sudden there came an overwhelming sense that I really had no idea how to pray at all. After a time of wrestling in my heart, I said, "Yes, Lord."

Thus began phase two, which is the basis of the teaching in this book. God furthered my education by introducing me to some of His great intercessors—living legends of prayer. Some of these have gone home to be with the Lord. Some are still at work for the Kingdom. We had marvelous times of prayer. A principle I learned during this time is that intercession is not so much taught as caught, meaning that I grew not so much by systematic teaching as by experiencing the power of the Holy Spirit at work and longing to be a part of it. Intercessors find it hard to analyze what they do, perhaps because they are committed to putting themselves aside and focusing on the Lord's will for their lives of prayer. So I observed and learned.

Many prayer giants are the most humble servants of God you will ever meet. One of these is Dr. B. J. Willhite. He finds the title "intercessor" tends to intimidate people, but anyone can be a "pray-er." Bob has received a legacy from pray-ers in his life. His mother was a mighty prayer warrior and actually went home to be with the Lord while kneeling in prayer. A short time after that his aunt was kneeling in prayer and stepped into eternity. I call that going from glory to glory!

At age nineteen, Bob began deeply seeking the Lord. During this time he attended the Glad Tidings Tabernacle in San Francisco and would slip into their prayer room. Not only did Bob meet God there, but day after day he listened to the prayers of a little woman agonizing in intercession. She would weep and weep. He was deeply moved as he heard her cry out to God for the nation of India. As Bob has said, "At that time I didn't know how eyes could hold that many tears." God had a purpose for his listening, for as I just said, intercession is not so much taught as caught. As that woman travailed before God for a nation she might never see, God opened the depths of intercession in Bob Willhite. As he cried out to God, he was filled with the power of the Holy Spirit and given a heart's desire to draw near to God.

Bob tells of his experience in his book *Why Pray?* He says:

> Up until that time I had never heard anyone pray for a nation to be saved. But as I studied the Word, I noticed that in Psalm 2:8 the Father speaking to His Son says, "Ask of me, and I shall give thee the heathen for thine inheritance, and the uttermost parts of the earth for thy possession."[1]

God took that nineteen-year-old and taught him to pray. Bob is the only person to have received a doctorate from Oral Roberts University as an "Apostle of Prayer." Many such "giants" of intercession have paved the way for the intercessory movements that we have today.

Another intercessor who has deeply touched my life is Dick Eastman. Like Bob Willhite, Dick's spiritual heritage is rich in intercession. Dick is the president of an organization called Every Home for Christ (formerly World Literature Crusade), headquartered in Colorado Springs, Colorado. Their vision is for the Gospel message to be distributed to every home in the world. This organization has had as many as 498,000 written decisions for Christ sent to its offices around the world—in a single month! Dick has also incorporated a prayer ministry, Change the World Ministries, into the evangelical thrust of EHC. I believe that this agreement of prayer and evangelism is the key element of God's strategy for global outreach.

In an interview with Dick and his wife, Dee, I asked him, "Dick, what event in your life most influenced your call to prayer?" A warm smile spread across his face as he answered, "When I was growing up I never needed an alarm clock. You see, each morning I was awakened by the sound of my mother's voice in prayer." Dick's mother, Lorraine, interceded faithfully for her son. She also invested her time in prayer for the nations, and God put feet to those prayers through her offspring.

Surprisingly, Dick was not a model youth. In fact, he was quite rebel-lious. As he explains in his book *Love On Its Knees*:

While I was a rebellious youth involved in serious stealing and burglary by age fourteen, my mother stood against the darkness enslaving me, praying that the light of Jesus Christ would shine into my heart.

I remember in particular the day that my mother's prayers seemed to catch up with me. Mike, my young partner in crime, was on the phone asking me to go with him to our local large swimming pool. We had developed a scheme that we carried out in the vast area where swimmers placed their towels along with beachbags and even purses and wallets. When swimmers went into the water, we would walk casually by, select-ing a neglected beach towel and purse or wallet and lay our blanket on top of it. After tossing a beach ball back and forth for a few minutes, we would pick up our blanket—with the purse or wallet now underneath it—and amble innocently off.

On this particular Sunday, however, when Mike called something came over me. I not only told him no; I told him that I would never do anything like that again. I couldn't explain why. I could only tell him my life was changing.

Mike decided to go alone that day and unknown to him a man sitting on a hillside near the pool would observe what he was doing and alert the police. Mike was arrested and taken to jail. That night, as it was a Sunday, I went to church. God had begun to answer my mother's prayers.[2]

Lorraine Eastman's prayers intensified when Dick went off to col-lege. While Lorraine prayed fervently for her son, God began to speak to Dick in what seems like an unlikely place—the large walk-in closet of his dormitory room. That large closet was the launching pad for a worldwide ministry of prayer.

We will meet these and other prayer warriors later as I describe star-tling episodes of God's work through them. Knowing them has been an invaluable experience. I listened and observed their methods and stood in awe at the answers to the prayers they prayed. They were patient as I asked them countless questions: "Why did you pray that way? Does that work the same way every time you pray? How do I know how long to pray?" This book is essentially a compilation of the golden nuggets mined from the depths of prayer of some of God's giants. I know that it would be their wish to pass on what they taught me and others in the school of prayer to future prayer warriors. These are lessons that must be applied in an ongoing way for us to maintain the place in intercession where God wants us. In order to war effectively, the sword must be sharpened constantly by His Word and presence.

Another aspect of my training during phase two was books by these and other writers such as E. M. Bounds and Andrew Murray. God spoke to me significantly through Norman Grubb's *Rees Howells, Intercessor*. I was so touched by the life of that Welshman in the early 1900s that I would read a chapter, cry and have to wait a week or so before I could read more because each chapter so awakened my ache to go deeper into this ministry. "As a result of a powerful meeting with God he was trained, chosen, and equipped by the Holy Spirit during the time of the great Welsh revival."[3]

God began to raise up those like Rees Howells during this great revival to be intercessors and teachers, to take the burden of the newborn babes, pray and lead them on. These young intercessors soon began to find out how mighty is the enemy of souls. As Rees Howells said later: "The intercession of the Holy Ghost for the saints in this present evil world must be made through believers filled with the Holy Ghost."[4]

God had still more to show me about intercession. Phase three tracks the founding of Generals of Intercession. It was then I learned—and over the course of this book I will share with you—about the gates of the enemy and how we can possess them.

---

1. B. J. Willhite, *Why Pray?* (Lake Mary, Fla.: Creation House, 1988), 34.

2. Dick Eastman, *Love On Its Knees* (Tarrytown, N.Y.: Chosen Books, 1989), 18–19.

3. Norman Grubb, *Rees Howells, Intercessor*, 3rd ed. (Fort Washington, Pa.: Christian Literature Crusade, 1983), 33.

4. Ibid., 34.

2

Generals of Intercession

Phase three of my training as an intercessor began on a quiet day in 1985. Mike was home working on our house when I felt a special need to be alone with the Lord to pray. Mike agreed to watch the children and went on his way singing as he often does.

Once alone in my prayer closet (which is also our bedroom), I knelt down beside our bed. I had been fasting and praying for three days, greatly concerned about the state of our nation. Finally things seemed to be coming to a head inside of me.

As I knelt, from deep inside me came a question: "Father, since Satan is not omnipresent or omniscient, how is he so effective in his war over the nations?" Quietly a still, small voice spoke to me. It was not audible but rather God making Himself known to me. You have probably experienced this. All of a sudden you know what He is expressing, and it settles deep within your heart. The Lord spoke this word to me: *strategy*. It became clear that the enemy has a strategy for every nation and ministry. I also realized that his army does not rest from the battle.

Have you ever noticed that when you come to the Lord with a problem He often asks you to be part of the solution? For seven years God had been training me, first in a hidden season in my prayer closet, then by putting me with people who were mighty in prayer. I had no idea then why those stages should be so intensive. In retrospect I can see that the early boot camp experiences were designed to teach me the clean heart principle, which we will discuss in the next chapter. Now, an entirely new expression and ministry was about to come forth—that of prayer leader.

In response to my question concerning Satan's inroads, the Lord impressed me to gather His "generals" of—or leaders in—intercession together. He wanted me to emerge from my more hidden time of training. As I waited on the Lord He gave me a strategy that would bring ministries together on a common battlefield for the nations of the world and our beloved United States.

In time of war it is the generals who make the battle plans. The Lord wanted us to meet together to hear His plan of strategy, as He revealed it through the different ministries, and learn how to put it into action. During this time I could clearly see that His Body was praying "shotgun prayers," mostly for their own ministries and purposes with a scattered effect over others and America, while God desired His body of intercessors to pray in unity. He gave me five key points:

1. No one ministry has all the revelation necessary to strategize over nations.
2. His Body must come together for the battle plans to be revealed.
3. When the ministers came together and each contributed his or her piece of the strategy, God would reveal His plans to us all.
4. The meetings would tear down barriers between ministries, and we would have a united front on which to wage war.
5. Those asked to be generals would be those Christians on staff with major ministries as prayer coordinators.

The basic assignments for the meetings were to be as follows:

1. We were to pray for the sins of our nation from its inception. These were sins of slavery, our treatment of the Indians, strife and division during the Civil War, the internment of Japanese during World War II and other like sins.

2. We were to use Daniel 9:3–19 as our pattern. In this passage Daniel confesses the corporate sin of his people. Some of the sins we were to repent for were prejudice, materialism, mammon, murder and idolatry.

3. After we repented of these sins, God would show us which rulers of Satan's kingdom needed to be called down from their high places and whose right to reign should be broken. By doing this we would tear apart Satan's strongholds.

4. We were to pattern ourselves after Jeremiah 1:10: "See, I have this day set you over the nations and over the kingdoms, to root out and to pull down, to destroy and to throw down, to build and to plant." We were not only to tear down, we were also to build and plant. The next step was to pray that the United States would return to its godly heritage. The planting would be that the "hearts of the children would return to their forefathers."

5. God would adapt and use this pattern for the various nations to which we would go.

The Lord gave this commission during that time of prayer and fasting in September 1985. Upon leaving my prayer closet I found Mike. "Mike," I asked, "will you help me gather the generals?" He looked at me for a minute and took a breath. "Yes, honey, I will." At that time he was not too surprised at anything I said when I came out of a season of prayer.

Let me add here that as a woman minister I cannot say enough for my husband. He is a good and godly man. He is totally supportive of me in the ministry and is my best friend and counselor. I know that I could not have accomplished the things that have happened in my years of ministry if it had not been for Mike's covering me in prayer, encouraging me not to give up, laughing with me and wiping away my tears when discouragement assailed me. Frankly, although God has given me the visions, it has been Mike's "Rock of Gibraltar" faith that has brought them into reality.

The next day after receiving this new assignment from the Lord I talked with a number of people as to how to proceed. One mighty prayer warrior named Margaret Moberly, who has since gone to be with the Lord, helped me greatly. She talked to our pastor and others who she knew could help. We gathered together and prayed, seeking God's wisdom. During these times of prayer the vision was amplified. We were to begin in Dallas, go to Tulsa, Los Angeles, Washington D.C., Canada, England and Australia, linking each in prayer as we went.

There is an interesting aspect to being a visionary. When the vision first comes, it is exciting—there is a lot of faith and joy. Afterward, however, comes the hard work, times of great stretching when you want to turn back and lay aside the vision. It is at those times that the devil mocks, "Has God said?" These are the battles that have to be fought through fasting and prayer—for instance, prayer that the right connections will open up, facilities will have space and people will not get upset over differences in doctrine.

The first Generals meeting was hosted by Bob Willhite at what was, at the time, the Church on the Rock in Rockwall, Texas, in November 1985. That night as we sat in a classroom in the educational space of the church we felt a sense of destiny. We felt other things, too. We had come from diverse backgrounds and doctrines. Some had questioned whether or not it was even possible for us to come together in unity and prayer.

As we went around the room and shared who we were and what ministries we represented, there was a sense that God was pleased with what we were doing. Then one gentleman, Bob Henning, shared his heart and the heart of God with us. With his deep, quiet voice he said, "God has called us together for a higher purpose than our differences in doctrine; there is something higher than doctrinal unity for this meeting. We need to rally around the cross of Jesus Christ. All of us can agree that our nation needs prayer and that Jesus needs to be Lord over America." God had spoken in our midst. It was as though each of us released a sigh inside and the walls came down. The tension left and a feeling of God's presence filled the room. Jesus Christ is indeed the Lord of the breaches and the repairer of the divisions among people.

From this first meeting we went from ministry to ministry in the Dallas area. Each time we met there was a stronger bond and greater agreement. The meetings took this shape: a focus on prayer for half an hour or so, and then a time when God used each ministry to bring forth a piece of the overall strategy. The corporate anointing was beautiful to behold!

God used the meetings to unfold His strategy for America and healing for the nations. The spirit of unity among the ministries pleased the heart of God, and after the times of prayer His peace would descend upon us.

From the Dallas area the Generals spread across America and to other nations. It seemed that each time we met, a particular need for prayer on the heart of God would evolve. Sometimes we would know that God wanted to heal situations between ministries or some particular aspect of the nation.

One example of this was our first meeting in Pasadena, California. As Dick Eastman concluded his speaker's remarks, the Lord reminded me of a direction I had received before the meeting. As I prayed for the meeting it became clear that the sin against Japanese-Americans during World War II was to be remitted so that God could move among them with the Gospel. As I shared this need one pastor from Torrance came forward and said, "That's why I cannot reach the Japanese-Americans in my community. May I pray?" He fell on his knees and began to ask God to forgive the American people for the loss of houses and lands and for hurting our fellow Americans. We did not know what was happening in the Spirit, but we all had a sense that God would move in some supernatural way.

Months later I was reading my prayer journal—that is, the daily newspaper—when I came upon an article dated April 21, 1988. The title of the article was "Senate Votes Compensation for Japanese-Americans." It went on to say that the Senate had voted the day before to give $20,000 in tax-free payments to each of thousands of Japanese-Americans who were forced from their homes and sent to internment camps during World War II. How much had our prayers affected this legislation? Others were undoubtedly praying, too. I earnestly believe, however, that the effectual, fervent prayers offered up to God on that day in Pasadena had a direct bearing on the Senate's vote.

I want to make it clear that we do not think we are the only ones praying! We are simply a part of God's strategy. The Word of God does say that He sought for someone to stand in the gap. The more we as intercessors use anointed times to pray against specific things, the greater the yoke that will be broken.

When it came time to open up different cities for new Generals meetings, I would fly in and pray until God opened a door at a ministry. Many times I did not know anyone there at all, but God would say, *Go.* He was faithful each time. The Lord also blessed us with intercessory support groups that prayed and stood with us for the doors to open.

One hindrance to our being received was the fact that so many Christian leaders had been "burned" by intercession and intercessors. They had seen so much abuse that they did not want to have anything to do with an intercessory prayer meeting. As I met with these leaders I began to hear stories of the out-of-balance praying that had turned them off to intercessory prayer as a whole. They knew that they needed this kind of prayer, but they were leery of groups holding meetings. In most every instance we were able to help them rethink the idea of intercession.

Because of the nature of Generals of Intercession, we became a kind of networking tool for people with problems and needs. We learned a lot about dealing with error, problems and needs in people's lives. Much of what we found came from sheer ignorance; when the people involved received proper instruction, they changed immediately. Some did not want to change and were not interested in being anything other than "lone rangers." This was difficult and grieved us deeply.

As we traveled from city to city, it became more and more apparent that these issues needed to be addressed with the balance of God's Word—not to throw out the real, but once again to draw ourselves back to the Word of God on a subject near to God's heart: intercession.

My desire to write came from meeting with the Generals. Many have asked searching questions about intercession; and although many excellent books have been written on prayer, books solely on the subject of intercession are relatively sparse.

From those initial meetings in 1985 until today, we have been in many, many prayer meetings and have put our feet upon the soil of nations all over the world. The ministry expanded to such a degree that our board of directors felt we should change the name to Generals International to reflect the scope of our calling to heal nations.

We are in a critical time in the history of our world. I believe that revival is coming, and that God is very much interested in raising up intercessors all over the earth. Isaiah 56:7 says, "My house shall be called a house of prayer for all nations." I believe that many, many people are about to be birthed into the Kingdom of God and that we can hear a call from God's heart: "Where are those who will be 'houses' of prayer for all nations?"

If we do not respond at this time and train and equip ourselves as intercessors, we will find that many babies are birthed into the faith with no one to stand in the gap for them to help them become mature. We will fail to help fulfill God's plans for nation after nation to come to the glorious light of the Gospel. I pray that God will not say of us, "I sought for a man . . . who would . . . stand in the gap . . . but I found no one" (Ezekiel 22:30).

Let's train for battle.

3

The Clean Heart Principle

Before He [the Savior] can lead a chosen vessel into such a life of intercession, He first has to deal to the bottom with all that is natural.[1]

Rees Howells

When I was a little girl my preacher daddy said something to me that has always stuck with me: "Honey, remember that the Holy Spirit is a gentleman. He will not intrude without our welcoming Him in." This simple truth is one that needs to be understood to become an intercessor. An intercessor is one with whom God shares His secrets to cover in prayer. The cleaner our hearts, the more welcome we can make Him. Then the more He shares, the more effective our prayers will be.

The Word of God says that there are things within our hearts that are wicked—desperately wicked. God will bring pressure upon us to change these things, but we must open the door by faith and say, "Lord, come in. Create in me a clean heart." As we open the door to all the dark closets of our heart, the Holy Spirit, the divine Gentleman, comes in and, as Rees Howells so aptly stated, "deals to the bottom with all that is natural."

The first step in praying this Davidic prayer, "Create in me a clean heart, O God" (Psalm 51:10), is simply to realize that we need to pray it. In a time of prayer once I sensed the Lord urging me to give all of myself to Him. It seemed God wanted to touch areas of my life that hindered His using me to intercede. After a time of reflection I was able to say, "Yes, Lord. Come in and deal with those things that stop You from having complete control of my life."

Rees Howells, speaking of the dealings of the Holy Spirit in his life, explained his own struggle in this area. God had asked him to give all of himself in exchange for all of the Holy Spirit.

> [It] was not sin He was dealing with; it was self—that thing which came from the Fall. He put His finger on each part of my self-life, and I had to decide in cold blood [because] He could never take a thing away until I gave my consent. Then the moment I gave it, some purging took place.[2]

At the end of the week Rees Howells experienced a glorious infilling of the Holy Spirit. The Lord dug out bitter roots and gave him a clean heart at the same time. For some people, like Howells, the cleaning up comes in a kind of tarrying before the Lord. For others the Holy Spirit comes in and begins to clean the person's heart instantly. I often wonder if we take the infilling of the Spirit too lightly. God wants to give us a clean heart.

The second step in asking God to create a clean heart in us is letting Him deal with what needs changing.

After asking God to fill me totally with His Spirit, I assumed that my wicked heart had been changed and would automatically be under His control. I guess I thought that being Spirit-controlled would be easy, that I would instantly become like Jesus, with His heart and attitudes. I could not have been more wrong! It seemed that from that day on every wicked thing I had ever done began to flash in front of my eyes. Plus, instead of becoming more Christlike, it seemed I was behaving worse than before. The difference was that within moments of sinning I felt deep conviction from the Holy Spirit, and my heart gradually became more pliable and soft before God.

One particular problem I had to deal with was pride. Funny how, before my prayer of surrender, pride would not have been on my list of besetting sins. I was oblivious to this deep sin in my life. I needed to realize that there was no good thing in me! My righteousness was as filthy rags. During this surrendering of all, the story of Joseph was precious to me. What does the story of Joseph have to do with the life of an intercessor? Joseph was used by God to bring divine intervention into the life of a nation. As such, Joseph was a type of intercessor. And God surely dealt with the wrong attitudes in his heart.

The story of Joseph begins in Genesis 37. In verse 2 we see Joseph as a young, prideful teenager:

> This is the genealogy of Jacob. Joseph, being seventeen years old, was feeding the flock with his brothers. And the lad was with the sons of Bilhah and the sons of Zilpah, his father's wives; and Joseph brought a bad report of them to his father.

Here was a proud peacock that God wanted to use to help change the course of a nation, but first He had to deal with some character flaws.

As young intercessors, Joseph and I ran neck and neck with pride. God would show me something about someone and I would run into that person and say, "God told me in prayer that you are filled with bitterness." Because I had not waited for God to show the problem to the person dealing with it, I caused him or her to be highly offended at me. At that time I thought the person was just rebellious and refusing to look at the issues in his or her life.

The next thing Joseph did was to wrap himself in his coat of many colors (symbolic of the anointing) and blatantly display his position. This is a real problem today as God is pouring out a spirit of prayer and many feel that they are "extra special" because they are intercessors.

When God trusts us to pray, He must first cleanse our hearts to the point that the reports we give in prayer are not tainted or biased. He wants to teach us to pray His will, not ours. Because of His Father's heart, He works at stripping us of "our anointing"—selfish desires, seeds of bitterness, rejections, doctrines and biased opinions.

As we saw earlier, Joseph had, at least on one occasion, given a bad report of his brothers. Here, when they saw this young brother wrapped in their father's favor, it was too much for them. "So it came to pass, when Joseph had come to his brothers, that they stripped Joseph of his tunic, the tunic of many colors that was on him" (Genesis 37:23).

This next verse is most interesting because of its symbolism: "And there was a company of Ishmaelites, coming from Gilead with their camels, bearing spices, balm, and myrrh, on their way to carry them down to Egypt" (Genesis 37:25).

The spices they were carrying were used in the time of Joseph for burial. God would use the events in his life over the next long years to bring death to the pride and selfish ambition that had kept this young anointed man from the high calling upon his life. There is a principle that is often painful to young intercessors who are full of zeal: God is not in a hurry. He takes the time He needs to build His character in us. He will patiently and methodically clean up our wicked hearts so He can allow us to pray His purposes into human affairs. Most of us want everything to happen immediately, but God loves to marinade. He wants tender hearts in His living sacrifices. The problem with living sacrifices is that they want to jump off the altar. They sit there awhile and begin to sniff; after a little longer they realize it sometimes hurts to be conformed to the image of Jesus. This is the point at which some decide that the price is too high to serve Christ in prayer.

God had more changes in store for Joseph as He cleansed his heart of pride. God began to give Joseph favor, and for a season things went well for him, culminating in his position as overseer of Potiphar's household. Then the finger of God touched on another area of his life—his physical attributes and abilities. "Joseph was handsome in form and appearance" (Genesis 39:6).

When we begin to have some measure of success, it is easy to fall into the trap that says God has placed us above our fellows because of our ability to pray with more authority or to hear Him more clearly. God has made us more "handsome" in prayer than the other prayer peons.

Even though Joseph resisted the temptation of Potiphar's wife, he still had an enormous problem with pride. Sometimes our words betray the attitude of the heart. Look at the number of personal pronouns and see who is at the top of his list of credits for his current position in his master's house:

> But he refused and said to his master's wife, "Look, my master does not know what is with me in the house, and he has committed all that he has to my hand. There is no one greater in this house than I, nor has

he kept back anything from me but you, because you are his wife. How then can I do this great wickedness, and sin against God?"

Genesis 39:8–9

Notice that the very last thing he said was "and sin against God." One day I shared a report about an answer to prayer. It was a totally dramatic answer to a prayer I had prayed. That night as I started to pray I sensed that the Holy Spirit was grieved. By this I mean that I felt sorrow and could not imagine what was wrong. As I prayed the Lord gently impressed on me that I had shared the testimony of answered prayer as though I had made it happen, as though He were an insignificant part of the answer. When I searched my heart I could see how out of line my time of sharing had been. I repented and felt clean before my heavenly Father.

One great thing about God is that if you flunk one test, He will think up another. Joseph had a hard head, and God had just the solution: another stint in prison.

Time went on, and God decided that it was time for semester exams. God gave dreams to two servants of the king of Egypt who were in prison with him. Joseph, trusting that God would reveal the meanings to him, asked about the dreams.

God did indeed give the interpretations to Joseph, and he saw this as his big chance to get out of prison. This statement shows his state of heart: "But remember me when it is well with you, and please show kindness to me; make mention of me to Pharaoh, and get me out of this house" (Genesis 40:14).

Joseph missed a great time to evangelize for the God of Israel and once more did not give the glory to God. Sentence: two more years in the refiner's fire. After those two years God gave Pharaoh a dream, and the chief cupbearer for the king suddenly remembered Joseph. Let's look at Joseph's response this time: "So Joseph answered Pharaoh, saying, 'It is not in me; God will give Pharaoh an answer of peace'" (Genesis 41:16).

Graduation day for Joseph: The glory had switched from him to God! God then touched Pharaoh's heart to put Joseph second in command over the nation of Egypt. When we let God strip those things out of our hearts that need changing, He will share with us the secrets that the kings speak in their chambers and entrust us to intercede over whole nations. And in the meantime, God will be working with us on the third step of the clean heart principle: letting Him clean up not only the sins of the heart, but the wounds of the heart. "See to it that no one misses the grace of God and that no bitter root grows up to cause trouble and defile many" (Hebrews 12:15, NIV).

I do not know anyone who goes through life without some wounding of the heart. Sometimes we take a little shower at Calvary rather than let God deeply cut and wash away the hurts with His atoning blood. Oftentimes we are unaware of the extent of the damage to our hearts until we are in difficult situations and our bitterness reveals itself in our words and actions. Unless we let the Holy Spirit shine His light on all the unforgiveness in our lives, our prayers will be tainted by the wounds of our hearts.

This lesson was driven home one time when God told me one of His secrets. A pastor, whom I will call Greg, was in deep trouble: If he did not mend his ways, he was in danger of having a severe heart attack. I realize now that God told me this secret for a twofold reason. He wanted the pastor to make adjustments in his life that would avert the heart attack, but He also wanted to expose bitterness in my heart toward Greg.

The problem with me was that this pastor had hurt me badly years before. I thought I had forgiven him and that it was all settled. My heart betrayed me, however, because my first thought after I heard this secret was, *Well, that will teach him not to hurt people and be so arrogant!* I began to envision him in the hospital bed and thought I would help pray him back to health after the heart attack. Fortunately I was jolted quickly by the Lord's rebuke. God did not want the pastor to suffer that heart attack, and I was to pray to avert it so that he would be dealt with in secret. What a wicked heart I had! My woundedness had festered into bitterness and I realized I had to let God cleanse the hurt and deal with my sin. After this, it was easy for me to forgive Greg for hurting me and to beseech God's mercy for him and pray that the adjustments would be made in his lifestyle. At the time of this writing he is being used by God and has never had the heart attack.

Many intercessors are praying amiss by not knowing their own hearts. They pray things spoken to them by their woundedness rather than the desires of their heavenly Father. This is particularly true in those who have been wounded by authority figures in their lives or rejected by those whose opinion is important to them.

As intercessors we are to cover the person or situation in prayer; it is God's job to convict and heal. There are times when we confront sin, but only after we have soaked the matter in prayer. Many people have gotten their lives straightened out, and many desperate situations have been changed because people have learned to pray. Maturity learns to fight battles in the prayer closet. When we pray, God does the impossible in ways we never could dream of.

In Genesis we see an example of intercession when a mighty man of God, Noah, fell in to drunkenness:

> And Noah began to be a farmer, and he planted a vineyard. Then he drank of the wine and was drunk, and became uncovered in his tent. And Ham, the father of Canaan, saw the nakedness of his father, and told his two brothers outside. But Shem and Japheth took a garment, laid it on both their shoulders, and went backward and covered the nakedness of their father. Their faces were turned away, and they did not see their father's nakedness.
>
> Genesis 9:20–23

This attitude of these two sons should be our attitude in intercession—to use it as a garment to cover the nakedness of another. As our hearts are cleansed we will be better able to discern the motive behind the prayers we pray.

I want to be like the psalmist who cries:

> O Lord, You have searched me and known me. You know my sitting down and my rising up; You understand my thought afar off. . . . For there is not a word on my tongue, but behold, O Lord, You know it altogether.
>
> Psalm 139:1–2, 4

Our prayer as intercessors is, "Lord, hem me in both behind and before and create within me cleanness and wholeness of heart, that I may be Your servant to stand in the gap."

As I have traveled the world teaching on intercession for over twenty years, I have often sat with intercessors who expressed their feelings of being unappreciated, misunderstood, maligned or just plain overlooked.

My friend, this is the life of an intercessor. It is also the message of the cross. Jesus didn't die for us because we deserved salvation; He did so because His was a message of unconditional love.

When God calls you to intercession, it is often a hidden place with little or no credit that will ever be seen on earth. However, I assure you your heavenly Father knows and sees your labor of love for your pastor, your church and your nation.

As intercessors, we need regular "spiritual check-ups," where we go through forgiveness to deal with the wounds we may receive in battle. A wounded heart cannot be entrusted with God's secrets because it does not pray with pure motives.

Why don't you stop right here and make a list of ways you may have been unappreciated, misunderstood or misinterpreted? Then forgive.

I know this: God sees, and that is all we really need to ask for, isn't it?

----

1. Norman Grubb, *Rees Howells, Intercessor*, 3rd ed. (Fort Washington, Pa.: Christian Literature Crusade), 88.

2. Ibid., 40.

4

The Enforcers

As intercessors we have an enormous responsibility: God will actually use us to enforce His will in what I call the earth realm. This comes about, as Bob Willhite has explained, because "the law of prayer is the highest law of the universe—it can overcome the other laws by sanctioning God's intervention."[1] Thus, God can act sovereignly over a world wallowing in selfish desires because of the "law of prayer," as Bob puts it, a law higher than rebellion and evil intentions. The means God uses are varied and often involve a whole series of prayer sequences.

One rather dramatic account of God's enforcers at work was told to me at a White House briefing banquet in Washington D.C. by Mark Ballard, who was at the time president of Mt. Vernon Bible College. His wife, Donna, later filled in more details. The story begins in a city in Virginia.

Residents of Christiansburg noted new construction going on in their city. After a while they saw a minaret take shape in the center of what appeared to be a school campus. Some Christians there looked into the matter and learned that a Muslim had obtained funding to build a campus to train third-world students about solar power and to send them back to teach their own people what they had learned. It was apparent, however, that the Muslims had a hidden agenda behind the building of the campus: They were building a mosque and planning to relocate Muslim families into the community to bring Islam into the area.

The people God alerted to the need for prayer were varied. Two intercessors who worked at a grocery store began to pray after getting wind of what was happening. They took a Bible and went to the construction site and asked the men pouring the concrete for the foundation of one of the buildings if they could put something into the site. The men agreed to turn their heads while they planted a Bible on the property and claimed it for the Kingdom of God. One doctor's daughter, age seven, would pray every time she saw the mosque that it would never open. The local churches prayed in their intercessory groups for God's intervention.

Because of the enforcers God called to pray His will, the law of prayer in action confounded the plans of the anti-Christian group. Remarkably, the backers of the Muslim campus ran out of funds, and the land and buildings went back to the bank. The facility sat empty and the pray-ers asked God to use it for His glory.

In the meantime, another group of enforcers in another state was at work on another God-inspired project. Mt. Vernon Bible College had been located in Ohio for thirty years. The board of regents felt a need to relocate the college because of the economic conditions of the local community. They prayed together and asked God to show them where they should move the school. The answer to this prayer came as Mark Ballard was driving to the Carolinas through Virginia. As he drove down Interstate 81 his attention was drawn to some buildings in Christiansburg, even though they were not easily seen from the road.

Through an amazing sequence of events Mark heard the story of how the Muslims had built the campus and how it now sat empty. The Lord led him to the very Christians who had prayed that God would use the facility for His glory. The only hindrance now was a financial one. The property was valued at $8 million. The bank agreed to sell it to Mt. Vernon Bible College for $2.5 million, but the college had nowhere near that amount available.

Back in Ohio, the students heard about the need and jumped into the gap. They began to fast and pray three times a week, and called early morning prayer meetings. God began to move on their behalf! In the end the seller bank was contacted by the buyer bank, saying that they could put a half million dollars into Mt. Vernon's account so that the college would have the line of credit necessary to finance the campus. During this transaction one of the bank secretaries came up to Mark with tears in her eyes and shared how she, too, had prayed that the campus would be sold to a Christian organization. God had called up His enforcers to intercede until His will was done. The property today is still being used by a Christian institution, and God used their prayers to allow it to be used for training for the Kingdom of God.

Why does God need us to function as enforcers in the earth realm? Why do we need to intercede at all? To answer these questions, we need to go back to the beginning.

The need for an intercessor began in a Garden. This might appear to be an unusual battleground—serene, beautiful, created by a loving Father for His children and filled with loving relationships. Adam loved Eve and Eve loved Adam; and they both loved their Father. They walked in the cool of the day, laughing, enjoying the Father's company.

During these walks there was one who watched with anger, jealousy and hate. All the time while this enemy watched, he plotted the downfall of that relationship. How Satan hated God's giving dominion to Adam! From that moment he searched among the very creatures Adam had named to find a vessel he could use to wrest from the hands of man what he himself coveted—power, authority, dominion, rulership of the earth.

Finally in his search Satan began to observe the serpent. He watched the serpent's subtlety and considered its beauty. The other created beings listened and smiled when it spoke. Satan waited for an opportune moment and cunningly took possession of that splendid creature. Once in control of the serpent he began to intertwine himself with its nature and abilities, twisting and perverting its giftings for his evil purposes.

Satan did not move in immediately to tempt God's supreme creation. He was patient and waited until the man and woman were comfortable with their role of dominion and were off guard. They knew how to tend the Garden inside and out and had enjoyed their relationship to the fullest. He schemed what he would say and how he would say it. He listened to their conversations and observed their likes, and one day he knew what to do. He would use the very words the Father had spoken to His children to bring deception.

The moment for which he had been waiting arrived. Eve had noticed his exceptional beauty, and he was talking with her, impressing her with his wisdom. In the midst of a delightful conversation he posed the question that he had carefully crafted: "Did God really say you must not eat from every tree in the Garden?"

The serpent, his verbal skills perverted and polished by the wicked Satan, convinced her quickly that God the Father had deceived her. She ate. Adam, fully trained by God about the tree before Eve was even created, brought no correction. Instead, he received the fruit from her hand and, with one bite, gave away rulership and was stripped of dominion. Satan then declared himself the "god of this world" (2 Corinthians 4:4, KJV).

Their communion with the Father broken, humankind desperately needed an intercessor. As a result of the Fall, humans were under a curse; generations forever would be under a curse.

The Father, having foreseen the demise of the human race, had prepared an antidote for sin—Jesus, the Lamb of God slain from the foundation of the world (see Revelation 13:8).

> He saw that there was no man, and wondered that there was no intercessor; therefore His own arm brought salvation for Him; and His own righteousness, it sustained Him. For He put on righteousness as a breastplate, and a helmet of salvation on His head; He put on the garments of vengeance for clothing, and was clad with zeal as a cloak.
>
> Isaiah 59:16–17

Jesus would bring salvation and deliver people from their sad plight.

Satan did not know what the Father God, Creator of the universe, would do to counteract his devious plan, even though God gave Satan a riddle. Genesis 3:15 says, "I will put enmity between you and the woman, and between your seed and her Seed; He shall bruise your head, and you shall bruise His heel."

Throughout the ages, God was preparing to bring forth salvation through His Son. This is certainly one answer to the riddle, but I believe it also refers to a further weapon, one that was hidden away, waiting to be unveiled after the resurrection. First Corinthians 2:8 explains it is a weapon that "none of the rulers of this age knew; for had they known, they would not have crucified the Lord of glory." It is the Church of the Lord Jesus Christ, a praying army. This mystery is alive in the earth today, "bruising" the works of the evil one.

One of the most dramatic cases I know of enforcers at work came during World War II and is taken from the pages of British history. It is described in Katherine Pollard Carter's book *Hand on the Helm*.

In September 1940 Churchill received intelligence reports of an impending Nazi air invasion. Since Nazi factories were able to produce planes more quickly than the British, there was little doubt the Royal Air Force would be badly outnumbered. The attack ensued with more than two hundred Nazi bombers droning toward England. Only 26 squadrons rose from British soil to oppose them.

Then inexplicably the discs on the wall chart began to move eastward. The great Nazi air flotilla had turned back. With 185 of their aircraft downed in flames they were in retreat! Miraculously, against all logistical probability, the Royal Air Force had won the battle. . . .

Amazing reports came from downed Nazi pilots. [Several were] quizzed as to why they had turned back when only two planes were attacking. "Two," exclaimed one pilot. "There were hundreds!" Another Luftwaffe officer asked them in perplexity, "Where did you get all the planes you threw into battle over Britain?" His British interrogators managed to mask their surprise. Actually, the powerful Nazi bomber force had been met by a mere handful of little outmoded Royal Air Force Spitfire and Hurricane fighters. There was no sky full of Royal Air Force planes! . . .

A Nazi intelligence officer captured still later came nearest to disclosing the divine source of the . . . mirages which had confused the Luftwaffe pilots. "With the striking of your Big Ben clock each evening at nine," the Nazi told the British intelligence officer, "you used a secret which we did not understand. It was very powerful, and we could find no countermeasure against it."

He was right! There was a powerful force set in motion each evening as Big Ben struck nine. It was the powerful force of a nation in heartfelt prayer against which no countermeasure could hope to prevail—a nation in prayer to the omnipotent God of creation. Each evening as Big Ben in the clock tower of the Parliament Building struck nine, the people of

the British Isles and of the far-flung English Commonwealth halted for
the famous Silent Moment of Prayer.[2]

The prayers of God's enforcers protected the British Isles. This was
made possible through Christ's sacrifice. Jesus became the supreme en-
forcer through His death, burial and resurrection. His death on the cross,
which broke the power of sin over humans, allowed divine intervention
in human affairs. Not only did His death, burial and resurrection give
us sonship by adoption into God's family, it gave us back the authority
through the name of Jesus to establish dominion once again. God is the
God of the second chance. Jesus said, "Behold, I give you the authority to trample on serpents and scorpions, and over all the power of the
enemy, and nothing shall by any means hurt you" (Luke 10:19).

There was a price paid by Jesus even before He went to the cross.
We noted earlier that God "wondered that there was no intercessor;
therefore His own arm brought salvation for Him" (Isaiah 59:16). God
wondered that there was no intercessor; thus, Christ has to "*pray* the
price" before He could "pay the price."

R. Arthur Matthews in his book *Born for Battle* says it well:

> The Soldier of the Cross had taught His disciples the need to pray,
> "Thy will be done on earth as it is in heaven." The obvious [implica-
> tion] is that God has limited certain of His activities to responding to
> the prayers of His people. Unless they pray, He will not act. Heaven
> may will something to happen, but heaven waits and encourages earth's
> initiative to desire that will and then to pray that it happens. The will
> of God is not done on earth by an inexorable, juggernaut omnipotence
> "out there" overriding or ignoring the will of people on earth. On the
> contrary, God has willed that His hand be held back while He seeks for
> a person, an intercessor, to plead, "Thy will be done on earth," in this
> or that specific situation. . . .
>
> In the quiet solitude of Gethsemane's olive grove Jesus appears in
> an active role. If He is acted upon on Golgotha, He is the lead actor in
> Gethsemane. It is here that He sets Himself to endure the travail pains
> of a demanding prayer warfare and actively wills for God to do His
> work through Him, regardless of the cost to Himself. His troubled spirit
> expresses itself in groans, strong crying, and tears. The battle is joined.
> The intensity mounts. Heaven's legions press forward to help, but this
> is not their battlefield; it is His alone. His will is assailed at every point.
> *"And His sweat became like great drops of blood falling down to the*

ground" (Luke 22:44). Here is God's work being done in God's way. God wills it in heaven, and a man wills it on the earth. The sacrifice at Calvary happened because first, out of His soul's depths in dark Gethsemane, the "Soldier of the Cross" willed with God for it to happen.[3]

In the battle of Gethsemane Jesus intentionally went to fight a war in the heavenlies to make way for His triumph at Calvary. Can you imagine what the battleground in the heavenlies looked like while Jesus travailed in the Garden? The angels of God blazing forth, preparing for the greatest war for the souls of humankind ever to be fought. Activity everywhere in heaven. I think Satan did not figure out what the assembling was about. Surely the thought must have crossed his mind that they were getting ready to save Christ from crucifixion. Meanwhile, in the Garden, Jesus won the victory and set His face toward Calvary.

It is interesting to note that just as the first battle for salvation began in a Garden, so this ultimate prayer vigil took place in another Garden. Jesus, the second Adam, was bringing a lost world back to its place of domination.

On the cross the request of the Son of God—"Father, not My will but Thine be done"—was accomplished. All sin, disease, unhappiness, disgrace, pain of the body and pain of the heart was paid for and canceled. With a last heart-rending cry Jesus declared, "It is finished!" Having won back the authority through His death and resurrection, He spoiled forever the evil principalities and powers, took back the keys to death and life and triumphed over them all. Hallelujah! When I get to heaven I want to see an instant replay of the look on "old slewfoot's" face when he lost those keys!

After the resurrection Jesus met with the eleven apostles and said to them:

"Go into all the world and preach the gospel to every creature. He who believes and is baptized will be saved; but he who does not believe will be condemned. And these signs will follow those who believe: In My name they will cast out demons; they will speak with new tongues; they will take up serpents; and if they drink anything deadly, it will by no means hurt them; they will lay hands on the sick, and they will recover."

Mark 16:15–18

Jesus Christ essentially tossed them the keys as He was ascending on high to His place of intercession and said, "Whatsoever you ask in My name, that I will do." He gave us the keys to the prison doors of earth—the keys to letting the captives free, whatever their captivity. We are the enforcers of His will in the earth today as we use His name and pray His will through His Word. Human beings can now fulfill their God-ordained position given in the Garden to subdue the earth and have dominion over it in the name of the risen Champion, Jesus Christ, while we at the same time discern and pray for His will. Through our taking dominion over the works of Satan in the earth and praying in the name of our King, we establish His will on earth as it is in heaven. We, in the act of intercession, are His ambassadors plenipotentiary, fully empowered with full authority to pray on behalf of the mighty, awesome God of this universe.

It is critical that intercessors in America rise up and enforce God's will in our nation. The Church must go to the war room in prayer to stem the tide of sin and decay that has come upon our land. We need this desperately.

The urgency for prayer for our nation hit many of us in prayer ministries in 1985. Since then many have taken up the standard of praying righteousness into our land and asking for God's mercy on America. We have been given numerous keys to understanding the current condition of our nation. One is that early in the '60s God poured out His Spirit on the Church, but we were so busy with the wonderful revival that we retreated from government. Essentially we gave the government to the humanists and atheists. In 1962, for instance, we slumbered while the Supreme Court took prayer and Bible reading out of our schools. We are currently reaping the whirlwind for our lack of accountability.

But God is showing us how to reclaim what we have given up. Take this issue of prayer in schools. In 1988 Generals of Intercession sponsored a seminar in the Phoenix, Arizona, area to shake that state for God. Its purpose was to systematically tear down strongholds that have hindered God's movement in Arizona. David Barton was the morning speaker. He shared how in the single year of 1962, 39 million students and more than two million teachers were barred from doing what public schools have done since our nation's founding—offering a few moments of prayer.

David said that the struck-down prayer simply stated, "Almighty God, we acknowledge our dependence upon Thee, and we beg Thy blessings upon us, our parents, our teachers and our country."

As he spoke we realized an awesome thing: Because of our sin of complacency concerning the government, our nation and our children were in a mess. He said that the Scholastic Aptitude Test (SAT) scores plummeted nationwide after 1962. Since 1963 the premarital sexual activity of students has increased more than 200 percent; pregnancies out of wedlock are up almost 400 percent; gonorrhea cases are up more than 200 percent; and the number of suicides has increased by more than 400 percent![4]

These statistics pierced our hearts. One who was particularly grieved was our evening speaker, Bob Willhite. He told us later that he went back to his hotel room and fell to his knees in prayer. He felt so convicted that his generation had allowed prayer and Bible reading to be taken out of our schools that he agonized in prayer all afternoon.

That evening as he stood to speak we all sensed gravity in his bearing. Bob is a tall, dignified man with a humble spirit before God. He spoke quietly. "For the past several hours I have been in deep repentance before God. As I listened to Dave share this morning, the sin of my generation came before me." He stopped. We felt the depth of God's convicting power upon him. "I have come tonight to repent before you for my sin and the sin of those of my generation. Will all of those fifty years of age or older please stand up?" All across that auditorium men and women began to rise. Each seemed to have had the same sense of God's speaking to and convicting them as Bob had had. Many had tears slipping down their faces. Bob continued. "We need to repent before the next generation for giving them an inheritance of a nation fallen into decay and sin." As he spoke, people began weeping. Some covered their faces as the cleansing power of the Holy Spirit swept across the room.

I believe something happened that day that in a measure caused the heart of one generation to turn to another. In other words, a wall between two generations was broken. The Bible speaks of it in Malachi 4:6: "And he will turn the hearts of the fathers to the children, and the hearts of the children to their fathers, lest I come and strike the earth with a curse."

God's will was accomplished that night. The enforcers had broken through with one of God's greatest weapons—forgiveness.

There are other excellent modern-day examples of enforcers all over the world. One of these groups rose up in Brazil in 1961. These particular enforcers were women—Deborahs and Esthers called by God to stand in the gap for their nation. They named themselves the Women's Democratic League, and formed under the threat of Communist takeover.

When propagandists from Cuba, Russia and China began working tirelessly in Brazil, feeding the people lies and false promises, these Brazilian pray-ers took up their "arms" and went to war. They not only prayed, they put feet to their prayers. Hearing that a mass meeting was scheduled in São Paulo with two Communist organizers from Russia as the featured speakers, they telegraphed the union officials that when the plane arrived hundreds of women would be lying across the airstrip to prevent its landing.

When the plane arrived, the women were there, singing, praying and refusing to be moved. The planes swooped low over them, but they were steadfast. Thwarted, the organizers never landed.

When one Communist leader did come to speak, women packed the hall and prayed so fervently that he could not be heard above the din of the prayers. The Communist leader left the hall in frustration.

Spurred on by these brave women and other resistance groups, the Brazilian army and navy rose up and routed a Communist attack with the leader slipping away in the night.[5]

Many of us are praying for women to rise up like this in many nations of the world—praying Deborahs, crying out to God for justice in their land.

Enforcers can function on many different levels, locally as well as nationally.

One way is to use output from the media as matters of intercession. Many prayer groups are now praying extensively for the media that God will raise up righteous reporting of the news in our land.

It has often been said that the newspaper is the Christian's report card. By reading the local news we can tell what kind of job we are doing as intercessors. I often encourage people to "pray the news."

Some intercessors in small towns tear out the pages of their telephone directories and pass them out in prayer groups. In Washington D.C., ministers like Jeff Wright drive prayer tours in vans and pray God's Word over the city each month. Others walk around their neighborhoods, as I have begun doing. You may have other ideas as well.

In what used to be my hometown of Weatherford, Texas, I became aware of an upcoming vote in the nearby small town of Willow Park. The county we lived in had been a dry county for years, meaning that liquor-by-the-drink is not allowed there. No beer is sold at the grocery store, and there are no bars. In Willow Park's upcoming election, some groups were trying to pass a liquor-by-the-drink law. I am not trying to pass judgment on those who wanted this law, but the atmosphere that would have come with the bars was one that many of us did not want. (Weatherford used to have half a dozen saloons around the city square. It is a real Western town!) I called several of my friends and we fasted and prayed for three days. At the end of the three days, two friends, Kurt and Laurie, and I went to a little church that overlooks Willow Park and prayed with the pastor's wife, Mary Gene. I am sure that God had raised up others to pray as well. We prayed against the bondage of addiction and prayed that people would come out to vote against the proposal.

It came as no surprise that liquor-by-the-drink was defeated by a landslide. When God establishes His enforcers to pray His will, He will hear their prayers.

Over the past years, God has been giving the Body of Christ deeper revelation of our role as enforcers in the earth and the authority we have to take dominion in our nations. We will explore this subject at length in the chapter on reforming nations through prayer.

---

1. B. J. Willhite, *Why Pray?* (Lake Mary, Fla.: Creation House, 1988), 91.

2. Katherine Pollard Carter, *Hand on the Helm* (Springdale, Pa.: Whitaker House, 1977), 4–5.

3. R. Arthur Matthews, *Born for Battle* (Robesonia, Pa.: OMF Books, 1978), 14–15.

4. David Barton, *America: To Pray or Not to Pray?* (Aledo, Tex.: Wallbuilder Press, 1988). Statistics in speech drawn from book.

5. Clarence W. Hall, "The Country That Saved Itself," *Reader's Digest*, November 1964, 133.

5

The Ministry of Intercession

An intercessor is a man or woman—or child—who fights on behalf of others. As such, intercession is the activity that identifies us most with Christ. To be an intercessor is to be like Jesus because that is what Jesus is like. He ever lives to intercede.[1]

Dick Eastman

There has been some controversy today about the ministry of intercession. Some say that there is no such thing as the gift of intercession—that God calls the whole Body to be intercessors. Others who feel a special call of God upon their lives to intercede are confused and say, "Where is my place in the Body if there is no gift of intercession? I know that I have a unique drawing from the Lord to stand in the gap. I spend hours every day alone with God praying for the nations of the world, my church, my own country and its leaders."

Which side is right? They both are. From the viewpoint of ministry we are all to pray and intercede like Jesus, our example. From the viewpoint of giftedness a vast number of people are also called specifically to be intercessors. The difference is that one level of intercession is the responsibility of every Christian, and the other is a gift that God bestows and is part of the biblical ministry of helps. Some who receive the gift of intercession receive a future gifting to become prayer leaders. God uses them not only to intercede but to teach others the secrets of intercession.

Personally, I have experienced all three phases, as I discussed earlier. At first I prayed a certain amount of time each day as I saw needs arising, my schedule busy with my duties as a homemaker and teacher. Then the Lord led me to spend more time during the day interceding, particularly when I gave up my job as a schoolteacher. I felt pulled to prayer and found myself on my knees mostly in the middle of the night, early in the morning, or while my children took naps or were at school. The third phase of my life is as a prayer leader and minister (of course, I have not stopped being a homemaker). Not everyone, however, will be called to intercede full-time.

The workings of these different aspects of intercession remind us how the Church can be likened to an army. Each rank in an army is significant and necessary. Although there are more privates than generals, each in his own place is critical to winning the battle. The same can be said for the army of Christ. We all follow behind Jesus, the Captain of the host, the great Soldier of the cross. It is not important to look at our rank; it is important only to be in the place God has called us.

Every believer is called to be part of the army of intercessors. We all will pray and intercede. For some it will be a full-time job; for others it will be an important part of a day that is focused on giftings more dominant in their lives than intercession. It is vital that we find our place in the Body of Christ in these end times and fulfill our calling and election.

In order to understand the ministry of intercession, whether it is a calling or part of Body ministry, we need to understand the work of Jesus, the greatest intercessor.

Jesus said, "I must work the works of Him who sent Me" (John 9:4). Dick Eastman says of this passage: "It was the expression *I must* that caught my eye. Jesus did not say, 'I hope to,' or, 'I intend to try to.' Rather, He declared forcefully, '*I must*.'"[2]

Jesus clearly understood that there were things He *must* do. As Christians we must be "little Christs," or imitators of Christ. Over and over in the Scriptures we see that Christ went away all night to pray in a solitary place. In fact, His whole life was intercessory. If Christ felt that it was important to intercede while He was on earth, then how much more should we consider intercession a priority? We must learn to intercede to become like Christ. We *must* intercede!

It is important to make a distinction between prayer and intercession. Not all prayer is intercession. In fact, many people never truly intercede. They simply pray prayers of petition asking God to meet certain needs. True intercession is actually twofold. One aspect is asking God for divine intervention; the other is destroying the works of Satan. This is illustrated in our now-familiar passage, Ezekiel 22:30: "So I sought for a man among them who would make a wall, and stand in the gap before Me on behalf of the land, that I should not destroy it; but I found no one."

One aspect of this verse involves coming before God with a specific, divinely inspired request. The other, discovered in the words *stand in the gap before Me*, has the connotation of actually destroying the spiritual strategies the enemy has devised. Most of the Body of Christ, unfortunately, stays on the defensive while Satan has a field day with governments, the Church and our families.

Satan is a master strategist. Many people go around and talk about how stupid the devil is. I cringe when I hear this. One of the most important lessons to learn for the day of battle is not to underestimate our enemy. Satan has been at this for a long time and, believe me, he wants you to think that he is stupid. He also wants people to think that he does not exist or have any power. But we hearken to the words of Paul and stay alert "lest Satan should take advantage of us; for we are not ignorant of his devices" (2 Corinthians 2:11).

Now why would Paul talk about Satan's devices if he did not have any? Satan also has storm troops who are highly trained and serve their master through fear. Paul defined our enemy this way:

> We do not wrestle against flesh and blood, but against principalities, against powers, against the rulers of the darkness of this age, against spiritual hosts of wickedness in the heavenly places.
>
> Ephesians 6:12

The Greek form of wrestling was to the death. Our warfare is hand-to-hand combat at close quarters with an enemy that wants to destroy us.

Ephesians 6:11 says: "Put on the whole armor of God, that you may be able to stand against the wiles of the devil." The word *wiles* in the Greek, as it is used in this passage, means "methodology." In military terms we could say that his battle plan is to rule the earth.

An intercessor, then, is a mediator. Hebrews 7:25 states that "He [Christ] ever lives to make intercession for them." For whom? Those who come to God through Him. Jesus paid the price so that we can come boldly to the throne of grace to obtain mercy in the time of need.

We can sketch it out as something like this. Someone comes to God with a request aligned with His will. Jesus, sitting at the right hand of the Father, says, "Father, do it for him." Touched by the need, the Father and Son send the Holy Spirit to prompt one of the members of the Body to stand in the gap in prayer. Many times we will just start thinking of someone over and over and not know why. After a little while we start praying for that person. We may sense danger or feel great sorrow when we think about another person. This is the Holy Spirit's prompting within us. It is at this moment that we stand in the gap, and the heart of God is expressed in intercession. God then begins to move on behalf of the one for whom we have prayed; His Kingdom has come into that person's life, and His will is done.

To be effective intercessors we must be like watchmen on the wall.

> I have set watchmen on your walls, O Jerusalem; they shall never hold their peace day or night. You who make mention of the LORD, do not keep silent, and give Him no rest till He establishes and till He makes Jerusalem a praise in the earth.
>
> Isaiah 62:6–7

Jerusalem is a walled city, and you can still walk on top of these walls. Watchmen used to walk up and down them, peer into the night and guard against potential attacks of the enemy upon the city. In these verses, God is telling us today to look into the distance through prayer to see potential harm that may come to our cities, churches or families. God is establishing His people as watchmen to give Him no rest until the Kingdom of God is established throughout the world. Here are several things you can do to develop a watchman's eye:

1. Sign up for the army! Tell the Lord that you are willing to be a watchman.

2. Keep your heart pure so that you can properly discern areas for which God wants you to pray.

3. Develop a God-consciousness in your life. Be aware at every moment that you are on call. Being a watchman is very much like being a doctor who carries a beeper. At any given moment he or she may be called up for an emergency. No matter what you are doing, God may call you to change your plans, pray and sound the alarm to stop the enemy's attack.

4. Pray that God will teach you the proper time and place to sound the alarm. God reveals to intercessors the intimate needs of those for whom we intercede. This is a precious trust. The things God shares with us are not to be told to others. Many prayer groups are nothing more than spiritual gossip sessions. If God reveals another person's weaknesses to you, you need to:

   • Ask for confirmation first to see if you have heard the need accurately. You do not want to pray amiss.

   • If you are sure you are praying accurately, then you need to ask God whether or not to tell the person what you have learned.

   • If you are to tell the person, then pray that God will prepare his or her heart to be receptive.

   • Many times you will never say anything to the persons for whom you have prayed. God will speak to them in His time and way. This is the most effective means of dealing with weaknesses in those for whom we have prayed. When God tells them they need to change, it does not cause them to feel embarrassed, rejected or wounded.

   • There are times to sound the alarm to others in your prayer group when you see a danger about to occur in your local church body. If this is the case, go to someone in a spiritual leadership position and share your prayer concern. Leave any further sharing in his or her hands.

5. Do not be afraid to pray prayers that may seem unusual to you. You may be praying, for instance, and all of a sudden you start praying for a pastor in South America whom you do not even

know. Many watchmen have averted disasters that threaten people they have never met. A good example of the watchman anointing is found in Luke 22:31–32:

And the Lord said, "Simon, Simon! Indeed, Satan has asked for you, that he may sift you as wheat. But I have prayed for you, that your faith should not fail; and when you have returned to Me, strengthen your brethren."

Vinita Copeland, an intercessor, stood as a watchman for many of her "spiritual children." One day the Lord told her that one of them, Beth, was under attack and that Satan had desired to "sift her as wheat." Vinita told her husband, A. W., not to let her be disturbed and she went to her prayer closet to do battle for Beth. One day passed, then two. A. W. was getting concerned for Vinita's well-being and called up intercessors to pray for the intercessor until, on the third day, she broke through the power of the enemy coming against her spiritual daughter. Thank the Lord for an intercessor who was willing to make an extended sacrifice. Beth now has an international ministry birthed and bathed in prayer by Vinita.

Sometimes, as we have seen, God calls watchmen to prayer in the middle of the night. A prayer warrior in Fort Worth named Naomi "Dutch" DuPuis woke up suddenly one night with a burden to pray for an evangelist named Hayseed Stephens. Hayseed was in Indonesia, and his preaching was causing quite a stir in the heavenlies: The madam of the local brothel and all the "girls" of the house were saved, and the local drug dealer came into the Kingdom of God along with the head of the gambling ring.

One morning around 4 A.M. Dutch woke with a start and saw a vision of Hayseed. He was in danger of being killed by angry villagers. Later she told him that she knew more about what was happening to him than he did. This is not an unusual occurrence with those who have the gift of intercession.

Meanwhile, back in Indonesia (it was 4 P.M. there), Hayseed was just coming out of a house where he had prayed for one of the local church deacons. There waiting for him was a frightening sight—some six hundred men with rakes and hoes. They were Muslims, angry because people had been turning to Christianity. The villagers, certain he had brought ill fortune upon them, were eager to see him destroyed.

Hayseed described what happened next. "At first a wave of fear hit me, and I cried out to God for help." I believe that this "flare prayer" prompted the Holy Spirit to awaken his friend Dutch in Texas to jump into the gap with prayer for God to protect Hayseed and give him peace.

Hayseed further stated, "After I called out for help I felt as though a mantle of peace had come down upon me. I walked forward and started to softly sing about the name of Jesus." Wrapped in the mantle of peace, Hayseed was able to walk through the angry crowd; it parted like the Red Sea. This event reminded him of Luke 4:28–30:

> All those in the synagogue, when they heard these things, were filled with wrath, and rose up and thrust Him out of the city; and they led Him to the brow of the hill on which their city was built, that they might throw Him down over the cliff. Then passing through the midst of them, He went His way.

Would it not be wonderful to see what happens in the unseen realm when God protects so supernaturally?

We are in a prophetic time concerning intercession. In the decade of the '90s a great harvest was reaped. South America, Asia, Africa, and other regions saw many come to the Lord. However, in this season of the 21st century we are seeing nations shaking as never before. We need to give heed to a new, fresh wind of a spirit of prayer that is being poured out on the Body of Christ.

God is calling us to pray that the Lord of the harvest will send laborers into the fields of society such as businesses, universities and media. Many are being called to pray who normally are not burdened to intercede. God is calling up His reserve troops! The revival we have prayed for in our nations will come if we pray and don't faint.

The spirit of prayer that comes upon nations and people actually constitutes the birth pangs of revival. In an interesting paper written for Intercessors for America, Douglas Thorson writes of Jeremiah Lamphier. Lamphier is an example of what God can do with ordinary people who answer the call to pray for revival. This took place in New York City around 1857.

Lamphier walked the streets, passing out ads for a noon-day prayer meeting to be held at the Dutch Reformed Church on the corner of

Fulton Street in downtown Manhattan. For 25 minutes he waited there alone, his faith tried. Finally at 12:30 six men came in, one after another. The next week there were twenty. Before long they decided to meet daily instead of weekly.

Within six months more than ten thousand businessmen were meeting every day for prayer in stores and company buildings. With hardly an exception churches worked together as one with no thought of jealousy.[3]

I believe that it is essential to the life of the Church today to prepare for revival by learning about prayer and intercession. Who knows how many Lamphiers are in business offices and classrooms obedient to what God has them doing presently, until one day He calls them to be prayer leaders who will dramatically touch nations for revival?

Martyn Lloyd-Jones is quoted in that same excellent paper. He says:

> The history of revivals brings out very clearly that God often acts in a most unusual manner and produces revival and promotes it and keeps it going not necessarily through ministers but perhaps through people who may have regarded themselves as very humble and unimportant members of the Christian church.[4]

The call is being sent out to each one of us. The next chapter will help you determine if you have the gift of intercessory prayer. It is exciting to see what God can do with a willing vessel!

---

1. Dick Eastman, *Love On Its Knees* (Tarrytown, N.Y.: Chosen Books, 1989), 21.

2. Ibid., 47.

3. Douglas Thorson, "Prayer and Revival: The Role of Prayer and Reformation Societies in American History" (Intercessors for America, 1989), 12.

4. Ibid., 4.

6

The Gift of Intercession

Certain Christians, it seems to me, have a special ability to pray for extended periods of time on a regular basis and see frequent and specific answers to their prayers, to a degree much greater than that which is expected of the average Christian.[1]

C. Peter Wagner

The gift of intercession has been something of a controversial subject because the Bible does not actually speak directly about it. Neither does it speak, however, about ushers, ministers of music or those who run the sound systems; intercessors have a place in the church along with those people with a gifting of helps. The difference between intercessors and those who have the ministry of helps is that intercessors serve in a spiritual manner, in "heavenly places," so to speak.

There are *indirect* references in the Bible to the gift of intercession. Luke 2:37 indicates that Anna, a widow, served God in the Temple with fasting and prayer night and day. In fact, *with fasting and prayer night and day* is a good description of the life of one called to intercede (although it is possible to get out of balance in the area of fasting and prayer, which will be discussed later).

The story of Aaron and Hur lifting up Moses' hands (during which time Israel prevailed in the battle with the Amalekites) is a type of gift of intercession in operation:

> But Moses' hands became heavy; so they took a stone and put it under him, and he sat on it. And Aaron and Hur supported his hands, one on one side, and the other on the other side; and his hands were steady until the going down of the sun.
>
> Exodus 17:12

Note that Aaron and Hur were supportive in lifting up Moses' hands but did not take the rod he was holding. Also notice that they did not go down and fight in the battle physically as Joshua did. People who have the gift of intercession love to pray. They would rather not do anything else. When people ask me how long I pray in a day, I reply, "As much as possible!" Some days, because of my travel schedule, I may not be able to spend as many hours in prayer as on other days, but whenever I have a day just to be alone with the Lord, I unplug my phone and put a sign on my door, "Praying, do not disturb." Those days are pure bliss to me! I have found this to be so with others who have the gift of intercession.

Earlier I mentioned the prayer meeting "Ninety Hours of Prayer for the Nineties" that was held in Florida. One morning around two A.M. we experienced a wonderful time of prayer for the Church in Russia. One of the intercessors leaned over and said with delight, "Isn't this just paradise?" I had to agree. For those called to the place of prayer, it is the most precious place to be.

The prayer movement has grown since that time in a measure we only dreamed about in the '90s. In looking back, I can see the decade was a launching pad for prayer movements around the world. Books were written such as Dutch Sheet's *Intercessory Prayer*, Peter Wagner's *Prayer Warrior* series and John Dawson's *Taking Our Cities for God*. Today it is more the norm to have a church with a prayer leader than one without. When I first wrote this book, I could hardly find a church that did have a prayer group. However, the need for committed intercessors is greater today than ever!

Intercessors often live unusual lives—at times it seems they are even recluses. In the last chapter I described Vinita Copeland standing as a watchman for her spiritual daughter, Beth, and praying for three days straight, not eating and hardly sleeping until God gave her peace that the prayer had broken through. This is something that those with the gift of intercession will sometimes do. It is not an everyday occurrence, but it does happen.

Our example here is Daniel. He had set himself aside to seek the Lord through fasting and prayer:

> In those days I, Daniel, was mourning three full weeks. I ate no pleasant food, no meat or wine came into my mouth, nor did I anoint myself at all, till three whole weeks were fulfilled.
>
> Daniel 10:2–3

Daniel must have been a sight to behold by the end of three weeks, but he did not care. God had given him an assignment: to pray for understanding of a vision. His prayers started a great war in the heavenlies, but the angel God sent to him finally broke through.

> Then he [Gabriel] said to me, "Do not fear, Daniel, for from the first day that you set your heart to understand, and to humble yourself before your God, your words were heard; and I have come because of your words. But the prince of the kingdom of Persia withstood me twenty-one days; and behold, Michael, one of the chief princes, came to help me, for I had been left alone there with the kings of Persia. Now I have come to make you understand what will happen to your people in the latter days, for the vision refers to many days yet to come."
>
> Daniel 10:12–14

The Lord sent an angel to Daniel because of his prayers and commissioned him to make this man understand.

Usually those with the gift of intercession will be given a focus from God for their prayers. Some will pray for a certain ministry or minister. Each day they will function as a "prayer guard" for the one for whom God called them to be a watchman. For example, our ministry, Generals International, has intercessors who cover us on a regular basis. We will go over this in more detail in the chapter on personal prayer partners.

While many would love to spend their lives in prayer, not all intercessors can pray full-time. When they are not working, though, they will give hours of their free time in prayer. Most consider prayer their recreation time. Do not misunderstand me. Prayer is hard work and we need a break sometimes, but for many it is refreshing to spend time in intercession for others.

Thankfully, today there are ministries that realize that while prayer is free, those who intercede must still pay rent on their homes—and while intercessors love fasting, they occasionally need to buy food and fuel for their cars. More churches are paying salaries to their intercessors than ever before.

Those with the gift of intercession may or may not have one focus of prayer all of their lives. The little lady Bob Willhite heard praying in Glad Tidings Tabernacle was called to pray for one nation. Many intercessors are called to pray for all of the nations. One of these is Sister Freda Lindsay of Christ For The Nations Institute in Dallas, Texas. Christ For The Nations is a Bible school that, as of 2008, has graduated approximately 34,000 students—not counting those from their 45 associated Bible schools.

Freda Lindsay spoke for a Generals of Intercession meeting in September 1986. Mrs. Lindsay, or "Mom" as many of her students call her, is a petite woman but a powerhouse for God. It is quite an experience to hear her call out to God the nations of the world, one after the other, not stopping until she has brought every one of them before the throne of grace. This precious saint of the Lord shared with us that day about the prayer life of her husband, Gordon Lindsay. The Rev. Lindsay has now gone to be with the Lord, but the effect of his prayer life is still felt around the world. She said that Gordon had this to say about prayer: "Every man ought to pray at least one violent prayer every day."

"And I think," she added, "that he had the world's record for praying the most violent prayers!" She cited the guideline of Matthew 11:12: "And from the days of John the Baptist until now the kingdom of heaven suffers violence, and the violent take it by force."

Freda then told this story:

I'll never forget when we were living in Shreveport, Louisiana, and I advertised for some help in the local paper. A small black lady answered. We were in the kitchen and I was telling her what needed to be done when all of a sudden she asked, "What's that, what's that? That voice, that man!"

I replied, "That's my husband. The first thing he does every morning is pray, and it sounds like a bomb explosion."

She asked, "Was he in Shreveport three years ago at such-and-such hotel on such-and-such a day?"

I told her that he traveled so much I didn't remember, but would ask him when he came out.

When he came out, I did ask him. "Were you in Shreveport three years ago at such-and-such hotel?" Gordon had a computer mind that never forgot dates and places.

"Yes," he replied, "I was there teaching at such-and-such a meeting."

The lady began to exclaim, "I knew it, I knew it! I stood outside your door when you were praying because I had never heard anyone pray like you were!"[2]

Wouldn't it be great if people remembered us for our praying rather than a lot of other things we are remembered for? What a legacy Gordon Lindsay left behind him! I believe that those prayers, along with those of his wife, have established a birthplace of revival. Their prayers have led the way for thousands of students to come and study at Christ For The Nations to prepare for the mission field.

Gordon and Freda Lindsay believed God's Word recorded in Matthew 9:37–38: "Then He said to His disciples, 'The harvest truly is plentiful, but the laborers are few. Therefore pray the Lord of the harvest to send out laborers into His harvest.'"

Intercessors call this "praying the harvest." Prayer ripens the harvest. God plants His intercessors in every place to pray for the nations.

This story also shows that the methods used by those with the gift of intercession vary. It is important that we look at the fruit of the prayers rather than the formula. God has many intercessors who pray in different manners. Some pray quietly in a prayer closet; some sing; some get loud. It is important to pray in the way that God has shown you and not think that others need to pray just as you do.

Many who feel the call to intercession begin praying with a system or discipline of prayer such as Dick Eastman writes about in his book *The Hour That Changes the World*. Sometimes prayer is a discipline even with those called by God to intercede. There are those days when heaven seems like brass, and you wonder if that five A.M. prayer time is accomplishing anything.

Another group of intercessors is prophetic intercessors. I will discuss this in more detail later, but basically they get up early every morning and "check in" with the Lord to find out what their prayer assignment is for the day (unless they were up all night with the last prayer assignment!). The way they begin to pray may vary. Many worship the Lord and then spend time just being still and listening until a name comes, or a Scripture or situation that needs prayer. I usually pray this way each day myself. It does help to be flexible, though. Sometimes in my worship time I find myself starting to pray for Romania and then a couple of hours later I come back to worship.

Although I have things for which I pray daily, God sometimes preempts these requests for others that are on His heart. I have found that God's daily prayer alerts may or may not be the same as those on my prayer list. Being an intercessor requires quite a bit of discipline in the emotional realm, because often I would rather pray my own concerns than the ones God will give me. This is when I "seek first the Kingdom of God" instead of my personal burdens. One wonderful thing I have found is that over and over in these instances God has others praying for the needs of my family. Thus, those needs are met by my being obedient to God's prayer agenda.

If you have the gift of intercession, you will find that God reveals in many different ways what or whom to intercede for during the day. Sometimes I will see someone who reminds me of someone else and I realize that I am to pray for him or her. Other times I will see the name of someone I know, or a similar name, and stop to seek the Lord's direction as to how to pray for that person. Any time my thoughts turn to someone I have not seen for years, I pray for that person. I am convinced that God is alerting many people to pray in this manner, but they do not recognize the signals. If in a day I begin to think over and over about someone in my church, I have found that this is God's way of telling me to pray. And as I ask Him how to pray in these instances, He will bring to my mind particular portions of Scripture. This is why it is so important for intercessors to know the Scriptures—so that God, by the Holy Spirit, can draw from the well of living water within us for prayer purposes.

As you grow in the gift of intercession you learn to walk and talk with Jesus, staying alert constantly for God's message that someone has an important need. Some call this learning to abide in Christ. We have a divine link by the Holy Spirit to the heart of God; when we realize that we are always on call, then we will know God's heart in intercession.

I find as the years go by, and I have grown in my gift, that God will give me intercessory assignments bigger in scope than the ones I had when I first began to intercede. For instance, now the Lord might wake me up to stabilize the economy of a nation, or give me a prophetic prayer directive for a president I have met in person.

Another way that the Holy Spirit alerts us for prayer is through dreams. The Bible has much to say about dreams and the use of dreams. The Lord appeared to Jacob in a dream when he was fleeing from Esau. God used dreams to display His glory and elevate Joseph in Pharaoh's eyes, as we saw earlier. Examples abound in the New Testament as well. God used a dream to warn another Joseph to take Mary and the Christ child and flee from Herod. It is not unusual for intercessors to have what I call "spiritual dreams." Spiritual dreams are different from pizza dreams, which are brought on by eating too much too late! For one thing, they are usually very vivid and very real. They are the kind that cause you to think about them for a while. Sometimes you wonder if you were awake or asleep when they occurred, because they seem so real. These dreams are often etched in your memory, although it is good to write down the details immediately. Notice from the biblical accounts that people remembered the details of dreams and would recount them. Many times God will speak or warn in a dream in ways we would not consider while we are awake.

When we have a spiritual dream it may be clear or it may need to be interpreted. If it is a dream of a disaster, we need to realize that this is a warning and not fate. We need to pray to either lessen, avert or eliminate what God has on His heart for us to deal with.

This often happens in my own family. Mike is much more of a dreamer than I am. For years he has had a dream of tornadoes coming toward our house, which warns of impending satanic attacks. We have learned to pay careful attention to the people in these dreams and pray both for their protection and against Satan's devices.

One morning Mike woke up and said that he had dreamed of five tornadoes coming toward us at one time. We did some heavy-duty praying that day! Thanks to the Lord's warning, what came was handled easily.

One of our most vivid accounts of averting a disaster because of a spiritual dream occurred as I was in Phoenix for a speaking engagement. Before leaving my room to attend a day of meetings, I felt that I should call Mike. His voice sounded kind of funny, and I pressed him to tell me what was wrong. He paused and then said, "Cindy, last night I dreamt that I was driving on a freeway behind two pickup trucks. Both were occupied by young couples and one of the women was pregnant. All of a sudden the traffic stopped. I pushed on the brake, but nothing happened; it was as though I were in slow motion. In the next instant I ran into the back pickup truck, pushing it into the front truck. When we came to a halt I jumped out to see if they were all right. I had particular concern for the pregnant lady and ran over and prayed for her."

After Mike finished recounting his dream, we prayed together for the safety of those driving his route on the freeway and for his personal safety. We asked God to give him wisdom as he drove to work that day.

Needless to say, as soon as I got back to my room that night I called him to find out what had happened on the way to work and to make sure that he was all right. (The year before he had been hit by an eighteen-wheel truck. He came away without a scratch, but you can understand my concern.) Mike was excited as he related the story of his morning drive. "Cindy," he said, "God is so wonderful! As I drove to work I was very cautious. I made sure that I stayed way behind the other cars, and I especially looked out for pickup trucks. Then, when I was near work, a car in front of me suddenly collided with the car in front of him. If I had not kept my distance because of the dream, I would have been involved in the accident."

The vehicles involved were not pickup trucks, and there was no pregnant woman. It makes one wonder if God completely protected the others in the dream as He did Mike so that none of them were harmed.

It seems to me that God is pouring out more revelation in dreams for this generation than ever before. For instance, some prayer movements such as The Call often have been given direction through dreams.

One particular dream influenced the whole movement of The Call. One of their young leaders dreamed that they put red tape on their mouths with the word "Life" on it as they stood in front of the U.S. Supreme Court to pray for the overturning of legalized abortion. Lou Engle and the leadership of the Justice House of Prayer associated with The Call obeyed what the Lord showed them through the dream and put red tape on their mouths as they prayed hour after hour to end the killing of unborn babies. Since then, thousands have stood in front of the courts of America wearing the same sign, crying out to the Lord in silent intercession for a generation in the womb without a voice to speak for themselves.

When you have had what seems to be a spiritual dream, ask God whether or not it was from Him. This is how the leaders of The Call responded to their spiritual dream. What if they had passed off the dream without seeking God's direction? Once you know your dream was spiritual, ask Him what He wants you to pray concerning it. If you do not understand the dream, pray that God will bring someone to help you interpret it. Be careful, for Satan can and does send tormenting dreams that are nothing more than nightmares. These dreams produce fear, not the peaceable conviction that the Lord's warnings bring. You can certainly also pray for protection against what you have seen in any nightmare.

Also, some people who have spiritual dreams on a regular basis keep paper and pen by their bed to jot down the details they received before they can forget them. Dreaming is part of God's intercessory language.

God is calling those with the gift of intercession today to make a huge net for harvest. Intercessors are coming together to pray in unprecedented numbers. The Lord is bringing together His Ruths and Naomis, Esthers and Mordecais, Deborahs and Baraks to do end-time battling.

One of the most precious to me was Vinita Copeland, whom I have mentioned. One day one of her relatives looked down and said, "Vinita, what's the matter with your knees? They look like camel knees." She answered that she was praying for her son. At that time he was running from God as fast as he could go. The relative said, "Well, Vinita, can't you pray standing up?"

She continued to kneel in prayer, and by doing so this mighty woman stood in the gap for thousands of members of the Body of Christ throughout her life. She got up at four A.M. every morning to go down to her basement to pray. At the end of her life, when she entered the gates of heaven, her body was literally worn out from her years of intercessory prayer.

One day when I visited her home we went down to the basement where she prayed. I noticed a little pallet with a shoebox on it to one side. I asked her, "Nonnie [her nickname], what's that pallet over there?"

She answered, "Darlin', that's where I pray."

The presence of the Lord washed over me as I knelt down on the pallet and picked up the shoebox overflowing with pictures. "Nonnie," I asked, "what are these?"

"Those are my prayer pictures."

"Who are they?"

"I don't know most of them," she said. "People send me pictures of their loved ones to pray over." She went on to explain that she would pray over them until God said, *It's done.* And then she would stop. There were tearstains on those pictures of people she did not even know. One thing I can tell you for certain, she will know them in heaven. I guarantee that if she prayed and stormed hell's gates for them, then Satan's schemes did not prevail in their lives.

The gift of intercession is a part of the Body of Christ that, although hidden, is mighty and produces great things for God. Some days when I am going through a particularly hard struggle, I will cry out to God, "God, raise up the intercessors!" Sometimes when I ask this I will take note of the time because later on someone will telephone and ask, "What happened to you at such-and-such a time?" I am thankful for the intercessors who are close to me who call me regularly whenever it seems as if all of hell's hordes have been assigned to me personally. My phone will ring and they will say, "Cindy, what's going on? I was praying for you a moment ago against discouragement."

What an encouragement to see how God is giving the gift of intercession to a people willing to receive it! May we all prove faithful with that precious trust.

---

1. C. Peter Wagner, *Your Spiritual Gifts Can Help Your Church Grow* (Ventura, Calif.: Regal Books, 1979), 74.

2. Taken from tape of Generals of Intercession meeting, Freda Lindsay lecture held at Christ For The Nations Institute, September 17, 1986.

7

Prayer Leaders

While many will be called to stay in the prayer closet and minister with the gift of intercession, some will find that the closet was their training ground and will move out to become prayer leaders.

Prayer leaders are those with what is called a gift-mix. The gift of intercession becomes coupled with a full-time ministry gift such as those in Ephesians 4:11—apostles, prophets, evangelists, pastors and teachers. According to Ephesians 4:12–13, these gifts are given

> for the equipping of the saints for the work of ministry, for the edifying of the body of Christ, till we all come to the unity of the faith and of the knowledge of the Son of God, to a perfect man, to the measure of the stature of the fullness of Christ.

Thus, prayer leaders are those who equip the saints regarding prayer and intercession. The focus of ministry will depend on the particular ministry gift that couples with the gift of intercession. Although a variety of intercessory ministries operate today, I will target a few that are clear-cut in their gift-mixes. Most of these leaders start out praying in a local church. Some stay there; others travel; and still others found organizations centered on prayer and intercession.

The danger of sharing about different gift-mixes and types of prayer leaders is that people might try to model themselves after certain ministries or become like a person they admire rather than seek God for their particular gift. It is good to have role models, of course, but we must be sure the call and gifting are from God.

Before I isolate examples of different prayer leaders, I would like to mention a few points that will help those with focused ministries survive the wear and tear that come with leading intercession.

A prayer leader must ask God what his or her particular sphere of responsibility will be. This is critical because prayer leaders are literally inundated with requests for prayer. The longer the leader functions as such, the more the word gets around that God has called that person to intercede; before long he or she is flooded with needs.

It is a rare day that I don't receive lists of prayer needs from individuals and organizations. If the prayer leader is not careful, this can become quite a burden and lead to frustration. Many intercessors experience burnout because they have not learned to ask God what to spend time on in prayer.

One of the greatest lessons in this realm came from a mighty prayer warrior who has now gone to be with the Lord. One day Mike and I visited her home. To tell you the truth, we had heard such outstanding reports of God's using her to pray that we were a little awed. Have you ever met someone whom you held in such high esteem that you really didn't want to say something utterly stupid in front of him or her? It wasn't that we idolized this woman, but we certainly respected her opinion highly. We were hungry to draw from her wisdom.

The time flew by, and we were given much good teaching on the subject of intercession. As we were walking out the door I hugged her and said, "I will be praying for you." With wisdom that comes from years of walking with God she looked at me and said, "Cindy, has God required you to pray for me?" To tell you the truth, I was a little taken aback. The offer had come from my heart, but had God indeed given me that direction? I was not sure.

As I went away from her home, I began to search and pray and ask the Lord what He wanted me to do concerning praying for her. Finally the answer came. I was to pray as the Holy Spirit brought her to mind, but she was not one for whom God required me to intercede on a daily basis. I thank the Lord for her great wisdom. This lesson has stood me in good stead as more and more needs press in on me as a prayer leader.

It is easy to find biblical substantiation for spheres of authority—particularly in the realm of territories. God called Adam to tend a Garden. God did not say to him, "Adam, I have created many lands and continents and you are to travel over all of them and see that they are taken care of." He called Adam to a specific task.

Abraham is another good example of God's giving one area of responsibility to an individual. We find in Genesis 12:1. "Now the LORD had said to Abram: 'Get out of your country, from your kindred and from your father's house, to a land that I will show you.'"

When God called the children of Israel to go in and possess the Promised Land, each was given an assignment as to what territory he was to take dominion over.

There are also New Testament patterns of specific assignments. Jesus instructed the disciples in Acts 1:8: "But you shall receive power when the Holy Spirit has come upon you; and you shall be witnesses to Me in Jerusalem, and in all Judea and Samaria, and to the end of the earth." These instructions were precise—first, Jerusalem; second, Judea and Samaria; and after that the end of the earth. This means that the prayer leader begins at home—his or her Jerusalem.

Many want to skip this part. This happens for a number of reasons, but mostly because this is where God works out the kinks in our armor. This is well said in Matthew 13:57: "They were offended at Him. But Jesus said to them, 'A prophet is not without honor except in his own country and in his own house.'"

God wants us to learn how to submit to leadership, to put our flesh under control, to be a servant. The best place for that to occur is in our Jerusalem, because it is there all our mistakes and slips are remembered as we grow in the Lord. Look at it this way: The sooner in the fiery furnace, the sooner out. As we allow God to polish us and our armor, we will grow to become vessels of honor in the house of the Lord. We will look back and see this as a time of great learning and blessing.

Years ago, in the midst of my fiery Jerusalem experience, a wise woman of God looked at me and said, "Cindy, you will bless God for this time in your life." I wish I could say that I had an appreciative response to her comment, but from my wicked heart came the thought, *You have got to be kidding!* But you know, she was right!

Local Prayer Leaders

For some, Jerusalem will be not only their training ground but also the place where God calls them to stay. Their gift-mix is pastor-intercessor. Although they may not be recognized as a pastor or have the title of pastor, they desire to tend the sheep in prayer. Nothing makes them happier than to see a little lamb grow and become a mighty prayer warrior. Many nights are spent in travail over the prayer group God has given them to watch over.

These prayer-pastors will find that much of their daily intercession centers around the particular church with which they have an affiliation. They are often found exhorting the people of the church to spend more time in prayer.

The intercessory groups they lead are the heartbeats of prayer for the local gathering of the Body of Christ. The need for such groups cannot be expressed enough.

The focus of the prayer meetings directed by prayer-pastors will be for the physical needs of the church membership, financial needs, the pastor and staff, direction for the church and ongoing local vision. There may also be prayer for the nations of the world, but that will not be the primary focus. Local prayer leaders may or may not do much teaching. Many teach as they pray, stopping to instruct as they go along.

As I look back at what I wrote about the '90s in regards to intercession, it is encouraging to realize that what I foresaw has happened and more! The Lord is making His Church a "house of prayer for all nations." We are seeing a fruition of the Isaiah 56:7 passage before our eyes. In that decade many churches did, indeed, realize the importance of local intercession and put people with the gift of intercession on church staffs.

In addition to putting pastors of prayer on the staff, churches are also building prayer rooms once again where their people can be alone with God. We have even seen a number of churches institute 24/7 prayer right onsite. However, there are still many churches that have rooms set aside for church dinners, recreation and the like, but do not currently have a place for prayer—the backbone of the Kingdom of God.

Many churches and ministries still have no staff to handle prayer needs. It is usually lumped in with counseling. I would encourage pastors to appoint someone in charge of prayer, if they cannot pay a full-time person at this time, just as they would a person as the head of the ushers.

Years ago when Mike and I planned the first gathering for Generals of Intercession, we called a number of ministries and asked for the person in charge of prayer. We were distressed to find that few even knew where to direct our call. We found that many of the representatives who came were not directly in charge of prayer, but were greatly burdened for God to move through intercession.

I also encourage ministries to include prayer in their budget as they plan for the year's expenses. Paying all the bills by faith requires belief, and what a ministry considers important is what is included in the projected spending. At our ministry, of course, prayer takes up a large portion of our budget as we lead the Global Reformation Prayer Network.

24/7 Prayer Rooms

One wonderful aspect of prayer that has risen up across the face of the earth is 24-hour prayer. The theme of many of these prayer rooms comes from Leviticus 6:13. "A perpetual fire shall burn on the altar; it shall never go out."

The Lord has many current prayer movements studying the Moravians and their 100 year, 24/7 prayer meetings. These meetings sparked a whole missionary movement. Among the leaders of these different movements are Pete Greig with his powerful book *Red Moon Rising*, as well as James Goll with his calling to establish Prayer Storms. Brian Kim, who is working with Lou Engle of The Call in Kansas City, Missouri, is raising up prayer on university campuses around the world. Bill Johnson's young leaders out of Redding are not only encouraging intercessory prayer, but are marrying the miraculous with the move—as are others. Many of these groups are loosely affiliated with each other. Jonathan and Sharon Ngai have 24/7 prayer at the Reformation Prayer House, located at the same site that the Azusa Street revival broke out.

Most of these spiritual movements, I am excited to say, are being spearheaded by youth movements like the ones being established by Jaeson Ma, with passion to see the fire of God spread across the face of the earth and nations changed for the Kingdom of God.

In the midst of all this prayer, we stand at a spiritual precipice where the destinies of nations hang in the balance. It seems as if many nations are in a state that Pete Greig and Dave Roberts describe in *Red Moon Rising* as "spiritual anarchy." In fact, I have spoken recently of how I see the United States as being at a turning point: We will either go on to become the "city set on a hill" of which our forefathers dreamed or go downhill and loose our greatness.

Of course, we in the prayer movement are not willing to accept the latter as an option, and we have great hope from looking back at the history of our nation. For instance, J. Edwin Orr described the American situation in the 1780s in which Chief Justice John Marshall wrote to the bishop of Virginia, James Madison, that the Church "was too far gone ever to be redeemed." The great philosopher Voltaire averred and author Tom Paine echoed, "Christianity will be forgotten in thirty years."[1]

Greig and Roberts go on to say that in a poll taken at Harvard not one believer could be found—and at Princeton only two believers were in the student body, and only five did not belong to the filthy speech movement of the day.[2]

Many people prayed in that day, and as a result revival movements began to sweep the land in such places as Kentucky.

The role of the prayer leader is critical to revival and to the changing of a nation. Perhaps you are reading this and feel strongly moved by God to give your life to prayer, like Rees Howells. Without prayer nations crumble, but with fervent intercession God awakens them to greatness.

Traveling Prayer Leaders

While those pray-ers with a pastoral gifting remain in their local battle-fields, those with other giftings move out into traveling ministries. Many of these are evangelist-intercessors, and their prayer focus is winning the lost. A prime example of this gift-mix is Dick Eastman of Every Home for Christ. Dick's first calling or first love was that of an intercessor; he then led youth prayer teams and established a round-the-clock house of prayer. Next he established Change the World Ministries, with the goal of winning the lost in every home in the world through Gospel literature.

Traveling prayer leaders are usually part of a local church. They may have an office in the church and be sent out as an extension of the local church body. Or they may minister full-time and consider the local church as the spiritual covering under which God has placed them. Both types give validity to the ministry, and the home church helps further by standing in the gap for their family members and financial needs.

Standing under the headship of a church also gives important protection to the intercessors in the area of accountability. A church body can watch to see that the traveling prayer leaders do not fall into gray areas in ministry. Gray areas are those that are not biblical or have little biblical substantiation. This is crucial for intercessors because of the very nature of our ministry. In intercession we listen for the voice of God through the Holy Spirit for prayer direction. Along with God's voice, many other voices speak to us, and some will try to deceive us. An intercessor once described it like this: "When we listen to the Spirit of God in prayer it is very much like turning on the television. There are many channels on that TV, but not all the channels come from the Holy Spirit. Simply because we have tuned into a channel and hear a voice does not mean that it is the voice of God. All of us need spiritual counsel to provide insight and to have the direction of God in our life judged." The local church is the place to submit a new vision.

Some larger prayer ministries have a board of directors who help keep the ministry centered on God's plumbline, but intercessors need to stay tied in to a local church as well. God has been faithful to provide Mike and me with our local pastors as well as a dedicated group of leaders in Generals International.

Another possible intercessory gift-mix is that of a prophet-intercessor. Those with a prophetic gifting have great insight into the discernment of spiritual strongholds over areas, and their spiritual assignment can be likened to S.W.A.T. teams. Doris Wagner calls these God's Spiritual Weapons And Tactics teams.

God will quicken these prophetic intercessors to pray for and often go to "hot spots." They tear down spiritual strongholds and fight principalities and powers over nations. They make breaches in the enemy's defenses so that God can move in and bring revival or send in missionaries. Just as in modern-day military strategy, they go in first to prepare the way for the Lord's purposes in an area. This will be discussed further in the chapter on prophetic intercession.

Those with the gift-mix of teacher-intercessor may become internationally known Bible teachers. They might teach on many subjects, but the primary thrust in their lives will be prayer and intercession.

A gift-mix that we have seen come to the forefront more and more since the early 1990s is that of apostle-intercessor. We have established a network of prayer coordinators by state here in the U.S., and have others partnering with us around the world through the Global Reformation Prayer Network.[3]

Seasons of Ministry

How do you know when or if you are to change from a local ministry to a traveling ministry? Start by realizing that the seasons of ministry can and do change. It is easy to get locked into a particular vision and not realize that God wants a new season to come into your life.

When God moves to change the season of ministry in which you are engaged, several things begin to happen. It begins with a transition period. Indicators that you are going through a transition can be varied, but generally your burden to pray for your present situation is not the same as it used to be. You almost have to force yourself to remember to pray for your current ministry focus. Oftentimes a restlessness comes with the transition time.

A word of caution is needed here. It may be that you experience these things not because God wants you to make a change, but because you have been wounded and no longer have the same heart to pray. You need to find the motive behind your lack of prayer for the current situation.

A sense of estrangement might come over you if you have been hurt, and it can seem very much like a release from God.

It is during the transition period that most people make mistakes in ministry direction. They sense that a change is coming and are vulnerable to accepting a counterfeit. Usually, right before God brings His best, the enemy throws out a proposition that looks incredibly good. This is another reason it is so important for prayer leaders to surround themselves with pastors and intercessors who will pray for them.

Remember, your heavenly Father is well able to make it abundantly clear that you are to make a change. Do not move until He gives you peace in a new direction.

This transition period often takes from one to two years. I experienced this after I had served an organization as director of intercession for seven years. I began to feel that a change was coming in my life. At the time there was no particular reason to make a change. Still, I took note when people began to come to me to say that they felt I would be resigning from the organization, that God had other things for me to do.

After a while I realized that God was indeed making a directional change in my life. I went to the board members and shared my thoughts. Most of them agreed that change was coming; one did not agree at all. Looking for unanimity, I went back to prayer and asked God to help me see if I was trying to leave because my heart was not right. In answer to my prayer the Lord showed me that I did have something in my heart against a board member. I went to the member and settled the offense.

For a time I felt that God had been trying to show me my wrong heart and that I was not to leave the organization after all. I loved the organization and the people on the board. They were like family to me, and we had worked hard together to raise up an international ministry. Another six months went by, during which I became convinced I was to leave. I brought it up several times, but the board was still not in agreement. Then the Lord showed me and the board the person who was to replace me. The day she joined the board was the day I resigned, with all in agreement.

The next week I received a call from another international organization asking me to join them. I rejoiced in the knowledge that because I had waited for God's time to leave, He had opened the door to the new direction in my life.

If Satan can't get a prayer leader to leave too soon, he will probably try to convince him or her that God doesn't want a change at all. Sometimes God will pour out new visions on intercessors and they will say, "No, God has called me to do what I am doing." This may very well be the case, but you need to be open to change.

Consider the story of Abraham and Isaac. God asked Abraham to sacrifice his son. Then God said to spare his son and sacrifice instead the ram in the thicket. The searching question is, what if Abraham had not heard the second word from God? Many people have dead visions because they cling to a vision that God wants to change.

One other safeguard in making transitions is to be sure you hear the voice of God and not the voice of another person. People who tell you to go here or there may be anointed, but they may not know their own hearts. In making decisions it is important not to let human emotions get involved with the decision-making process. Obey God and not man.

Traveling prayer leaders often experience great change in their lives and ministries and need to be especially sensitive to the Lord when He wants to change them. The Lord may just as well switch them from a traveling ministry to a local pastoral role.

I believe that in the coming days we are going to see new organizations rise up and enter spiritual warfare to make way for great moves of God in nations. God already has "generals" in many places who are sensitive to Him and who are praying the path clear for the other ministers of the Gospel, such as evangelists, to come in to reap the harvest.

I have a word of caution for those in traveling ministries: Be careful to stay connected to a local church. There is a reason for my mention earlier in this chapter of being under accountability. A pattern I have seen in traveling ministries in general is that they are not submitted to any leadership anywhere on a local level. Then when they face trouble or get into some kind of sin, there is no one close enough to help them, or anyone they can trust to intervene for them. If you call my pastors, they will tell you that I value my local church and am there almost every Sunday when I am home—whether I am tired or not.

While I am on this subject, it is also critical for those in traveling ministries to have a working board of directors who watch over not only the soul, but financial accountability. The Generals International board of directors sets our salary and we give audited reports to them each year—at our expense, I might add! And it is worth it. As leaders, we cannot be unethical and expect God to hear our prayers.

While this is all true, prayer leaders need to be open to change and transition as God directs. Their gift-mixes put them in a unique position to lift the needs of the world in prayer. They will be most effective in that calling by being in the places the Lord wants them to be.

---

1. Pete Greig and Dave Roberts, *Red Moon Rising* (Orlando, Fla.: Relevant Media Group, 2005), 9.

2. Ibid.

3. The United States branch is called the U.S. Reformation Prayer Network.

8

The Language of Intercession

Sunday morning—what an exciting time for a new believer! Susan is thrilled with all that God is doing in her life and with the new things she is learning daily. After taking her seat she scans the weekly announcements and stops at the line that says, "Ladies' Intercession Group Tuesday Morning! Please come and join in a time of prayer for your family, the church and our city."

Susan feels a stirring in her heart. Could she pray for others' needs? She puts the announcement in her purse, eager for Tuesday to arrive.

Tuesday morning she arrives at church, takes her son to the nursery and slips into the room where the prayer meeting is being held.

The prayer leader calls the group to order and Susan waits eagerly for instructions. She is ready to learn. But then she listens in confusion to something like this: "Pastor Todd wrote me a note this morning about a serious stronghold coming against the finances of the church. This financial yoke has been strangling the church all summer, and we need to bind the enemy's control of the funds we need to pay our bills. Let's pray the prayer of agreement, loose the will of God and intercede until we have prayed this through and the power of the enemy is broken."

By the time the leader begins to pray Susan is in a panic. *What makes me think that I can be an intercessor?* she mulls. *I don't even understand half of what she was saying.*

This scenario is not uncommon in churches today. Eventually, if Susan doesn't give up, she will begin to break the "language code" of intercession and start to grasp what phrases like *the prayer of agreement* and *binding and loosing* mean. Sadly, in many instances, these words become no more than a prayer chant because they are understood only vaguely. Many prayer groups lack real authority because they do not have proper teaching on the biblical meaning of the words they use in prayer. When prayer becomes jargon, misunderstanding, misinterpretation and confusion are the results.

As 1 Corinthians 1:10 implores us:

> Now I plead with you, brethren, by the name of our Lord Jesus Christ, that you all speak the same thing, and that there be no divisions among you, but that you be perfectly joined together in the same mind and in the same judgment.

This chapter is written, then, to give clear definition to terms of belief so intercessors can speak the same language and pray with greater understanding and authority.

The Prayer of Agreement

> "Again I say to you that if two of you agree on earth concerning anything that they ask, it will be done for them by My Father in heaven."
>
> Matthew 18:19

The eyes of the world were fixed on the Berlin Wall. Unbelievable events were occurring, and media people everywhere were expressing their surprise as history was being made in Germany. It seems that this tearing down of the Berlin Wall was a "not-to-be-predicted event." To one group of people, however, the demise of the Berlin Wall was not only prophesied but also expected. God's intercessors all over the globe had prayed in agreement for this. I suspect that most of the prayer warriors had no idea that anyone else had been given the amazing assignment to pray that God would tear down this political wall. They just prayed what the Lord gave them to pray.

Years ago, some of the top prayer leaders in the world came to a meeting of the Spiritual Warfare Network in Pasadena, California. The topic of the Berlin Wall came up in the circle of thirty people that I was a part of, and it was interesting to hear the stories many of those pray-ers related concerning its destruction.

Dick Eastman shared, for instance, that he had prayed at the wall one bitterly cold day, laying his hands on it and praying that it would come down. He said that he didn't think it would fall down immediately, like the wall of Jericho, but that eventually it would indeed crumble. Another prayer leader, Sister Gwen Shaw of the End-Time Handmaidens, had been in Berlin with a group of intercessors two years before the wall fell. She, too, stood and prayed that the wall would fall. More than a year before it came down, I prayed for a missionary our home church was sending to East Germany. I was surprised to hear these words come out of my mouth: "And I will cut asunder the gates of brass and the bars of iron, and the wall will literally be disassembled piece by piece and brick by brick, and I will let my people go." I knew that others must have been receiving a similar revelation, but I was not aware of who they were at the time. When I spoke this prophetic declaration about the taking down of the "iron curtain," I did not understand legislating in the heavens as I do now, and I have dedicated a whole section to it later in the book.

Another report that came to me, independent of that meeting, was that students at Christ For The Nations in Germany had prayed consistently for the wall to open up and for the Gospel to go in. Those students have special faith to believe in such miracles: The building purchased to house their Bible school was built to train some of Hitler's top S.S. troops! This makes me wonder who was there praying during the time of Hitler that the building would one day be used for the glory of God.

All this is an example of praying in agreement. In this instance the Lord had His children all over the world pray for His will to be done concerning the nation of Germany. This is not at all uncommon. In fact, I believe that every time history is made that moves circumstances toward the will of God, intercessors have been there first. This is true on a smaller scale as well, whenever two or three intercessors agree together. An interesting concept is found in Amos 3:7: "Surely the Lord GOD does nothing, unless He reveals His secret to His servants the prophets."

When we read of the prayer of agreement bringing such change to nations and people, a number of questions may arise.

First of all: *What does agreement prayer mean and to what can it be likened?*

The prayer of agreement is one of the most powerful weapons that can be used in prayer. The word *agreement* in the Greek means "to be harmonious or to symphonize." We can understand this using the illustration of a symphony. When a symphony plays, many instruments perform, each adding its own quality to the blend heard by the composer. In a similar manner, Scripture tells us, God uses many types of prayers and people to orchestrate His divine melody of prayer. God does not place the responsibility or authority for His will to be done on earth on only one believer. This also shows how important it is to take our place in prayer. We can help shoulder a burden that may be too much for someone else to bear alone.

Agreement can also be likened to filling a bottle with water. One person may pour in 20 percent, another 30 percent, still another 10 percent, and the last person 40 percent until the bottle is full. When the bottle is filled to the brim or is overflowing, then agreement is complete and the task is finished. This is an important principle to know because some feel that their prayers are so small they do not amount to very much. The truth is that those little prayers may make up the one percent that is needed for the bottle to be full.

Another important point to remember in filling the bottle is that you never know how many others are also praying. We each need, therefore, to pray as fervently as we are able.

Some people might use the fact that many others are praying as an excuse not to be fervent in their prayers. Remember that in God's symphony each instrument is an integral part of the whole. I like what I heard one pastor share with his congregation: "I want you to pray as if you were the only one praying and as if the answer to the prayer depended upon your faithfulness." If you don't pray when it's your time to intercede, God will move upon someone else to fill the gap, but it may delay His purposes and timing.

It is interesting that when intercessors get together, they often find that God has had them concentrate on prayer in the same areas.

Another question about the prayer of agreement is: *Why do I feel such a great urgency when others are also praying?*

Sometimes it is because you are praying a prayer that will fill the bottle up with the last bit of water—a prayer God is using to break the final resistance to His will being done. This is often accomplished through a travailing prayer (which I will describe in the next chapter), or perhaps through supplication. The person involved in the last part of the process may have an anointing as he or she prays to stop or avert a disaster. Sometimes in this instance God makes the crisis known to the person praying. An example of this is Nehemiah's prayer for the children of Israel in Nehemiah 1.

Another important question concerning the power of agreement is: *How many people does it take to pray until a certain need is met?*

Several factors determine the number that God will call to pray:

1. What kind of stronghold are you dealing with? (See the explanation of *stronghold* later in this chapter.) Is the situation concerning an individual or power coming against a group of people? The stronger the resistance or higher the territorial power, the more people will be required to break the stronghold.

2. What level of authority does the person praying have in the Spirit? This is not to say that every prayer counts or does not count, or that one is more important than the other, but we have seen veteran prayer warriors, those who have experienced God's moving many times in answer to prayer, have a quick breakthrough when they stand in the gap for certain situations. This is because they believe wholeheartedly that God will move as they pray according to His will. There is an authority that comes with such prayer, and the enemies of God know they are in trouble when this authority rings out in a prayer meeting. For instance, when the apostolic council for the Reformation Prayer Network convenes and begins to pray for certain "stuck" situations in our nation to "shift" or change, it happens very quickly. Why? We have moved in faith in prayer, both separately and corporately, for many years.

One other critical component to the number of pray-ers that it takes for God's will to be done is that of fasting coupled with prayer. Fasting multiplies the effect of prayer at least several times. This is why we often ask for fasting chains along with prayer requests for serious issues. Fasting will touch things that prayer alone will not affect.

A final question is: *How do I actually go about agreeing in prayer with someone else who comes to me with a need?*

When asking someone to pray the prayer of agreement with you, you need to consider these points:

1. How are you to pray concerning a need? You may be praying, for instance, for a sick relative and believing God for a miracle. The person with whom you are praying, however, may be asking the Lord only to comfort that person. I usually ask people who call me with a request, "How has the Lord led you to pray in this situation?" I may or may not be able to agree with the way they are praying.

2. If I don't agree with the way they are praying, rather than tell them so, I will sometimes mention the way that I do feel led to pray. If they agree with that approach I pray with them right away. That way I don't have to remember it later, or feel overburdened with needs.

3. Has God given you Scripture concerning this need? Are you in unity with the other person about it?

4. If you are in agreement, you might pray a prayer something like this:

   Father, I agree with what my friend has asked You for this day. I thank You that Your Word declares "that if two of you agree on earth concerning anything that they ask, it will be done for them by My Father in heaven." Now, Father, according to Your Word, I thank You for answered prayer. Your Word says that "faith is the substance of things hoped for, the evidence of things not seen." So I am praying with faith asking You to do this thing now. In the name of Jesus, Amen.

Praying Through

Praying through is persistence in prayer until we have the assurance from God that His will has been accomplished in the earth realm.

One of the most often-asked questions by those just beginning to intercede is, *How do I know when I have prayed enough?* There are several ways to know when the prayer is answered:

1. When we no longer are reminded repeatedly by the Holy Spirit to pray. God will continue to prompt us through thinking about the person or situation until His will is accomplished.
2. When we try to pray about a certain matter and there is absolutely no desire to pray. The best way I can describe this is that there is no unction given by the Holy Spirit for more prayer on the matter. We may or may not see the answer happen in the natural, but as far as God is concerned it is a finished matter.
3. When God begins to lead us to Scriptures that tell us victory is won.
4. When God speaks to us through circumstances, letting us know that the matter is finished or taken care of in the natural—for instance, the person is healed or restored.

A good illustration of how a concern was prayed through and how God let me know without a shadow of a doubt that it was finished in the heavenlies came to me as I was driving one day. For some time I had been greatly concerned, along with many others, about the necessity for prayer and Bible clubs to be allowed back into our public school systems. We felt a great urgency about this because of the tremendous decline shown in the morals of the schoolchildren themselves and prayed to the Lord to change the situation through legislation. It was interesting how God let me know that it was accomplished, because when the assurance came I was not even thinking about prayer in schools; rather, I was seeking God's direction about my traveling as a minister.

While I drove the presence of the Lord filled the car. Have you ever noticed that during your quiet times God often chooses to answer previous prayers rather than those you think need an answer most urgently? His ways are mysterious but never boring! All of a sudden I saw a picture of lawyer Jay Sekulow standing before the Supreme Court in Washington D.C. Now this was not particularly outstanding because I knew he had brought a Jews for Jesus case before the court previously and had won. But I did not know Jay personally and had no reason to think of him. In the vision I heard him arguing the case for prayer to be allowed back into schools and for the students to be allowed to pray. The force of the vision filled me with such joy and awe that I started to weep. I wept so hard that I thought I would have to pull off the road because I could barely see.

Later on in the day I called David Barton. I told him the good news. I was as excited as if I had read the account in the newspaper. To me God had already answered, and it was done in the heavenlies. There was still a lot to be done to win the case in the natural, of course, but God had answered and given His will in the matter. The interesting part about my calling David to share the news was that he later wrote the Friend of the Court brief that helped the school prayer case to be won!

My family was on vacation in June 1990 when I picked up the newspaper and read about Jay's winning the case that allowed Bible clubs back into schools. What was won in the heavenlies became an accomplished fact in the Supreme Court of the United States of America. Today there are numbers of prayer groups and Bible clubs on campuses across the country. We still have a long way to go and are still embattled regarding prayer at public school meetings; it is only a matter of time until we win that battle as well.

I have a caution to insert here: Many people stop praying when they see a partial answer to their prayer or a breakthrough. What happens next is that, in essence, we have "swept the house clean," and then the enemy comes back into the empty house and fills it with seven worse situations or strongholds. Don't run on to the next thing in intercession without making sure you have finished your last assignment—or do both, praying for the new thing and praying through your previous assignment until you see the answer is completely secured.

Breaking a Yoke

> By your sword you shall live, and you shall serve your brother; and it shall come to pass, when you become restless, that you shall break his yoke from your neck.
>
> Genesis 27:40

Yokes are spiritual oppressions and heavy loads that Satan puts on people in order to hold them in bondage. It is not uncommon to hear the term *breaking a yoke* used during most intercessory meetings. In order to get a clear picture of the meaning, you need to know the nature of yokes in biblical times. They were usually double yokes, made for a team of two oxen. A strong or lead ox would take the larger side and the younger, weaker ox the opposite side. Thus, as they worked, the weaker ox had to plow or track with the stronger ox. This is one reason Matthew 11:29–30 is so beautiful for us as believers: "Take My yoke upon you and learn from Me, for I am gentle and lowly in heart, and you will find rest for your souls. For My yoke is easy and My burden is light."

When we are in the yoke with Christ, the burden is light because He is pulling the weight and making the way as the stronger one. Satan has counterfeited this principle by putting heavy yokes on people to oppress them and bring them into bondage to sin, law, occultic oppression and wrong relationships.

Samson is a good example of one who had the yoke of Satan upon his neck. He was a mighty man but became bound by his affair with the woman Delilah. This yoke brought great spiritual blindness to Samson, and he could not free himself from her embrace. This happens today to modern-day pastors and leaders. The Bible is clear that we are not to be yoked to unbelievers: "Do not be unequally yoked together with unbelievers. For what fellowship has righteousness with lawlessness? And what communion has light with darkness?" (2 Corinthians 6:14).

How do we pray for those who have been enslaved by Satan's yokes? There are several effective weapons:

1. Fasting. Isaiah 58:6 says: "Is this not the fast that I have chosen: to loose the bonds of wickedness, to undo the heavy burdens, to let the oppressed go free, and that you break every yoke?" I usually suggest a 21-day fasting chain for leaders involved in known sin. Different people sign up to fast through different days or meals until the whole time is covered in fasting. Each person needs to understand exactly why he or she is fasting in order to have proper agreement.
2. Binding and loosing. Pray a binding prayer against the power of sin, legalism, occultic practices and so on in a person's life. Forbid Satan from holding him or her in his grasp.
3. Commanding Satan to stop blinding his or her eyes to the glorious light of the Gospel (see 2 Corinthians 4:4).

4. If a relationship with fornication or adultery exists, praying that the tie be broken. Pray a loosing prayer wherein you command the people involved to be loosed from the wrong relationship. An interesting passage, Ezekiel 13:18–23, describes the women who hunt for men's souls through witchcraft. This still happens today; and if that is the case and the people are thoroughly deceived like Samson, fasting and prayer will be needed to break the yoke from their necks.

5. Praising. Praise releases captives from their captivity, as Psalm 149 relates; it binds the king with chains and his nobles with fetters of iron. We will learn more about this at length in a later chapter.

6. Receiving the anointing. One of the most powerful weapons in breaking yokes is the anointing itself. The Holy Spirit will move through us in intercession and tear apart the yokes of Satan. Isaiah 10:27 says in the King James Version: "And it shall come to pass in that day, that his burden shall be taken away from off thy shoulder, and his yoke from off thy neck, and the yoke shall be destroyed because of the anointing."

A sample prayer concerning breaking yokes is:

> In the name of Jesus I thank You, Father, that every yoke that the enemy has put on [name] is being broken. Satan, you will no longer cause him to participate in sin. Lord, I thank You that the blindness is falling off his/her eyes concerning this sin right now and that the glorious light and truth of Your Word is being revealed to [name].

Tearing Down Strongholds

Strongholds are fortified places Satan builds to exalt himself against the knowledge and plans of God: "For the weapons of our warfare are not carnal but mighty in God for pulling down strongholds" (2 Corinthians 10:4).

The ancient city of Pergamos was a stronghold of the enemy in biblical times. Revelation 2:13 says this of Pergamos:

> I know your works, and where you dwell, *where Satan's throne is.* And you hold fast to My name, and did not deny My faith even in the days

in which Antipas was My faithful martyr, who was killed among you, where Satan dwells (emphasis mine).

Unger's Bible Dictionary has this to say about the city:

The city [Pergamos] was greatly addicted to idolatry, and its grove, which was one of the wonders of the place, was filled with statues and altars. It was a sort of union of a pagan cathedral city, a university town, and a royal residence, embellished during a succession of years by kings who all had a passion for expenditure and ample means of gratifying it. It was according to pagan nations a sacred place, a city of temples, devoted to sensual worship.[1]

You can easily see that Pergamos was a wicked city, a place where Satan could establish his reign.

There are several types of strongholds. Gary Kinnaman gives excellent definitions of three types in his book *Overcoming the Dominion of Darkness*. Here is a paraphrase of those three:

1. *Territorial Strongholds*. These represent the hierarchy of dark beings who are strategically assigned by Satan himself to influence and control nations, communities and even families. Certain demonic forces mass to different regions to fortify particular kinds of evil. Certain cities will be strongholds of idolatry, sensual sin or certain types of religious spirits.
2. *Ideological Strongholds*. These concern Satan's dominance of the worldview through philosophies that influence culture and society. Charles Darwin's theory of natural selection, for instance, which opposes biblical creation, is considered to be an example. These strongholds are portrayed in 2 Corinthians 10:5: "Casting down arguments and every high thing that exalts itself against the knowledge of God, [we bring] every thought into captivity to the obedience of Christ."
3. *Personal Strongholds*. These are things that Satan builds to influence your personal life—personal sin, your thoughts, your feelings, your attitudes and your behavior patterns.[2]

Edgardo Silvoso of Harvest Evangelism gives another definition of a stronghold: "A stronghold is a mindset impregnated with hopelessness that causes the believer to accept as unchangeable something that he/ she knows is contrary to the will of God."[3]

A rather dramatic account of the effects of tearing down a stronghold over a city through intercession and spiritual warfare occurred in the city of Mar del Plata, Argentina, in September 1990 when Generals of Intercession met with a group of intercessors in that city. We discerned four major ruling, territorial spirits over the city with a strongman, or demon ruler, who reigned over them all. The intercessors had fasted and prayed, and about three hundred people had gathered in the plaza to pray for their city. With pastors from the city present, we began with repentance and prayer. Near four P.M. we began to pray against the ruling spirit—witchcraft. Right at four o'clock we noted the time as the cathedral bells chimed and we went on praying against witchcraft.

Later on, after our time of prayer, one of the local pastors received a phone call asking what we had been doing at four o'clock. It seems there was a Macumba witch who had been joining the witches to pray against the pastors of the city for two years, and right at four o'clock she dropped dead.

We were stunned when we heard this report. While we were not happy that the woman had died, we were acutely aware that God was sending a clear message of judgment upon witchcraft. The Lord most high had drawn a line in the sand and said, "No more, Satan!" When Satan's strongholds are pulled down his kingdom cannot stand. This reminds me of Luke 11:21–22:

> When a strong man, fully armed, guards his own palace, his goods are in peace. But when a stronger than he comes upon him and overcomes him, he takes from him all his armor in which he trusted, and divides his spoils.

We will go into much more detail on particular kinds of strongholds that affect our nations in chapter 17, "Reforming Nations through Militant Intercession."

Supplication

Supplication is an earnest beseeching of God to the point of begging. In fact, according to *Strong's Concordance of the Bible*, the word *supplica-*

tion means "to beg."[4] This type of intercession is not widely taught. It is the kind of praying that took place prior to Pentecost and is spoken of in Acts 1:14: "These all continued with one accord in prayer and supplication, with the women and Mary the mother of Jesus, and with His brothers."

Supplication and travail (which will be discussed later) are closely related. Supplication can be likened to a woman who is ready to have her baby at any moment; there is no holding back the birth. It is a "God-this-must-be-done-now" type of prayer. This type of prayer is often prayed for people in life-and-death situations. The Lord may arrest people in their tracks to pray an "SOS" prayer of supplication. For me these types of SOSs often come from the Lord in the middle of the night when I wake with a start and begin to pray in earnest for a person whose face I suddenly see before me.

This happens on a fairly regular basis with me, and it often occurs when people are in serious situations and need divine intervention. God looks for one to stand in the gap, and I have given the Lord full liberty to awaken me at any time for this purpose. In fact, if you will recall, supplication prayers were my clues that God was offering me the gift of intercession.

Binding and Loosing

> "Assuredly, I say to you, whatever you bind on earth will be bound in heaven, and whatever you loose on earth will be loosed in heaven. Again I say to you that if two of you agree on earth concerning anything that they ask, it will be done for them by My Father in heaven."
>
> Matthew 18:18–19

Two of the most powerful weapons of spiritual warfare are binding and loosing, or forbidding and permitting. There has been some confusion as to what it means to bind and loose and the scriptural precedents for such. Let's look at the meaning of binding and loosing first and then give some practical examples. Gary Kinnaman offers this theological basis for binding and loosing:

> The use of the phrase *binding and loosing* did not, in fact, originate with Jesus. It was a frequent expression of first-century Jewish rabbinical

dialect. According to Alexander Bruce in *The Expositor's Greek New Testament*, to bind and loose (Greek: *deo* and *luo*) meant simply "to prohibit and to permit," that is, to establish (Vol. 1, p. 225). The Jewish religious authorities at the time of Christ retained the right to establish guidelines for, or keys to, religious practice and social interaction.

But *deo* (to bind, tie) also expresses supernatural control. In Luke 13:15–16, Jesus rebuked a Jewish leader,

"You hypocrites! Doesn't each of you on the Sabbath untie [Greek: *luo*, loose] his ox or donkey from the stall and lead it out to give it water? Then should not this woman, a daughter of Abraham, whom Satan has kept bound [Greek: *deo*, bind] for eighteen long years, be set free [Greek: *luo*, loose] on the Sabbath day from what bound her?"[5]

The Jewish leaders in the day of Christ understood only the natural part of binding or loosing, and He was showing them through the encounter with the woman bound by infirmity that binding and loosing had a supernatural side. Notice that Jesus said specifically that it was Satan who had bound the woman.

It is understandable that the Jewish leaders were furious with Jesus for telling His disciples that they had the authority to bind and loose since they were not part of the prescribed Jewish religious/political system. They felt He was giving them authority He had no right to give. They did not understand that He was giving them authority in the unseen realm of heavenly places. This is the realm where the real binding and loosing occurs and from which all things on the earth can be bound or loosed—disallowed or allowed.

Binding

There are two kinds of binding—positive and negative. Both are important in spiritual warfare. Let's look at negative binding first.

Negative Binding

One of the easiest ways to understand negative binding is by using an illustration drawn from the town of Weatherford, where we lived when this book was first written. Weatherford is full of the things you might expect in a small Texas town. We have, for instance, an annual rodeo. Cowboys come from all over to compete in typical cowboy activities such as roping, bronco-busting (wild horse riding) and calf-tying (a calf being a young cow, for all of you city people!). The event that best depicts binding is the calf-roping and tying. A cowboy chases and ropes a calf from his horse, pulls it to the ground and ties the calf's legs together so it cannot move around. This done, the cowboy throws up his hands in a gesture of victory.

This is the picture of what happens in the realm of the Spirit when we pray and bind or tie Satan from having anything to do with a given situation. How does this work?

First, we become aware of a certain situation in which Satan is trying to cause problems. Let's use disunity as an example. Satan tries to get into the midst of a church group and whispers into people's ears things like, "Your pastor doesn't really love you. Remember when you were sick that time and he didn't come to see you?" or, "The organist didn't speak to you today. She has probably been talking about you behind your back." He begins to sling his ugly slime around and if people don't realize what is happening, they begin to distrust one another and become distant.

Second, as intercessors we begin to notice the disunity and go to our place of prayer. Using the illustration of the cowboy, we take our rope, which is the Word of God, and ride the vehicle of prayer out to stop the works of Satan.

Third, we release our rope by speaking the Word of God: "Satan, I bind (or tie) you in the name of Jesus! The Word of God says that whatever I bind on earth will be bound in heaven, and whatever I loose on earth will be loosed in heaven. You will stop bringing disunity to this church body!" We can say with scriptural accuracy, "Satan, according to the Word of God, I forbid you to cause any more strife, in the name of Jesus Christ of Nazareth!"

Some situations require more than one person to do the binding, and the weapon of binding needs to be coupled with the weapon of the prayer of agreement. Using the previous illustration, we could say one calf might be easy to subdue, while a crazed bull would probably drag one cowboy around the arena. Prayer may be offered by a group gathered together or by people who have been notified to pray at the same time, such as a prayer chain. Each person who prays throws a rope until the prayers stop the wild bull, or the attack of Satan.

The weapon of binding is just as effective long-distance as it is close-range because there is really no distance in the realm of the Spirit. In other words, we don't have to be with the person being attacked for the prayer of binding to stop the enemy's work.

A couple of years ago I was awakened by an emergency call early in the morning from a sobbing woman. I finally figured out who she was and what was wrong. She answered between sobs that someone close to her had been taken to a mental hospital, and would I please pray. I was awake immediately and began to pray with vigor and bind the enemy from her friend's mind. I "felt" something, as though a big chain had been broken from her friend's mind, and great peace came upon both of us. About a week later she called to say that her friend had been completely restored that night and released from the hospital the next morning. The enemy's hands were tied from distressing her mind any longer and she was set free.

Positive Binding

One interesting aspect to the power of binding is often overlooked by intercessors. This is the power of positive binding. Positive binding occurs when we speak the Word of God over a given situation. Spoken words are powerful. We are made in the image of our Father, and He literally spoke the world into existence. Proverbs 18:21 says: "Death and life are in the power of the tongue, and those who love it will eat its fruit."

Positive binding by speaking God's Word makes the enemy weaker and able to put up less and less resistance against the purposes of God.

The most powerful example of positive binding was given by Jesus Himself when He battled against Satan in the wilderness. Jesus spoke the Word of God over and over against the enemy until he was so weakened that his power to tempt Jesus was broken.

Notice one aspect of positive binding: It does not always stop the enemy immediately. Many times the struggle will be intense and can last a long time, such as the forty days that the Lord wrestled against Satan in the wilderness. We will discuss this in greater depth later on.

Returning to our illustration of a church in disunity, we could use positive binding by quoting Psalm 133:1, where the Word of God says,

"Behold, how good and how pleasant it is for brethren to dwell together in unity!"

As you pray over loved ones, those in rebellion or those who need the Lord, the Scriptures will begin to speak to them in their hearts. God's Word will begin to live in them and combat the words of evil companions and the things that exalt themselves against the knowledge of God.

Proverbs 6:20–21 has something very interesting to say about words: "My son, keep your father's command, and do not forsake the law of your mother. Bind them continually upon your heart; tie them around your neck." It is interesting that the words of a father and mother, when bound upon the heart, actually lead the son.

Whenever we use negative binding to stop Satan in the area of someone's life by using words like, "Satan, I bind and forbid you from operating in my child's life," we need to do some positive binding and plant the Word of God back into the person's life. Jeremiah 1:10 says: "See, I have this day set you over the nations and over the kingdoms, to root out and to pull down, to destroy and to throw down, to build and to plant."

When Jesus went into the Temple to drive out the money changers, He spoke the Word, which had the effect of positive binding: "It is written, 'My house is a house of prayer,' but you have made it a 'den of thieves'" (Luke 19:46). Jesus had many reasons for speaking this Scripture at this time, but one of them was to bind or speak the Word of God over the Temple and establish it as a house of prayer once again.

Loosing

Loosing in prayer is a type of intercession that sets the captive free from the hands of the enemy. Let me give you an example from an intercessory team and end with an examination of the techniques used in the example.

The intercessory team at the Lausanne II Congress on World Evangelization, held in July 1989 in Manila, was gathered for a prayer watch. Prayer warriors like Robert Birch, Ben Jennings of the Great Commission Prayer Crusade and Joy Dawson prayed along with other mighty prayer giants gathered there who, with swords honed from years of warfare, cut quickly through Satan's devices. There were several requests about which we were praying when a special one came through for a missionary named Bruce Olson. To understand the importance of this request, it is important to know the scope of what God has done through Bruce Olson.

Bruce Olson is world famous for his work as a missionary to the Motilone Indians in Colombia. His life has been a well-known encouragement to those God calls to the missionary field. He had gone to the field at the age of nineteen with no prior experience as a missionary but with a deep call from God. His first attempts at reaching the Indians almost cost him his life as the Motilones had the dubious distinction of killing everyone who came near them.

After years of reaching out to the Indians, learning their language and refusing to give up, Bruce had seen many of the Motilone come to the Lord; he has also brought much good by introducing methods of farming, health care and education.

The knowledge of his prior sacrifice was in our hearts as we listened to the request: Bruce Olson had been captured nine months before by enemy guerillas who wanted to use him against the Indians. The guerillas had issued a statement that Bruce Olson would be killed.

We received this request with a sense of gravity. We knew that it was not an idle threat, as others had already been killed by the group. We were also aware that Bruce was ready to meet the Lord, but this did not seem like God's time for him to go home. As we went to prayer each of us sensed that the Lord wanted to stop the guerillas and use Bruce further in ministry. The enemy had to be halted and the captive loosed.

It was Wednesday afternoon, July 12, 1989. Joy Dawson was asked to lead the group in prayer for Bruce. Joy is a general's general in God's army and has a no-nonsense approach to intercession. She is a petite and lovely former New Zealander with expressive green eyes. Joy stood and waited on God before praying anything. During those moments I felt that God was poised for action and that we were about to participate in it.

She started by praising and thanking God for His sovereign and complete control over the situation. Following this, she committed Bruce into the hands of God and declared her trust in Him that He was acting on Bruce's behalf. She then asked God to do something to bring the maximum glory to the Lord Jesus in this situation with Bruce and his captors, and released faith that this prayer would be answered.

Next she asked God to dispense ministering angels to Bruce and to keep his mind in perfect peace.

Joy stood in the gap between Bruce Olson and satanic forces. The intercessors were in agreement as she began to war in the heavenlies with the authority that comes from knowing she had a right given by the heavenly Commander-in-Chief to do so.

She wielded the sword of the Spirit boldly by binding the forces of darkness operating against Bruce Olson according to Matthew 18:18—"Whatever you bind on earth will be bound in heaven." She then declared the shed blood of the Lord Jesus as the grounds for Satan's total defeat and she exercised faith in the name of the Lord Jesus Christ, loosing Bruce Olson from all of the enemy's power and plans. She concluded by praising God for His almighty power and plans that were in operation.

I did not hear the story of Bruce Olson's release until after returning home from Manila, when I received a Christian magazine that carried a story about him. As I read the article and saw the date of his release, I was deeply touched to find that it occurred exactly one week after the intercession that took place in the prayer room in Manila. We know that many, many people had been praying those nine months for his release but felt that the intercession on that particular day helped to loose a captive to fulfill the destiny of God upon his life.

This is also an example of using both binding and loosing in order to accomplish the desired answer. The intercession first prohibited or forbade the guerillas from killing Bruce Olson, who was then permitted or allowed to go free through the prayer.

A loosing prayer can have the following effects:

1. It can actually cause the physical release of a captive as in the case of Bruce Olson.
2. It can release a person from sickness or disease as in the case of the woman whom Satan had bound with an infirmity.
3. It can loose or declare the will of God to be done in a certain situation.

4. It can loose God to move in and change situations. The Word of God says, for instance, that He has chosen to move into needs that we have presented in prayer: "He saw that there was no man, and wondered that there was no intercessor" (Isaiah 59:16); "You do not have because you do not ask" (James 4:2).

To sum up binding and loosing, we could say the following:

1. Binding stops the enemy's attacks.
2. Loosing releases or permits God's will to enter the situation because God has willed that His purposes be carried out by asking in prayer.

I hope these scriptural precedents and examples help you better understand the language of intercession and think through its application. Let's look now at another misunderstood aspect of intercessory prayer, one that may seem to depart from rational thinking because it calls on our emotions.

---

1. Merrill F. Unger, *Unger's Bible Dictionary* (Chicago, Ill.: Moody Press, 1957), 844.

2. Paraphrased from Gary Kinnaman, *Overcoming the Dominion of Darkness* (Tarrytown, N.Y.: Chosen Books, 1990), 54, 56–58.

3. Edgardo Silvoso, taken from a memorandum to supporters and friends on "Plan Resistencia," September 15, 1990: 3.

4. James Strong, *Strong's Exhaustive Concordance of the Bible* (Nashville, Tenn.: Thomas Nelson Publishers), Greek Dictionary ref. no. 1189.

5. Kinnaman, 162–63.

The Manifestations of Intercession

We have seen that our prayers have great impact when they are inspired and directed by the Holy Spirit. One of the ways He manifests Himself in our intercession is through our emotions. This evidence of His power at work has been greatly misunderstood. Many Christians seem almost to scorn emotion, fearful perhaps that a lack of control follows closely on its heels. If we deny emotion in prayer, however, we lose some of the depth of intercession, for we cannot pray the heart of God fully without joining in His expression.

There will be times when we are interceding that we seem to feel or identify with the sorrow of the person for whom we are praying, or we will know the grieving of the Holy Spirit over a person's sin. When we enter into this kind of prayer we will experience manifestations such as travailing, weeping and laughing. Sometimes these strong emotions take the intercessor quite by surprise. They cannot be forced to occur—it is as the Spirit wills.

Remember my describing in the first chapter an incident in which a young child was being prayed for and I cried as though the child were my own? Perhaps you also recall when I laughed out loud and wondered why I did such a thing. In this chapter we will learn the different ways the Holy Spirit will affect us as we pray. It will give you insight as to whether you are experiencing a feeling from God or from Satan, or simply your own human emotions aside from the Holy Spirit.

Travail

In the mid-1950s a young Englishman named John White was in training for the Lord's service at the New Tribes Mission's Boot Camp in Pennsylvania. The participants were given folders each day containing prayer letters from various missionaries. At seven A.M. they were to pray for the names they had been given.

One particular morning John opened the folder and found a letter from a missionary in the Philippines by the name of Loretta O'Hara. John had never met Loretta, nor did he know anything about her personally. The letter in his hand contained a life-and-death prayer request from her. She was writing from a hospital in Manila where the doctors were telling her she had either cancer of the cervical spine or tuberculosis of the cervical spine.

Something happened to John as he read the request, and he began to pray in a most unusual manner. He began to demand that God heal Loretta. In fact, not only did he demand that the Lord heal her but he absolutely insisted that He do so. At the end of the prayer, John sat back and marveled at what he had been saying. He felt great peace in his heart at first, but then he started thinking about the way he had talked to God! Prior to this experience he had prayed only proper petitions, and the words that had just come out of his mouth did not fit into his theology or his idea of the respect one was to give God in prayer—based in large part on his British upbringing. Unbeknownst to John, he had entered into travail in prayer—travail that produces the will of God in a given situation in a miraculous way.

This travailing prayer brought dramatic results in the life of Loretta O'Hara. At the time John was praying, Loretta was in Nova Scotia. She was traveling to a tuberculosis sanitarium, as the doctor had concluded her condition was cervical tuberculosis. God had other plans for her life, however. It happened that a Christian group heard she would be passing their way and asked her to speak about missions before she went into the sanitarium. This seemed impossible to Loretta because of her condition but they persisted, telling her they would provide a deep, comfortable chair from which she could address the group.

Upon their insistence, she agreed to go speak. As she was sitting describing missions she suddenly felt that the sitting position was not the best way to be addressing this group, and she took hold of a table to pull herself to her feet. Loretta did not know it at the time, but she had just stepped into the supernatural healing power of God.

As Loretta stood she felt stronger. The pain left her body. She knew before long that something dramatic had happened to her. Rather than go to the sanitarium, she went back to the doctor who had diagnosed her condition. When he saw Loretta, he was upset with her because he had worked hard to get a bed for her in the sanitarium. She insisted that he perform the tests that would show her free from tuberculosis. He was reluctant but finally consented to do so. The tests showed her to be completely healed. Loretta rejoiced not only for her healing but also for her ability to return to the mission field.

When she decided to visit the New Tribes Mission's Boot Camp, Loretta had no idea she was entering a new assignment with the man who had prayed for her.

When Loretta arrived at the camp, John was not aware at first that she was the missionary for whom he had prayed, but he was very conscious that she was an attractive woman! John had heard from the Lord that he would meet the woman whom he would marry at the camp, and prior to that time no one had looked like a candidate for marriage. Within a short time they both knew that God brought them together for a lifelong commitment. As John and Loretta came to know each other, they marveled at God's intervention in their lives. John proposed and called her by the new name she is known by today, Lorrie White.

What actually happened when John prayed? Was it something he decided to do, or was it really a burden from God for the life of Loretta O'Hara? Why did he pray with such fervor and intensity? These questions are answered when you understand the type of intercession called *travail*.

In Galatians 4:19 Paul speaks of travailing in birth until Christ is formed in His spiritual children. The word for travail in the Greek is *odino*, which means to experience the pangs of childbirth. There are times when we are called by God to pray strong prayers and help to birth the will of God into that area. Usually there is a sense of wonder after the prayer, and a sense that God has done something through it.

We want, of course, to be certain it is God who is working through us, and not a counterfeit or false travail. Here are four points to help you recognize the work of the Holy Spirit:

1. Travail is given by God and is not something we can make happen. Travail is often a deep groaning inside, which may be audible or which cannot be uttered, as described in Romans 8:26. There are those who try to make themselves travail and moan and groan loudly. But God's moving on us in travail is not something that can be turned off and on like a water faucet.

2. Travail sometimes comes as a result of praying in an area that others have prayed about before you. God then chooses you to be one of the last pray-ers before the matter is accomplished. You are the one who gives birth to the answer.

3. Those with the gift of intercession will often pray more travailing prayers than those who are not as open to the Lord's using them in this manner. As in the case of John White, however, God may call upon any believer at any point to travail in prayer for His purposes.

4. The travail may be short or extended. Some prayers will be accomplished quickly, and some will be like labor pangs at different times until the birth of the answer comes.

The Old Testament speaks prophetically about Jesus' travailing for us: "He shall see of the travail of his soul, and shall be satisfied" (Isaiah 53:11, KJV).

We read in the New Testament that Jesus did travail. One time was in the Garden of Gethsemane when He prayed with such anguish that He sweat drops of blood. Another was at the tomb of Lazarus. John 11:33 says: "Therefore, when Jesus saw her weeping, and the Jews who came with her weeping, He groaned in the spirit and was troubled." Many have taught that His groaning is simply a form of indignation at the situation and the death of His friend. I am sure He was grieved about the wailing going on around Him, but something also happened in the Spirit in intercession as He groaned.

Many times travail can be so strong that it seems to overwhelm the intercessor. Those around need to intercede for the one in travail if this happens in a group situation. We need to help bear the burden in prayer. Remember that travail is like giving birth, and in a way we are acting as midwives when we help the intercessor in travail. We also need to watch after that one by binding the enemy from entering into the travail.

One word of caution. The Holy Spirit will rule over our emotions in a time of travail. We must be sure that we don't let our emotions run wild. Intercessors need to walk in the fruit of self-control. I have heard of planned meetings where everyone is coming to "travail" and they all, at a signal from the leader, start wailing. This kind of expression does not match my understanding of biblical travail. In my opinion, it is a God-given expression of intercession that comes in God's timing, rather like the moment ordained for a baby to be born. The woman might want to have the baby, but the "push" is timed by God Himself.

Weeping

In August 1990 Dr. C. Peter Wagner was addressing the North American Renewal Congress in Indianapolis, Indiana. He began to share about the burden of prayer he felt for Japan. He then took a moment to ask for prayer as he was leaving the next day to speak at a conference for leaders in Japan. One of the leaders of the workshop, Jim Bevis, asked me if I would lead in prayer for Peter. As I prayed I was suddenly drawn to the hurt and devastation caused by the bomb dropped on Hiroshima. I prayed that Peter would be used like a bomb in the Spirit to break apart the darkness that Satan had worked against the nation of Japan and the Japanese people.

At the end of the workshop, Peter left Indianapolis for Los Angeles to get ready to leave for Japan. The next morning was Sunday. Peter was having his morning time of prayer when he began to think about the Japanese people and the pain they had gone through in Hiroshima and Nagasaki. All of a sudden he started to weep and weep. This puzzled him because he had been only fifteen years old when the bombs were dropped in Japan. He had not participated in the dropping of the bombs nor had he anything to do with the decision to drop the bombs. God showed him, however, that as a fifteen-year-old boy he had hated the Japanese and that there had been fifteen-year-old Japanese boys who were killed during the bombings. Because of his own hatred he was just as guilty as those who had made the decision to drop the bombs. He later realized that in his weeping God had moved him into a time of deep intercession for the nation.

When his wife, Doris, phoned later that morning he shared what had happened. Doris said to him, "Peter, perhaps the Lord would have you repent for Hiroshima and Nagasaki." As soon as Doris spoke the words, Peter knew that this was exactly what the Lord was calling him to do.

Upon arriving in Japan he spoke to the leaders of the conference and asked if they would gather a group of people whose relatives died when the bombs were dropped on Hiroshima or Nagasaki. They were able to do so and arranged a time when he would do what the Lord had told him to do—ask forgiveness publicly for his sin.

When the time came to repent, Peter spent quite a bit of time preparing the people—telling them about the Scriptures that speak of forgiveness for nations, passages from Daniel 10 and Nehemiah 1. Both Daniel and Nehemiah repented on behalf of their nations and for their own sin, and he explained that this was what he was about to do. Just like Daniel he was going to say, "Father, I have sinned." He was not trying to make a judgment as to whether or not the bombs should have been dropped, but rather he wanted to be used by God as an instrument to heal broken, devastated people.

Peter asked those who had lost loved ones when the bombs were dropped to come forward. Then this servant of God knelt to ask forgiveness for his sin and wept big tears asking God to heal the Japanese people. All across the room the Holy Spirit swept into broken hearts, and that room with one thousand people was filled with the sound of weeping—some loud and anguished. The pain of a people was being released and washed away with those tears.

When Peter finished and stood to his feet, a Japanese representative rose to speak and declared that their sin as a people was much greater than that of the Americans and asked the Lord to forgive them of their sins against the United States in World War II. Through that experience the Holy Spirit moved into the heart of a nation to bring healing and restoration.

As we weep in intercession, life comes into situations that God wants changed and made whole.

I used to call my husband "Mr. Spock" (a television character from outer space) because he showed so little emotion. One day I was weeping for a church that was not experiencing revival. The prayer went something like this: "Lord, if they knew how to have revival, they would; show them how to have revival. Let Your Spirit fall and renew them and break their strong hearts."

Mike came in while I was crying and sat and prayed and watched me. After a time I went over and laid hands on him and prayed. He says that I prayed, "Get him, God," but what I really said was, "Lord, give him Your compassion and Your tears."

Later that night he awoke weeping profusely. I guess it was like a time-released capsule that took awhile to act. He wept all the next morning when he ministered to men about their duties as fathers to their children, and we have it all on videotape! Today Mike weeps freely when the Holy Spirit moves him to do so.

Dick Eastman was speaking at Christ For The Nations in Dallas one day when he announced that God wanted him to show the students something very personal. He reached into his pocket and drew out a little round tin. As he held it in his hand he said that it was full of eye salve. It seems he had gone to the doctor because his eyes were "crusty" all the time. The wise doctor told him, "Dick, it is because you weep so much in prayer."

Dick was not bragging about the fact that he weeps in prayer. Nor was he suggesting that the students go around weeping all the time. The Lord wanted to use that little tin of eye salve to show them that it is all right to weep.

It is particularly difficult for men to weep before the Lord in some cultures. The American culture frowns on men weeping, although there is some change in this today. "Real men don't cry" is the general feeling. I remember asking my daddy one day why he never cried. He said, "Honey, men don't cry." My son once told my daughter that men hide their emotions. Pretty insightful for someone who was only nine years old at the time! I explained to him that God was the Lord over his emotions, and that he didn't need to hide them inside in an unhealthy way. Today, as an adult, my son Daniel has become a Jeremiah in the Lord and is unashamed to weep when God gives him tears.

Jesus was certainly a strong man, and was the greatest intercessor of all time. "Jesus wept" (John 11:35) is the shortest verse in the Bible, yet one of the most powerful. His weeping broke the yoke of death around Lazarus and prepared the way for the command of resurrection, "Lazarus, come forth!" (verse 43). We also see Jesus weeping over the city of Jerusalem in Luke 19:41: "Now as He drew near, He saw the city and wept over it."

Sometimes weeping in intercession will fall on groups of people as well as on a single individual. This occurred in the church we attended in Weatherford, Texas. We had not planned that the whole church would weep, but God Himself orchestrated this unique, holy time.

Linda Gossett, our children's church teacher, was taking her first trip to Russia. It was exciting for her because the Lord had shown her twelve years before that she was called to go to Russia to minister, and this was the first time the door had been opened for her to go. Her call was to teach the children, and she had spent many hours weeping over the little ones in a faraway place whom she had never seen with her natural eyes, but had visited on her knees many times.

Linda is a small, beautiful lady who looks rather like a China doll. She has a deep knowledge of the Word and loves to laugh. Our pastor, Don Connell, had asked her to speak to the congregation that Sunday morning so we would all know how to pray for her on her trip. Beside Linda on the platform was a brown suitcase full of "Holy Cargo," as she called it. The Holy Cargo was stuffing the suitcase to the straining point with Bibles, children's materials and gifts. At the end of the service Pastor Don asked that she open the suitcase in the front of the sanctuary so that we could pray over every article she was taking to the Soviet Union.

As he shared Linda's need for prayer support, something unusual started to happen in the room. At first it was almost imperceptible—rather like a holy hush—as solemnity fell on the room, from grandparents to the youngest child. This feeling grew as we took up an offering.

The offering baskets were passed from person to person and child to child and when the ushers brought the baskets back to the front, one of the ushers began to weep. Pastor Don reached into the basket and pulled out a small jar with a slit in the top full of pennies, and then another, and another. The children were giving to Miss Linda. There was something about the sight of that sacrifice that brought a spirit of intercession and weeping into the service. The people came and held each of the Bibles in the suitcase and wept over them. They held the flannelgraph materials and asked God to bless the people who would use them. Two- and three-year-old girls and boys wept as they held the children's materials in their little hands.

God had called a whole church to pray; and when the spirit of weeping and intercession flowed, it touched and enveloped us all on behalf of the children of a nation. And later, as Linda went into what was at the time the Soviet Union, she was able to go through the checkpoints without any threat to the Holy Cargo. The tears washed away any schemes that the enemy might have planned to keep out God's Word, and seeds of life were planted across Russia in the hearts of a future generation.

Laughing

Laughter in prayer is a sign that God's will has been accomplished or that the answer is on the way or that the enemy's plan has been averted. "He who sits in the heavens shall laugh; the LORD shall hold them in derision" (Psalm 2:4).

I have read this verse many times, and it has always been a great blessing to me. But it recently became a greater source of wonder after a spiritual warfare campaign in Argentina.

In June 1990 four of us went down to assist in "Plan Resistencia"— Doris Wagner, Dave and Jane Rumph and me. We flew down to South America after Peter and Doris Wagner had returned from meetings in April in the city of Resistencia. Our interpreter was Marfa Cabrera, a powerful woman of God. Marfa and her husband, Omar, were pastors at the time of the Vision de Futuro Church with ninety thousand members.[1] Doris had been greatly burdened that there needed to be more intercession over Resistencia, which had been targeted with a brilliant strategy for church growth and evangelism by Harvest Evangelism president Edgardo Silvoso.

Plan Resistencia attempts to modify a city on levels that will affect the physical, emotional and spiritual levels of its people. It calls for the complete unity of all pastors—evangelicals, charismatics and Pentecostals alike. It strives to plant six hundred "lighthouses" in private homes with the purpose of ministering to the needs in their neighborhoods. Massive rallies follow. Finally the lighthouses are turned into churches and the people who have received Christ as Lord and Savior are funneled there. This is a thumbnail sketch of an involved plan.

We had spent the week teaching 750 leaders about spiritual warfare. In addition, we had a time of battling spiritually the spirits that had laid claim to the city. Great release had come through that time of warfare. Some of the spirits had been strong—especially a nasty one called San La Muerte, or the spirit of death. It seems that some of the people actually worshiped this spirit of "good death" as they called it.

Our involvement in the plan completed, we were relaxing on the plane coming home. We were flying on an Argentine airline, which has a map displayed for passengers showing the flight route and the spot on the route that you are currently flying over. Underneath the map appears the name of the city closest to your current location.

Doris Wagner and I watched this map with interest but lost track when our dinner was served. All of a sudden the plane shuddered and started to bounce up and down as though with severe turbulence. Doris looked at me and started laughing right out loud! I said, "I think we should pray," and started laughing, too. We looked at each other and suddenly had a strange thought at the same time. Could we be over the city of Resistencia? A quick glance showed us the story: At that moment the city of Corrientes, a large city next to Resistencia, came up on the map. After ten minutes the turbulence just stopped. We had a smooth ride the rest of the way home.

Coincidence? Possibly. But the knowledge that we were right above the city where we had wrestled against territorial spirits made us wonder. Did the laughter have something to do with the plane ride's becoming smooth? And if so, what place does laughter have in intercession and spiritual warfare?

When I first became aware of this, one verse that spoke the clearest to me was Psalm 2:4, which I mentioned earlier. It speaks of the Lord laughing and holding the enemy in derision. When Doris and I laughed on the plane, the Lord was actually laughing through us and mocking the enemy for thinking he could hurt us while we flew through the heavenlies. The laughter clearly came as a sign that we had nothing to fear from Satan's devices and that the angels of the Lord surrounded us. This kind of warfare through intercession lets the enemy know who is in charge of our lives. It is a sign that we have nothing to fear from him.

Two other Scriptures speak of laughing at the enemy in the context of mocking. Psalm 37:12–13 says: "The wicked plots against the just, and gnashes at him with his teeth. The Lord laughs at him, for He sees that his day is coming."

The second is Psalm 59:7–8: "Indeed, they belch with their mouth; swords are in their lips; for they say, 'Who hears?' But You, O LORD, shall laugh at them; You shall have all the nations in derision."

Another Scripture that has been important to me in this regard is Psalm 126:1–2:

> When the LORD brought back the captivity of Zion, we were like those who dream. Then our mouth was filled with laughter, and our tongue with singing. Then they said among the nations, "The LORD has done great things for them."

Gwen Shaw relates in her book *God's End-Time Battle-Plan* that there is a time when we must let the laughter of the Lord fill our hearts. She gives Ecclesiastes 3:4, "A time to weep, and a time to laugh," as an example of this. She says, "If we are to allow God to laugh, then He must laugh through us, just as He speaks through us."[2]

It is not unusual for people who have not experienced this to be quite surprised that we are so joyful in our praying. On more than one occasion people have expressed this sentiment: "We did not know that prayer could be so refreshing. We thought that we must always be very solemn or else God would not be pleased." Others have said with joy on their faces, "We must go home and tell our churches and prayer groups that we can be joyful in our petitions. No wonder we have been so weary as we pray!" They learned the wonderful truth that all intercessors need to draw from life: "The joy of the LORD is your strength" (Nehemiah 8:10).

These emotional displays of travailing, weeping and laughing are God-inspired and God-directed. As we let Him lead He will take us to a new place of expression.

Letting Him lead is always the key to intercession. In the next chapter we will discuss what happens when we take matters into our own hands.

---

1. Omar and Marfa Cabrera, my good friends, have now gone home to be with the Lord. Their son, Omar Jr., is now the pastor along with his wife, Alejandra.

2. Gwen Shaw, *God's End-Time Battle-Plan* (Jasper, Ariz.: Engeltal Press, 1984), 107.

10

Flaky Intercession

flak*y (flākē) *adj*. Exhibiting eccentric, unbalanced or irrational
behavior.

The phone rang early one Monday morning. The caller was a young
Bible student whom I'll call Pam. She had told me before that she was
attending a large church that emphasized prayer.

"Cindy," she said, "I don't want to criticize unfairly, but something
isn't right with my prayer group." As Pam told her story I realized that
she was involved with "flaky" intercessors.

How did it happen? What makes an intercessor flaky?

One Sunday morning at church a woman whom I will call Estelle
approached Pam with a "word from God" that she was to join a select
home prayer group and intercede for their pastor. Estelle shared excitedly that as the pastor's personal intercessors the group would be asked
to travel with him when he was on the road.

Estelle neglected to tell Pam, however, that neither the pastor nor the
church leadership knew of this select group. Pam discovered later that
Estelle was expecting God to reveal it to them supernaturally.

Without checking its validity, Pam decided to join the group. At first all went well, but after a few meetings they began praying in a direction exactly opposite to the vision of the church.

They began to pray fervently that the pastor would "see the light and get aligned with God"—which was synonymous with getting aligned with them. They also prayed that God would lead him to consult them regarding direction for the church. This made Pam uneasy and prompted her to call me.

I recommended that Pam leave Estelle's group and join one of the church-sponsored intercessory meetings, for reasons that I will discuss later in this chapter.

Pam's situation is fairly typical of the problems Mike and I hear frequently as leaders of Generals International. She was sucked into a group of flaky intercessors—men and women who, for a variety of reasons, drift outside biblical guidelines in their zeal for prayer. They bring reproach on their ministries and confusion and division in the church. Flaky intercession could become a widespread problem, for many prophetic voices are proclaiming that God is calling the church to intense prayer as a prelude to revival.

Studies of past revivals indicate that they were birthed and bathed in prayer, but that the move of the Holy Spirit was short-circuited by the inability to sustain effective intercession. In many instances it was flaky intercession that undermined true prayer and destroyed revival.

In a planning meeting for the Spiritual Warfare Network (a post-Lausanne II consultation on spiritual warfare), I sensed the Lord impressing me with the idea that in the time of Luther, the rallying cry was "The just shall live by faith." In the coming reformation the watchword will be "We wrestle not against flesh and blood, and the weapons of our warfare are not carnal."

Satan—crafty, evil serpent that he is—undermines revival through one of his most effective weapons—deception. Through clever lies that appeal to the flesh he draws people away from God's purposes for revival prayer. In other words, he works overtime at making flaky intercessors. So how do we avoid flaky intercession?

The answer is actually quite simple: Use clear, biblical guidelines as your plumbline for intercession. This chapter will explore problems that arise with intercessors and prayer groups, problems that cause confusion and give intercessory prayer in general a bad name. This is especially sad because true intercessors are servants of God who sacrifice for others daily. Those who get off balance do so generally from a lack of teaching or else by learning from others who are off balance. Most people make corrections immediately when they understand the areas in which they have become extreme.

There are two safeguards for intercessors. The biggest is spiritual accountability. If intercessors are afraid of having their prayers and what they believe God has shown them judged, then they are on flaky spiritual ground, as we saw with Estelle's group.

Let me interject here that when intercessors pray for ministries outside of their local churches, they need to be submitted to the other ministries for which they intercede as well. If they are not related on an intimate basis, they should have some way to make sure their prayers are in keeping with the vision of the ministry. Intercessors who are called to pray for parachurch ministries still need to have the covering, as I mentioned earlier, that a local church provides.

The second safeguard to flaky intercession is abiding by the clean heart principle, which we discussed in chapter 3. Psalm 51:10 says, "Create in me a clean heart, O God."

Estelle, by not knowing her own heart, violated this principle in several areas. For one, she had pride in her heart. She was convinced she needed to be a leader rather than submit to the leadership of church prayer groups. She felt that her "revelations" were superior to what the pastor or elders heard from God. This is a common trap for some people when God begins to share His secrets with them through prayer.

Estelle also had a critical spirit, which is closely associated with pride. She was critical of the way intercessory groups had been set up by the pastor, especially since she had not been asked to lead one, and so she started her own. She should have become involved with an established prayer group in the church, proven herself trustworthy and let God promote her (or not promote her) to leadership.

As intercessors we need to ask God to reveal our heart motives. I have observed that many aspiring intercessors pray out of bitterness and woundedness. What I find remarkable is that they are unaware of these heart conditions. They are drawn to intercession because of its great power and, subconsciously, because they see it as a means of getting their way. Only God's Spirit can reveal the true condition of our hearts. A good prayer for intercessors, therefore, is "Lord, show me my heart so that I can remain pure before You always."

Estelle was in further danger of violating the clean heart principle by developing what might be called an Absalom spirit. This happens when an intercessor starts to act toward others as Absalom did toward his father, King David. Absalom was bitter because after he came back from exile his father did not talk to him. So Absalom began to undermine his father's kingdom. His works in doing this appeared to be good, and he even helped the people; but his heart attitude was wrong. Absalom desired attention from his father even if it was for wrongdoing. He pursued vengeance, forcing communication.

How do we recognize an Absalom spirit in someone else—or ourselves? First of all, he (or she) starts saying things that cut down the minister: "I know the pastor means well, but I have been praying and I think that he just cannot see what the people really need." Then in conversation he gives his wisdom. He may even comment, "Now, if I were the pastor, I would do such-and-such," not realizing he sounds just like Absalom, who said to the people, "If I were king, you would be treated right." Intercessors need to judge their hearts constantly to determine why they say what they say, pray the way they pray and react the way they react.

An Absalom spirit left unchecked and uncorrected has caused many church splits because the people start to look to that person for guidance and vision rather than to the pastor. Usually the person affected with the Absalom spirit is sincere about his Christian walk and has no idea what has happened. If he is ultimately rejected, he goes away hurt, and the church is left wounded. This is not to say that every person who has a different philosophy of ministry and makes changes in churches is an Absalom, but that the heart always has to be checked before suggestions are made to change.

Some of you prayer leaders may be saying right now, "Cindy, my pastor doesn't ever talk to me or listen to what God is saying to our prayer group. I'm extremely frustrated!" We will discuss this further in the chapters on leading corporate intercession and personal prayer partners. This is a real problem and often leads to great heartache on the part of those giving of themselves to intercede for their churches.

There may be a time when you have prayed and prayed but yet still feel that you cannot go with the direction of the church. If that is the case, I suggest that you go with your spouse, if you have one, or another person and explain to the pastor that you are being led another direction. This should be done without a critical spirit or feeling that you have to dramatically drive your point home as to what you believe should be changed. The Holy Spirit is well able to get through to the leader in a way he or she can receive it.

Gary Greenwald has a section about manipulative intercessors in his book *Seductions Exposed* that is a classic example of the Absalom spirit. He writes:

> It has been my observation that intercessors often have a tendency to share their revelations with one another when they get together and before long find themselves agreeing with one another. Some time ago a group of intercessors in my church exhibited this truth in a damaging way. The Eagle's Nest had gone through some strife, and many of the people along with a large portion of the pastoral staff had left the church.
>
> One of the intercessors had received a revelation that God's judgment was about to fall upon me because of my supposed disobedience in leading the church in a certain direction. After sharing her views with a few others, they all agreed that if I did not repent, I would be judged like King Nebuchadnezzar, who grew hair like an animal and ate grass in the field.
>
> Because those intercessors had stepped out of their calling as supporters and prayer warriors, they had been deceived into believing they had more vision for the church than their pastor. Their pride had opened them up to a spirit of error. The role of intercessors is to birth the vision received by the leadership through prayer—not to discuss what they may see in the spiritual realm with others. Those intercessors were trying to manipulate me with their warnings and in doing so had fallen into fleshly manipulation. When they confronted me, I exhorted them telling them they had overstepped their calling. One strong intercessor had led them into their deception. Most of them left the church over the incident.[1]

I do not desire here to make any type of judgment as to what led up to this confrontation, but only to comment on the actions of the intercessors.

First of all, the word the group gave to Greenwald was a harsh correction. Nebuchadnezzar was a king who led his kingdom into abject sin. Even if Greenwald were getting into pride, this offered a rather stiff punishment for it. This isn't to say that God does not deal with pastors. Sometimes, though, intercessors' home lives affect their judgment. Those who are constantly receiving harsh words from God usually come from dysfunctional home situations. This taints what they hear and leads them into legalistic ways of hearing from God and applying what they hear.

Secondly, if God did tell them He was going to judge Greenwald, their attitude should have been a grieving one, as with Daniel when he interpreted the king's dreams: "O king, I pray that this is not for you but for another." Remember when I heard God say that a pastor was in danger of having a heart attack? I had been hurt and desired that judgment fall upon him. My heart was deceitfully wicked, and my sin was greater than his.

Thirdly, if they had heard from God accurately, rather than speak to others about the word of correction, they should have taken it to their prayer closets and cried out to God to warn the pastor. The Word of God says that we are not to rebuke an elder (see 1 Timothy 5:1). An intercessor is not to rebuke his pastor but to pray for him, to ask God to send those into his life who would speak a balancing word to him. Many times the Holy Spirit will speak quickly to pastors about the things that are prayed from a pure heart in the prayer closet.

Fourthly, having done all of this, intercessors who are still concerned might ask the Lord if He has given them a release from the church. They must never, however, speak out against the pastor to members of the congregation. This causes confusion and dissension. An intercessor and particularly a prayer leader is responsible to cover in prayer the vulnerabilities and heart attitudes that God needs to correct in leadership. It goes without saying, of course, that sexual sin and other deviant behaviors need to be shared with the elders in the church.

One other point to keep in mind. It is quite possible that the minister wants to go deeper with God but feels his people are not ready to be led in that particular direction. Maintaining spiritual accountability and following the clean heart principle will keep you from pushing him to move too fast or in the wrong direction.

"Strike-'em-Dead" Prayers

A number of years ago I sat in a prayer meeting in a room filled with intercessors. The leader stood up to pray about a political situation and started to give details concerning a politician who was not behaving in a godly manner. After elaborating on a needed change she asked us to bow our heads and pray. Her prayer for the politician took a compassionate tone, but in a few moments I was startled to hear her say these words: "God, either save him, get him out of office or *kill him*!" I could hardly believe my ears. She was a godly woman. How could she pray such a thing?

After this I began to hear other intercessors praying in a similar fashion all across the country. They were cursing pornographic bookstores and asking God to burn them down. They were calling on Him to destroy X-rated movie theaters—and to strike down those who would not repent of running them. Other times I listened as intercessors picked up the Psalms of David and read the parts where he asked that his enemies be eaten up with worms and die.

I even heard reports of witches cursing Christians because they thought that if they didn't the Christians would curse them, and they would burn to death.

When I first heard these types of prayers I felt they did not line up with the New Testament pattern for intercession. As I studied I became convinced. Several examples from God's Word leaped out at me, particularly this one:

> And when His disciples James and John saw this, they said, "Lord, do You want us to command fire to come down from heaven and consume them, just as Elijah did?" But He turned and rebuked them, and said, "You do not know what manner of spirit you are of. For the Son of Man did not come to destroy men's lives but to save them." And they went to another village.
>
> Luke 9:54–56

Many times as intercessors we do not know what is influencing us. We can be caught up with a spirit of power and step over into intercession that is far from the heart of Christ. Once again, we need to examine our motives. Here are two reasons not to pray "strike-'em-dead" prayers:

1. Strike-'em-dead praying is a bad witness to nonbelievers. I have a friend who used to own a bar before she was born again. She was deeply hurt by Christians who were cursing her bar, hoping it would burn to the ground. As she said, "I, or a member of my family, could have been hurt in a fire. Why didn't they pray that I be saved and sell the property to be used for the Kingdom?"
2. Strike-'em-dead praying violates the principle of mercy that is the stance of an intercessor. By definition an intercessor is one who stands in the gap on behalf of another.

This second point came from the wise teaching of Bob Willhite. It was one of the greatest lessons ever taught in a Generals of Intercession meeting. It helped me understand how intercessors should respond when God gives a word of judgment for a people or nation.

Bob explained that God never changes His nature or His character, but He does change His mind. And because He does not desire to bring judgment, He seeks those who will stand in the gap.

Bob then brought this to life with this example: Jeremiah was one of the greatest intercessors in the Bible and he prayed incessantly for Israel. But at one point God told Jeremiah to stop praying for Israel because He was going to judge it. What was Jeremiah's response? He prayed for God's mercy for His people. Ten chapters later Jeremiah was still praying for mercy and God's anger was averted. We as intercessors should stand before God when we receive a word of doom and gloom and pray from Habakkuk 3:2: O God, in judgment, remember mercy.

This teaching changed my life and also changed the way I pray when I see someone in error or when God speaks that He is going to bring severe correction on a person or ministry. As I have jumped into the gap on behalf of the person about to be judged, I have consistently seen God move, the judgment stayed and the person in error do a complete turnaround.

I realize that sometimes we may be in an emergency situation when it might seem like a very good idea for God to destroy the enemy—if a robber were about to shoot your children, for instance. The point that I am making, however, is that while we do rebuke Satan from controlling people, we are not to curse people. We are to cry out to God and let Him decide the judgment.

The point is this—let God judge! In praying for those in political office it is all right to pray, "God, save them; get them right or remove them." We need, however, to leave it to God as to how He removes them.

Bearing Others' Sickness

Over the past years we have received a number of sad reports from pray-ers across America. One of the saddest involved an intercessory prayer group leader who had become sick. As she prayed she felt that this sickness was not hers but that she was bearing it for another friend. She said openly that this sickness could not touch her because it was not real and was only something she was carrying for the weaker person. As time went on, however, she got sicker and sicker. When finally she went to the doctor, she learned that she had an advanced case of diabetes. She was in such serious condition that the doctor could do nothing for her, and she died. This woman took on false burden-bearing and stepped into an area of presumption and deception that killed her.

In studying about this problem I reread a section in Norman Grubb's book on Rees Howells that shed some light as to where the idea might have developed that intercessors should actually take on another's sickness. I share this not to attack a man whom I consider to be one of the greatest intercessors who ever lived, but to make the point that although Rees Howells was a pioneer in the area of intercession, his written explanation might not convey exactly what the Lord meant when He spoke to him about "identification."

> Mr. Howells had already known something of the groanings of the Spirit in him for the needy and afflicted. . . . But what would it mean to intercede for a consumptive? As an intercessor, he must enter into the sufferings and take the place of the one prayed for. He knew that a bed-ridden consumptive could have no normal home life, was confined to one room, and was cut off from everything that once comprised the interests and pleasures of life. So during this time of "abiding" the Holy Spirit went much deeper in identifying him with the suffering of others. And as he did so, it was not just this one woman, but the consumptives and sufferers of the world whose burden came upon him.

Mr. Howells had not gone very far on this path before the conviction took definite hold of him that before he was through, the Lord would literally let this disease come upon him and that only as an actual consumptive would he fully be able to intercede for consumptives. That this was not a foolish imagination but a practical possibility will be seen later in his life when, after taking great personal risks to care for a consumptive, it looked as though he had contracted the disease. Moreover, in all the earlier intercession he had literally had to take the place of, and live like, the ones prayed for.[2]

This passage opens some dangerous areas for intercessors because the idea of identification could be stretched and taken out of context until intercessors feel that they are the ones who bring salvation and change, that their works bring healing and wholeness.

God's Word tells us that Jesus bore our sins in His own body on the cross and that we are healed by His stripes (see 1 Peter 2:24). Nothing in our carrying sickness brings healing. Only the work of Christ, which we appropriate as we pray, can do that. To say that we bear someone's sickness physically in intercession is a false fellowship of suffering. It is true that we will suffer certain things as we intercede, such as hunger when we fast. Isaiah 58 says that fasting afflicts the soul, and I believe it; it surely does afflict mine. Other times it might mean giving hours of your time when you want to be out doing something else. For many intercessors it has meant being misunderstood or thought of as kind of crazy.

I am sure that many intercessors are saying at this point, "But the same sickness afflicting the person I was praying for hit my body, too." Others might be thinking, "Sometimes I didn't even know that the people I was praying for were afflicted with the same kind of sickness I had. Why did that happen if I was not bearing their sickness?"

Please remember that when you stand in the gap for another you place yourself in prayer between the person for whom you are interceding and whatever the devil is trying to inflict upon him or her. Thus, the very sickness that is hitting the person for whom you are praying will sometimes hit you, too. The important thing is to resist immediately what Satan is trying to do not only against the person for whom you are praying but also against you. If the enemy cannot kill the person he has targeted, he does not mind afflicting an intercessor instead. Remember, Satan comes to steal, kill and destroy (see John 10:10).

At other times you may not even know at first that you are supposed to be interceding for a person who is sick, but discover later that your symptoms were exactly the same. There are times that the Lord puts us in the gap, and we are not aware of what has happened at first. This is another reason always to resist the fiery darts of the enemy and ask the Lord if those darts were meant for you or someone for whom you are supposed to be praying.

Witchcraft Praying

Now the works of the flesh are evident, which are: adultery, fornication, uncleanness, licentiousness, idolatry, [and] sorcery [witchcraft].

Galatians 5:19–20

Quite a number of years ago I was home on a lovely spring day when Leslie (not her real name) called me on the phone. Leslie was very excited as she shared that a friend had just confirmed to her during a time of intercession that she would marry a well-known single televangelist. She was ecstatic as she told about the detailed "word" her friend had given her.

The more Leslie talked, the more I prayed for wisdom. What Leslie did not know was that just that morning I had received a call from Phoebe (not her real name) living in California telling me exactly the same news—about herself. Phoebe's revelation was so similar it was eerie. After Leslie stopped bubbling I sent a quick prayer to God to give me the right words to say so as not to offend Leslie or discredit my other friend.

Thinking that my pause was prompted by pleased shock, Leslie exclaimed, "Cindy, I want you to pray and agree with me that he will meet me and that the marriage will happen quickly thereafter."

Well, I really was in quite a predicament! I knew I could not pray that way for a number of reasons:

1. God had not confirmed to me that they were to be married.
2. More importantly, God had not spoken to the evangelist that they would be married.
3. If I put those two points aside to agree with Leslie in prayer, I would be getting into the area of witchcraft, praying in a manipulative

fashion if I prayed the prayer of agreement with Leslie to marry the evangelist.

This is what I could do:

1. I affirmed that I also desired that she find a godly husband.
2. I told her that I had not heard a direct word from God that this evangelist was to be her husband but would be glad to pray with her for God to bring His best to her, and that if this evangelist was His best, that God would cause them to meet.
3. I told her about the call from California. She knew that since God does not condone polygamy, one of them was wrong.
4. I prayed and agreed with Leslie for God to bring the husband into her life who would best suit God's gifts and purposes for them both.

Why was Leslie in danger of getting into witchcraft praying? It was not her desire to do so, but in her loneliness she was stepping into the realm of manipulation and control in her prayers. This is the basis of what witches do in their unholy intercession: They produce curses and false bindings on those for whom they pray. This is why witchcraft is listed as a work of the flesh in Galatians 5:20. These are actually psychic prayers out of our own human minds and not ones prayed from the mind of Christ. The psychics and witches sometimes call this mind control.

Throughout the years Mike and I have seen variations of witchcraft praying as we have ministered in Generals of Intercession. Some people run around and "claim" houses and property, which puts bindings on other people's property. We have known people who were unable to sell property for long periods of time because some Christian decided he wanted it as his own and prayed accordingly. We always suggest to people who pray over property (or whatever they hope to possess) that they pray like this:

Lord, I believe that You have spoken to me in my heart that this will be my property. If it is the land You have set aside for my use, please hold it for me and bless the people who own it financially while we are making arrangements to buy it.

One day a man called me and said that God had told him that his wife did not have a strong enough anointing to match the call on his life. He said, therefore, that she was going to die and that God was going to give him another wife. Even more astounding was the fact that he had convinced his wife that this was true. Fortunately, he was open to instruction and soon saw the error in his thinking. I told him, "Since God can do anything, why not just pray that God will increase her anointing also?" He thanked me and hung up the phone happy in this decision.

Believe it or not, stories like this are fairly common in intercessory circles. We have heard many variations through the years, as have most prayer leaders. Let me explain what happens when someone prays manipulating prayers.

When someone prays a prayer out of his own mind, will or emotion, he is releasing tremendous psychic (and many times demonic) forces to work against the one for whom he is praying. Proverbs 18:21 says: "Death and life are in the power of the tongue." Words are powerful. Consider the words of the Hebrew spies in the book of Numbers. The evil report given by the spies defiled the whole camp. Our words spoken in prayer can work in much the same way; if the plan prayed for others is not God's will for their lives, they can find themselves confused.

Intercessory groups that operate out of an Absalom spirit pray in this manner quite often: "God, our pastor has stayed in this pulpit past his time. We ask You to remove him, Lord, and bring in the right one who will bless Your people."

If it is not the time for the pastor to move, their prayer opens a door for Satan to attack the pastor's thought life and begin to create confusion. Whereas the pastor was once sure of being called to that church, he or she may suddenly feel troubled and may sense heaviness or bondage when delivering sermons or ministering to needs. The works of the flesh, or witchcraft, will afflict the pastor, but it will rebound against the person praying as well. The Bible says in Galatians 6:7 that what you sow, so shall you reap.

If you have been praying wrong prayers, repent and ask the Lord to remove the deception from your life. Ask God to show you any wrong praying you have done. Then, in the name of Jesus, release each one for whom you have prayed amiss and manipulated in prayer.

If you sense that you have had intercessors pray manipulative prayers over you, consider this: Are you experiencing confusion or heaviness for no known reason? If the problem is not physical or related to sin or strife, then pray in this manner:

> Father, in the name of Jesus, I now break the power of every work prayed for me that is contrary to Your will for my life. I thank You now that all bondage is broken from any manipulating prayers.

The Bridal Chamber

There are some incredibly flaky things going on in intercessory circles—such as shooting at the devil with cap guns and shocking visitors (not to mention pastors!) by squatting in the Sunday morning services and groaning as if giving birth. (As I said earlier, most intercessors are humble, balanced people of God; it is the few who are flaky who give the intercessors a bad name.) But a few deceptions that flaky intercessors fall into compare with what I call the "bridal chamber experience." This is a physical relationship with spiritual beings.

Before I wrote this chapter I deliberated as to whether or not I should bring up this subject at all. In recent years not much has been said about sexual relationships with evil spirits, although with the rise of the New Age and satanism we are beginning to hear more about it. Yet it is not something new—even among Christians. St. Augustine and Thomas Aquinas discussed the subject. They wrestled with, among other things, the meaning of Genesis 6:1–4, which states that the "sons of God" bore children to the "daughters of men." It was a common topic among church leaders in the Middle Ages. Since the Enlightenment, however, the debate has shifted as to whether or not demons even exist; investigation of their activities has assumed a lower priority.

Recognizing that some may say, "It looks as though Cindy has now joined those flaky intercessors she is describing," I nevertheless feel that discussing this is worth the risk. We may not like it (I certainly do not), but we cannot escape the fact that either something is happening or certain individuals are so convinced it is that it makes no difference to them if it is real or not. My desire is not to be lurid but to be very clear that there is a problem out there that must be exposed. Having said this, let me describe the phenomenon as discreetly as I can.

I first became aware of this problem in a conversation with an intercessor. We were talking about something totally unrelated when Louise (not her real name) began talking excitedly about how God blesses mature intercessors with special intimacy with Him. The word *intimacy* triggered something inside of me. A red flag went up. As I asked her to tell me more about what she meant by intimacy, she described how Jesus would come to her in the night and take her into the bridal chamber. When she said, "Jesus would come in the night," three red flags went up. Thinking that I must be mistaken about what she was implying, I said, "Louise, you mean that the Lord lets you know in your heart He loves you?" At this point Louise began to stammer.

When the whole story came out, it was apparent that she was in grave deception, which, I am happy to say, she is no longer involved in today. Evidently those experiences began when she was awakened in the night and felt that every part of her body was charged and alive and a voice told her that it was Jesus coming to take her to the bridal chamber. She would become aroused in ways that the Holy Spirit does not do but that were purely demonic. But because the voice was so beautiful and said that it was Jesus, she felt that she must be having some unique experience in which the Lord was loving her in a special way.

Louise was actually being attacked by evil spirits that come generally in the night, although sometimes in the daytime, with tormenting sexual dreams. These spirits are called the *incubus* and *succubus*. Webster's dictionary gives the following definition for *incubus*: "A spirit or demon thought in medieval times to lie on sleeping persons, especially women, with whom it sought sexual intercourse: see also succubus."

After this encounter with Louise I began asking other prayer leaders if they had ever dealt with people who had similar stories and was told over and over that they had. Many did not know what to call it, but they knew it was demonic.

How did I minister to Louise? First I asked her to renounce as sin her actions in participating with the demonic spirit. She asked God to forgive her for believing a lie from Satan and attributing to Jesus what was from the devil.

Second, we asked the Lord to show us what opening had allowed the deception and attack against her. Louise said that her husband did not give her what she needed in their relationship and that she was bitter toward him for his lack of attention. This left her an easy mark for the enemy.

Third, we looked at the biblical precedents for intimacy in the Word and saw that those given by God touch us deeply with joy in the spirit, not physical arousal.

Fourth, in prayer, I took authority over the demonic incubus spirit, commanding that it no longer visit her in the night. She did the same and told the incubus spirit that she wanted it to leave.

One day this subject came up among a group of intercessors and friends. They were asking me some of my concerns as I was writing this book and I shared my struggles with them in writing on the topic of the false bridal chamber experience. One of them told me this story of a woman to whom she had ministered who was deceived by the incubus spirit.

A young worship leader named Gloria (not her real name) had been deeply in love with a handsome young man. They were engaged to be married when he died suddenly. Naturally this broke Gloria's heart, and she missed him desperately. One day as she was playing her guitar and worshiping the Lord she sensed someone in the room with her. To her shock and delight a spirit who looked like her fiancé entered the room. At first it was unbelievable, but it was so wonderful being with him that she let her defenses down. After all, she reasoned, he had come when she was worshiping the Lord. Perhaps God was allowing this because of her deep grief.

As time went on the deception deepened. She shared the experience with a friend, who took the matter to her prayer closet. The friend asked God to show Gloria who the spirit really was so that she would be free from its influence.

A while later Gloria was again worshiping the Lord when she felt the presence in her living room. As she went into the room she saw him lying on the couch, but to her utter shock his form was disgusting and revolting. Only his eyes looked like those of her fiancé. The Lord had revealed the incubus spirit for what it really was. She went for ministry to be set free from its influence.

Safeguards against Flaky Intercession

The surest way to avoid falling into any of these areas of flaky intercession is to focus your prayer on God's living Word.

When I first learned to "pray the Word," I had a little book with topic headings and related Scriptures for almost any situation. If someone had a need, I just turned to the appropriate section of the book and prayed directly from it.

One day a woman phoned with a dire financial need. Would I pray? Boy, would I! I prayed every prosperity Scripture in my little book and any other verses I could think of. I also told the devil to get his hands off her finances. I felt quite satisfied with my spirituality.

On hanging up, however, I sensed that the Holy Spirit was grieved; so I prayed again. God began to show me that He had been dealing with the woman about getting a job and that she was resisting Him because of laziness. Her financial need had resulted from disobedience.

I realized that she was unrepentant, and that I had prayed against the dealings of God in her life! I was shaken and quickly asked for God's forgiveness. Since then I have sought God for His *living* or *rhema* word for each situation in which I minister.

This is a critical point to grasp. We must learn how to pray God's living Word. Some people pray cafeteria-style: They go through the Word of God searching for a part that will fulfill their appetites. "God," they pray, "I want a new house, the neighbor next door as my spouse and please throw in a new car for good measure."

God's Word is full of promises and blessings and in many specific instances He may want to give us a home, spouse or car; but assuming that everything we want is God's will is not the same as praying God's Word.

If you have participated in any of the flaky practices in this chapter, why don't you repent right now and begin to intercede in a fresh way? For instance, if you prayed witchcraft prayers over anyone, break the power of the prayers and release blessing.

As we try to listen more closely to the way God directs us to intercede, coupled with the knowledge of ways the devil may try to lead us astray, we can continue to intercede with confidence, sure that flaky intercession will never be a part of our lives.

---

1. Gary Greenwald, *Seductions Exposed* (Santa Ana, Calif.: Eagle's Nest Publications, 1988), 22.
2. Norman Grubb, *Rees Howells, Intercessor*, 3rd ed. (Fort Washington, Pa.: Christian Literature Crusade, 1983), 79.

11

Prophetic Intercession

When a team from Frontline Ministries landed in Guatemala City, Guatemala, they felt anticipation for the task ahead as they went into the city to stay for the night. Among the team members was our good friend Dutch Sheets. He and the others had come to build a ministry center in Penten Jungle on the Passion River. Little did they know that they were stepping into a situation in which their lives depended on the obedience of an intercessor from Ohio named Linda Snelling, who was aware of the trip.

The group arrived on a Friday night, planning to fly out on Saturday to their ministry destination in the jungle. The next morning Dutch and the group went to the airport and found that their flight had been canceled. For those of you who are not familiar with travel in Central America, this is not unusual. The airport authorities simply told them that they would have to come back on Sunday.

The team went to prayer asking the Lord for His direction. Was Satan keeping them from leaving, or did God want them to stay in the city one more night?

Finally, the group in Guatemala felt that they should try to leave, and negotiated back and forth with the Guatemalan Airlines representatives. Meanwhile, back in Ohio, Linda Snelling was on her knees.

For over three hours she agonized in prayer for the team. She prayed and prayed until finally she received a release from God. This prayer helped turn the stony hearts of the airline people; suddenly, for no reason, after three hours of arguing, they changed their minds, threw up their hands and said, "Get on the plane. We will fly you now!"

The next morning at three A.M., one of the worst earthquakes in the history of the nation hit Guatemala City. It killed 30,000 people and left one million homeless. When the team returned from the jungle, they went to the hotel and homes where they had stayed the previous Friday night—and would have been on Saturday night. To their shock they discovered that many of them would have been crushed to death had they stayed that second night, when ceilings fell in and beams landed on top of the very beds in which they would have slept. How they praised God for His intervention and grace!

When they returned, Dutch heard about Linda Snelling's prophetic intercession on their behalf, and a sense of wonder filled his heart along with gratitude. His amazement increased when he found out she had prayed during the exact three-hour period when they were in the midst of negotiations with the Guatemalan Airlines representatives.

Thank God for the "extra" team member whom God sent with the Frontline team! And thank God for a faithful prayer warrior who said, "Here I am, Lord, send me; I will go on my knees." We may never know how much work for the Kingdom of God was affected by her prayers.

What exactly is prophetic intercession and how do you feel when God is calling you to pray such a prayer? Linda obviously felt strongly that she was to pray for the team. How did she know what to pray?

Prophetic intercession is an urging to pray given by the Holy Spirit for situations or circumstances about which you have very little knowledge in the natural. You pray for the prayer requests that are on the heart of God. He nudges you to pray so that He can intervene. Remember the chapter on God's enforcers? God will direct you to pray to bring forth His will on the earth as it is willed in heaven.

There are many different kinds of prophetic prayers, and not all are made by those who have the gift of prophecy. God will call upon anyone in the Body of Christ to pray prayers that go beyond natural knowledge because the Holy Spirit Himself desires to use all believers to pray. There are those, however, who will pray such prayers on a regular basis. These prophetic pray-ers are usually those with the gift of intercession.

This chapter will discuss two aspects of prophetic intercession: the believer's role in prophetic intercession, and the role of those with the gift of intercession—prophetic intercessors.

The Believer's Role

What is the believer's role in prophetic praying, and how do you hear the Holy Spirit's promptings?

Begin by telling the Lord that you want to pray for the things on His heart. Following the steps to develop a watchman's eye is also helpful (see pages 61–62).

In your quiet times with God ask Him to stretch you and enable you to pray beyond your natural knowledge about situations that come either directly into your thought life or from prayer requests.

Spend time worshiping the Lord. As you praise Him He will sanctify your natural reasoning.

Open the Word of God and ask the Lord to give you a living Word for the prayer request. Sometimes a Scripture will seem to jump out of the page as you read, or you will read devotional material that just fits the situation you are praying about.

Listen to God and trust the Holy Spirit to fill your thoughts with His words.

If you are open, you will begin to realize that thoughts about others are occurring to you. It might be that a name comes to you over and over. Or you might find yourself thinking things like "pray for protection" or "Lord, keep so-and-so safe." These will seemingly spring up from inside you.

You will sometimes enter into identification with or feel the emotions of the one for whom you are praying. The Holy Spirit might move through you with the emotions we discussed in the chapter on the manifestations of intercession.

You might weep or feel sad. Sometimes people feel agitated, and don't recognize it as the need for prayer for someone other than themselves. If you are agitated, ask the Lord why you are feeling uneasy and trust Him to speak to you. First John 2:20 says: "But you have an anointing from the Holy One, and you know all things." Dick Eastman tells of such intercession in his book *Love On Its Knees*. He had heard that 153 Dutch grade school children were being held by terrorists in Holland. The terrorists threatened to execute the children one at a time if their demands were not met. As Dick began to pray his mind was filled with a picture not only of the Dutch schoolchildren, but also of his own children in the picture with them. He put it this way:

> In the natural I knew this could not be. Both the girls were fewer than a hundred feet away, fast asleep in comfortable beds. But I had forgotten that. I had slipped into the intercessor's role of identification and the Holy Spirit had ushered me into an intensity of prayer I had never before known.
>
> Indignation swept over me and I began to command the terrorists to let the children go. I hit my fist into my palm as I prayed. I pointed my finger with authority, shaking it repeatedly at the terrorists as I demanded they release the children. I wept. I shouted. I trembled. And suddenly I sensed victory. As abruptly as the prayer had begun, it concluded.[1]

Dick later heard that all of the schoolchildren had been released.

What if Dick had shrugged off the feeling? Perhaps he could have decided that he had more important things to do than pray for Dutch children he didn't even know. There are 153 children alive today in large part because he paid the price to identify with the pain of parents in a land far away.

When you finish praying you might want to record your prayers in a journal along with the time and date you prayed. Ask God to confirm what you have prayed. If you seem to receive bizarre requests, do not pray them until you have had them judged by someone more mature than you in intercession.

Even a little child can be taught to pray prophetic prayers. This has occurred repeatedly with our own children, Mary and Daniel. One of the more dramatic examples occurred on a balmy spring day. Daniel was six years old at the time and suddenly came bursting through the door. I was busy fixing supper when he came over to me. "Mommy, Mommy! I feel funny in my tummy," he murmured. I looked at him and suddenly felt that what was happening to Daniel was not what it appeared.

"Daniel," I said, "is it in your tummy or is it something that God is trying to tell you?" The Bible says that rivers of living water will flow out of the belly (see John 7:38, KJV), and I have found that children will point to their tummies when they feel God touching them to pray. (Of course, sometimes they're just sick!)

Daniel said, "Mom, something is wrong with someone."

I sat down with him and said, "Honey, let's pray and ask God to show you what is wrong and who is having the problem, okay?"

He agreed, and we prayed together for a while. Finally he said, "Mom, could someone be killed?" I told him, "Yes, sweetheart. Ask the Lord to show you who is in danger." We prayed again and asked the Lord to show him when suddenly he exclaimed, "Mom, could the president of the United States be killed?"

I explained that this would be called assassination, and we needed to ask God to stop it from taking place. He prayed and asked God to stop the killing and protect the president. After the prayer he hopped up, feeling great, and went back outside to play until supper.

The next week I received a call from a friend who lives in Washington D.C. I was told about a plot to assassinate President Reagan that was uncovered the previous week by federal investigators. God had a heavenly investigator on the case before it happened, and partly through the obedience of a little boy, the plan of the enemy for our president was foiled. I explained to Daniel that God touches many people to pray and that he was probably one of many who prayed at that time for the president's protection, but it really increased Daniel's faith that prayer works.

Children can be especially used by God to pray prophetic prayers because they trust God so easily. They don't have the same inhibitions about listening and trusting what they hear. When children are reared to know the ways and character of God and His Word, they move easily in this type of prayer.

Over the years we have had many times of praying prophetic prayers over the nations of the earth as we have traveled. One of our most powerful times came as we traveled into Iraq to intercede during the war in U.S. President George W. Bush's administration.

I am aware that the war was extremely controversial, but whether or not one agrees with the premise, there comes a time when one has to hear from God as to what plan of action should currently be taken.

As I interceded for the soldiers involved in the fighting, the Lord strongly spoke to me that I was to go in and bring some people to pray about the way the war was going. In fact, what I heard was, "This war is going to result in another Vietnam War for the U.S. if there isn't a shift in the spiritual warfare strategy."

When strategy shifts, it is often up to the generals to make a plan of action and, at times, lead in its execution in the battle. As a result, we made plans to go to Iraq.

The team that ended up traveling there was small but mighty: Greg and Sharon Stone, a young Arab leader whom I feel it is best not to name, and Mike and me.

I must admit that I had some trepidation the night before we left from another Middle Eastern location to fly to our destination. Satan was working on my emotions. My husband, Mike, told me with a smile on his face, "We have been married for thirty-three years so if I am going to die, I might as well die with you!" Now that is true love.

As I watched Mike sleep the night (how do men do that?) before our long flight, I paced the floor and prayed. "God, keep us safe!" and other strong pleas went up to the throne of God from that hotel room surrounded by palm trees and sand.

The next day we arrived in Iraq in the dark of the night. There are enough details to the journey to write a whole chapter, but let me just say this: God led us to pray at a city about sixty miles away from ancient Nineveh. We decreed prophetically that the war would shift and take on a new battle strategy, among other things.

Not long after we arrived home, there was a shift in leadership on the U.S. side, and a new general was put in place with a battle strategy that included a surge in the number of troops.

What is the lesson in this? First the spiritual and then the natural. There are times when God wants us to put "boots to the ground," so to speak, to release His will from heaven to earth and the Lord will physically call us to pray, as some say, "onsite with insight."

God may not have you go all the way to Iraq and pray—and, I might add, that should only be done with seasoned prayer warriors under the inspiration of the Holy Spirit—but He might ask you to pray in a place of spiritual darkness in your city.

Results in prayer can be part of every believer's life as we are open to the Lord's leading. Those with the gift of intercession will find this happening frequently.

The Intercessor's Role

Those with the gift of intercession will find that prophetic praying is part of the call of God on their lives. As prophetic intercessors, they actually prophesy as they pray. Most have stumbled into this type of intercession and don't know why they pray as they do. They only know that they are able to pray for extended periods of time and that they see frequent answers to their prayers.

Peter Wagner gives this definition of prophecy in his book *Your Spiritual Gifts Can Help Your Church Grow*:

> The gift of prophecy is the special ability that God gives to certain members of the Body of Christ to receive and communicate an immediate message of God to His people through a divinely anointed utterance.[2]

We could adapt this to say that the gift of prophetic intercession is the ability to receive an immediate prayer request from God and pray about it in a divinely anointed utterance.

Daniel was a prophetic intercessor and his prayers are powerful to study. He was a prophet of governments and prayed prayers that changed history. Look at Daniel 9:2. The Lord wanted to release His people from captivity in Babylon and so He touched Daniel to pray to remind Him of His Word given through Jeremiah the prophet:

> In the first year of his reign I, Daniel, understood by the books the number of the years specified by the word of the LORD, given through Jeremiah the prophet, that He would accomplish seventy years in the desolations of Jerusalem.

Daniel took this promise of God and went to war in the heavenlies with it so that the Israelites would be released from their seventy-year captivity. Daniel 9:3 says: "Then I set my face toward the Lord God to make request by prayer and supplications, with fasting, sackcloth, and ashes."

This shows us that prophetic intercession comes about not only when God gives an intercessor awareness of a problem to pray about, but also when God gives a sense of urgency to words that have been spoken previously through the mouth of a prophet. First Timothy 1:18 says: "This charge I commit to you, son Timothy, according to the prophecies previously made concerning you, that by them you may wage the good warfare."

A wise prayer warrior, Margaret Moberly, once said, "Not all intercessors are prophets, but all prophets are intercessors." Intercession is the training ground for people God will use to speak prophetic words on a regular basis.

Years ago I was teaching at a retreat in Hemet, California. There was a certain pastor's wife over whom I prayed; and as I prayed the Lord started speaking a specific word to her about her family situation: "You have a daughter who is about this tall [I pointed to the top of her shoulder], and the Lord says that she is yours."

Now, even as the words were coming out of my mouth they seemed strange to me. Why would the Lord tell a mother that her daughter was hers? It made a lot of sense, as I discovered later, to the pastor's wife who was actually the stepmother of a daughter just as tall as her shoulder. The girl wanted to live with a relative in a situation the couple did not approve of and they were involved in a court case to determine the custody. The couple used the prophetic word to war in intercession. They reminded God that He had said the daughter was theirs, and proclaimed that Satan had no right to try to interfere. They had a living-word promise that she would come to live with them.

The next time they walked into the courtroom, the daughter was saying, "I will not live with you, Dad. I want to stay where I am." In the middle of the hearing, however, she said that she had changed her mind and wanted to live with her dad. She is now serving the Lord.

The prayer closet is the place where the prophet learns to hear the voice of God. Jeremiah 27:18 says: "If they are prophets, and if the word of the LORD is with them, let them now make intercession to the LORD of hosts."

Every single one of the prophets in the Bible was an intercessor. Abraham interceded for the city of Sodom. Isaiah, Jeremiah, Ezekiel—the list of prophets who prayed for Israel throughout the Old Testament is extensive. Examples in the New Testament include Simeon and Anna. No doubt God had told them to intercede because it was time for His Son to be born.

> And behold, there was a man in Jerusalem whose name was Simeon, and this man was just and devout, waiting for the Consolation of Israel, and the Holy Spirit was upon him. And it had been revealed to him by the Holy Spirit that he would not see death before he had seen the Lord's Christ.
>
> Luke 2:25–26

Anna served God day and night with fasting and prayer, and she also recognized the Child (see Luke 2:36–38).

A word of prophecy may be a form of intercession because it brings divine intervention into the life of the one who receives it—which is exactly what happens when we stand in the gap. Revelation 19:10 says: "Worship God! For the testimony of Jesus is the spirit of prophecy."

This brings us to an interesting point. Have you ever wondered how Jesus "ever liveth to make intercession" on our behalf (Hebrews 7:25, KJV)? His work on the cross was intercession, of course, but perhaps another way is through the prophetic word and prophetic intercession.

It could very well be that Jesus sees a need, touches someone to intercede and through the power of the Holy Spirit prays through that person in order for His will to be done on earth as it is in heaven.

In 1987, while flying home from a time of ministry in Jerusalem, I was praying for America. I was suddenly burdened overwhelmingly for the economy of the United States. All at once the words came to me: *I want you to fast as soon as your feet touch the ground in the United States because the stock market is going to crash. It cannot be averted, but it can be lessened.* Needless to say, I went on an extended fast when I got home. The stock market did crash, but I believe the effects were lessened through the prayers of intercessors.

Since I have given the Lord permission to change my schedule any time He wants to put me on special SOS assignments, this kind of prayer assignment is not necessarily a one-time event. During a worship service at our church, Trinity, (located in Cedar Hill, Texas), I once again heard the Lord call me to develop a prayer strategy for the stock market.

At the time, we had just finished a prayer assignment where we had seventeen 24-hour prayer rooms up and down Interstate 35. The highway runs from Laredo, Texas, to Duluth, Minnesota. We prayed for 35 days for a new holiness movement and called the prayer time The Highway of Holiness.

We had just concluded that massive project, and, frankly, I was ready for a vacation. (I know that our staff at GI concurred with this idea as well.) Right in the middle of a powerful moment of worship, the Holy Spirit spoke to my heart: *Cindy, I want you to take prayer teams to New York City and be there on October 29 to pray for the stock market.*

Most of you probably know that Wall Street crashed on that date in 1929, on what is known as Black Tuesday. Processing this was difficult for me; especially since I was going to have to explain to Mike why we had to go to New York for a massive prayer campaign on his sixtieth birthday!

We called a meeting of our U.S. Reformation Prayer Network council and went to work. The plan was to have people pray at stock markets around the world on that day, partnering with Graham Power and the Global Day of Prayer, and intercede on the floor of the stock exchange, all twelve regions of the U.S. Federal Reserve and at the Reserve in New York.

What should you do if you think you might be called to prophesy in prayer on a regular basis? First of all, don't call yourself a prophet. God Himself calls prophets in the Body of Christ. Simply pray the prayers He gives you and have them judged by those in authority over you. If you receive revelation in prayer, share it if you can. In due time those in leadership will recognize the anointing on your life and help you develop the gift.

If your church or pastor does not understand prophecy and/or prophetic intercession, don't try to force anyone to receive a revelation God has given you. Pray, be patient and let God open a door for you to speak.

If you ask the Lord to guide you, He will make a way for you to describe what is in your heart. God is a big God; if He wants you to speak what He has told you, He will enable you to do so. Proverbs

18:16 says: "A man's gift makes room for him, and brings him before great men."

Years ago I was in great frustration because I seemed to be receiving a lot of revelations as I prayed and had no one with whom to share them. The impression came to me finally that I was to believe that the above verse applied to me. I put it on my refrigerator and tried to wait, but I was chomping at the bit. As long as I was pushy the Lord made me wait. There were certainly others He could speak through besides me! He was more concerned that I learn to be patient and to have a quiet spirit.

It was difficult to wait on His timing. I used to think that *wait* was God's favorite word. One day when it seemed that He would never let me tell the things He was showing me in my prayer closet, I heard Him say, *Cindy, I don't waste My anointing. When it is time I will open up the doors for you.*

And open the doors He did. I have now led prayer teams across the face of the earth—from the tip of the world to the top of continent after continent.

When God thought that there was sufficient tempering in my life to enable me to say things the way they needed to be said, He flung the doors to ministry wide open. He will do the same for those who feel the call of God to minister the prophetic word.

---

1. Dick Eastman, *Love On Its Knees* (Tarrytown, N.Y.: Chosen Books, 1989), 34–37.

2. C. Peter Wagner, *Your Spiritual Gifts Can Help Your Church Grow* (Ventura, Calif.: Regal Books, 1979), 228.

12

Personal Prayer Partners

Almost two hundred years ago a shoe repairman in England became concerned about the world's heathen. As he pounded away on his shoes, looking at a map he had placed above his workbench and on which he had written the few facts he could garner from *Captain Cook's Travels* and other books, he would pray for the salvation of people in distant lands.

William Carey, who described himself as a self-educated, ungifted plodder, went on to become the father of modern missions. Through his influence Britain's first missionary society was formed—but only after Carey overcame great reluctance among his Baptist brethren. Soon afterward he went as a missionary himself to India, where he spent 42 years. Carey and his co-workers translated the entire Bible into 26 Indian languages and the New Testament, or parts of it, into 25 more.

Many books have been written about William Carey, but to my knowledge not one has been written about his little-known sister, a bedridden cripple. She and Carey were close, and he wrote to her from India relating all the details and problems of his work. Then hour after hour, week after week, she would list those concerns to the Lord in prayer. It makes me wonder who was really responsible for the success of William Carey's ministry!

Carey and his sister tapped into a source of spiritual power about which more and more ministers are becoming aware—personal prayer partners. How does God apportion credit to this team? Both apparently share equally in the responsibilities and rewards of a successful ministry or life lived for Christ. As 1 Samuel 30:24 explains, "As his part is who goes down to the battle, so shall his part be who stays by the supplies; they shall share alike."

Today it seems that ministers are experiencing serious attack and are going through much turmoil. When ministers come together for fellowship this is often a topic of conversation. And many whom they have respected as mentors are having serious problems. One of their greatest cries is, "How can I avoid having these sorts of things happen to me?"

Whenever those in ministry call me with tremendous burdens on their shoulders, one of the first questions I ask is, "Do you have personal prayer partners?" They will invariably say, "I have people who tell me that they pray for me on a regular basis." And I say, "But do they know your needs on an intimate level?" Only a handful have even thought of mobilizing personal intercession.

Is it biblical to have personal intercessors? Without question. Paul wrote to the church at Ephesus asking for personal intercession and stated that he was sending Tychicus for that very purpose, so that they might know his affairs (see Ephesians 6:21–22). Over and over at the closing of his letters to the churches he asked them to pray for him and told them his needs.

Have you felt hesitant to start or become part of a prayer partnership? You don't have to be in a public ministry to need prayer! Every intercessor needs the support of a prayer partner and many ministries are quite eager to find those who will support them in prayer.

Peter Wagner is sold on having personal prayer partners, and he has a good reason for this. He believes that he would not be alive today if not for an intercessor's prayers. In fact, on March 25 every year Peter and Doris Wagner get together with this prayer partner and her husband for an anniversary dinner to "Celebrate the Fall."

On March 25, 1983, one of Peter's prayer partners was attending a concert at a church near Temple City, California. At exactly 8:30 P.M., she experienced a great feeling of evil. She began to pray and ask the Lord what it meant. As she prayed she sensed that someone close to her—though not one of her children—was being attacked by death and destruction and that she was to pray for legions of angels to protect this person. During her intercession her back hurt so intensely that her husband put his hand on her to pray against the pain. She prayed for nearly twenty minutes before she sensed a release. The feeling of darkness lifted. She went home feeling fine, not knowing what her intercession had prevented.

Unknown to the prayer warrior Peter was in grave danger when the Lord called her into intercession. He had crawled up a ten-foot-high ladder in his garage to retrieve something from the loft. His head was twelve feet off the ground. He had climbed up the ladder many times before and knew that it was very secure. Right at 8:30 P.M., however, something pushed that ladder out from underneath Peter's feet, and he fell down to the cement floor of the garage, landing on the back of his head and neck. He called out for his wife, Doris, and she came running and telephoned for an ambulance.

After being rushed to the hospital, Peter was examined only to find that he had no broken bones or internal injuries other than severe bruises. There was absolutely no damage to either his back or his head. He was sore for a couple of months but recovered completely. He is certain that without those prayers by his prayer partner, Satan would have neutralized his ministry.

If you lead a ministry, I would like to encourage you in the pages that follow to start a fellowship of prayer. Tips follow as well for those curious about becoming prayer partners.

The prayer partners for Generals International are all top-notch intercessors, and we are greatly touched by their labor of love on our behalf. Since they have been praying for us, our ministry has exploded in growth and Mike and I know why—our prayer partners pray that God will anoint us as we speak and give us wisdom in ministry.

Once you make a commitment to your partners and ask them to commit to you, be aware that God will show them your weaknesses. Some days I pick up the phone and one of my partners will say, "Cindy, what are you anxious about? I have been praying for you in the area of fear and anxiety off and on all day long."

Personal prayer partners give us good accountability and are a comfort when we are desperately in need of direction from the Lord. Recently invitations to speak have been piling up on my desk, and some of them are to minister in troubled areas of the world. There are times when I simply write them down and send them to my prayer partners and ask them, "What do you think?" Invariably, three or more of them will call with the same word from the Lord—either not to go at this time or to accept the invitations.

Generals International has not always had personal prayer partners. Frankly, Peter Wagner has taught me how to mobilize partners in prayer from his teaching on intercession for Christian leaders. We were becoming exhausted from going into nations to minister before we had prayer partners. It was not that we didn't ask people to pray for us, because we did. After we asked people for a commitment to pray in ways that will be described later in this chapter, however, we began to see some marked changes in our lives and ministry.

Why do Christian leaders need personal prayer partners? Years ago I heard it explained that high-visibility people are bigger targets for Satan because he knows that if he can cause them to fall many others will fall with them in a domino effect. Satan comes after them with greater vengeance than he does the average Christian in the pew. Remember that it was the prince of Persia himself who battled to keep the word from getting through to Daniel.

As Dr. John Maxwell said in his prayer manual, *The Pastor's Prayer Partners*, "Any battle worth fighting calls for more resources than the leader possesses by himself."[1]

This was true of Moses. In the battle with the Amalekites, Joshua's army prevailed as long as Moses stood on the hill above and held up his hands. But his hands became heavy, so Aaron and Hur helped hold them up. Likewise, many Christian leaders are not able to finish the course given them by God because they are not strengthened by adequate prayer coverage. The enemy pressures them, distractions hit, persecutions come and they simply give up. Frankly, pastors are dropping out of the ministry like flies. Whatever your service to God, you need someone who will help you and cry out to God on your behalf.

Another reason that Christian leaders need personal intercession is that the warfare of the enemy has become sophisticated. His people are engaged in unholy fasts and unholy intercession. The following is an excerpt from a letter written to Peter Wagner from a Baptist Christian leader:

> During the flight from Detroit I had a man sitting next to me who seemed to have little interest in conversation. As we crossed the halfway point in the trip, he bowed his head as though he was praying. After his lips stopped

moving and he raised his head I inquired, "Are you a Christian?" I had given him no indication that I was a Baptist pastor and a university professor.

He looked shocked at my question and commented, "Oh, no. You have me all wrong. I'm not a Christian. . . . I'm actually a satanist." I asked him what he was praying for as a satanist. He answered, "Do you really want to know?" Assuring him that I did, he said, "My primary attention is directed toward the fall of Christian pastors and their families living in New England." He was serious about his mission and didn't care to discuss it further.[2]

Do these satanic prayers and unholy fasts have any real power? The Bible indicates they do. Jezebel called an unholy fast against the righteous Naboth:

> She wrote in the letters, saying, "Proclaim a fast, and seat Naboth with high honor among the people; and seat two men, scoundrels, before him to bear witness against him, saying, 'You have blasphemed God and the king.' Then take him out, and stone him, that he may die."
>
> 1 Kings 21:9–10

Naboth, a godly man, was put on trial and sentenced to death. The elders of the city believed the scoundrels' lies rather than the word of a righteous man. This particular attack seems to be in force today as more and more Christian leaders are being sued and accused by their brothers. Christian leaders need to face the fact of direct satanic attack, which can be stopped by means of prayer partners who pray on a regular basis.

Getting Started

Many leaders would like to have personal intercessors but don't know how to mobilize them or, after they are mobilized, how to communicate with them on a regular basis. The next part of this chapter discusses some practical steps for mobilizing intercessors, communicating with them and protecting yourself from possible traps as you receive their intercession. I have also included a section on knowing if you have enough prayer coverage. Let's look first at the types of prayer partners.

1. *Inner Circle.* This is a small group knitted to you by God. Moses had Aaron and Hur. Jesus seemed most intimate with Peter, James

and John. Some intercessors will be especially faithful in calling and praying, and these are your inner circle group. They will stand with you.

2. *Outer Circle.* These committed intercessors resemble Christ's other nine disciples. They will not pray as often but do pray for you on a regular basis.

3. *Congregation.* These are members of your congregation or people who tell you that they pray for you every day, but with whom you do not have close personal contact. They are nevertheless important to mobilize. This is done not through a letter, usually, but by describing your needs from the pulpit or platform and asking for prayer.

4. *Pentecost or Crisis Intercessors.* There are times when you will have a spiritual assignment that is particularly trying or be surrounded with more spiritual warfare. God will raise these up to pray for you until the job is accomplished. These can be mobilized by newsletter, media appeal or other announcements.

Traveling ministries would do well to develop intercession from this group since they do not usually have a church congregation to pray for them. Dick Eastman has mobilized these intercessors for years by stopping and asking for prayer for his family members by name at the end of each of his seminars. He gives each of their names and asks for special prayer for them after he leaves.

Another way to mobilize for traveling ministries is to send out prayer needs in your regular newsletter. These are not as intimate but will prompt people to pray.

Yet another way to communicate is to be open from the pulpit concerning your needs and those of your family. Some people are reluctant to be this vulnerable in a public arena, but it has always helped rather than hindered me. After all, the people to whom I am speaking are for the most part my brothers and sisters in Christ. I treat them like my family because that is what they are.

Mobilizing Prayer Partners

First of all, let's look at Luke 11:9: "So I say to you, ask, and it will be given to you; seek, and you will find; knock, and it will be opened to you."

1. *Ask.* The first step is to pray and ask the Lord to set aside personal prayer partners on your behalf.
2. *Seek.* Make a list of those whom you feel might pray for you on a regular basis. Listen to what people tell you as they go out the door of your church or after you speak. Some will say repeatedly, "I pray for you and your family every day." Take time to interview some of these as to what they hear from God as they pray for you. If you are in the ministry, God has already set aside some who are praying for you. Mobilizing them for effectual intercession is usually a simple matter of recognizing what God has already done.
3. *Knock.* Write a letter to those whom the Lord brings to your heart, asking them to be personal intercessors. Some you may want to call personally.

When I first learned about mobilizing personal prayer partners, Mike and I were going through some rough times. His boss was constantly threatening to fire him; our children were getting hit with all sorts of harassment; it seemed that everywhere we turned we were putting out fires. Finally one day I said, "Enough is enough! I have had it with this attack!" I sat down to pray and seek the Lord's will in providing personal intercessors.

After I made a list of intercessors my next step was to write a letter and ask for a commitment from them to pray for us. This letter stressed the confidentiality of the requests. It explained that we would be sharing intimate details that were to be revealed to no one other than our prayer partners. At that time we did not ask them to pray for us on a daily basis, although most indicated that they would do so. Instead, we asked them to pray as the Holy Spirit led them.

The response was tremendous. Within a week after sending the first letter explaining our needs, our lives began to turn around. Mike's boss stopped harassing him. Through an amazing sequence of events we received some clear direction from the Lord, and our children found relief from their trials.

What are some of the important qualifications to consider in choosing personal prayer partners?

1. A commitment to pray
2. Confidentiality
3. Ability to listen for God's direction and share in a way that is not intimidating
4. A call from the Lord to pray for you and your ministry

Communicating with Your Prayer Partners

Generals International sends out a prayer packet on a regular basis. It includes our itinerary, a personal letter and a sheet of prayer and praise requests. When we participate in an outreach we send a detailed report of the trip or meeting. The packet also includes any articles written about the ministry, or articles relating to the ongoing life of the ministry. We used to send out hard copy—and we still do to a few people—but now we find that using email is faster and more cost-effective.

The way you relate with your intercessors may depend on your type of ministry. Pastors, for instance, will be able to develop different relationships than traveling ministers will.

While Dr. John Maxwell pastored a local church, he related to his personal prayer partners on a number of different levels. For instance, he had one hundred personal prayer partners, all men. They got together every quarter for breakfast and he communicated by letter and phone. He also joined them for an annual prayer partners' retreat with food, fellowship and fun as well as heart-to-heart talks and prayer for each other. This is a good way to have healthy bonding with your prayer partners.

Peter Wagner gives this key to relating with his prayer partners: total accessibility! He says that his partners can reach him any time, day or night. He also stresses the need to be open and vulnerable to our partners and allow them to pray for our deep needs. This is extremely important. Your partners will not be able to pray for you effectively if you do not reveal your intimate needs to them. I cannot think of one time when any prayer partner betrayed my trust.

Relationship is the key. The more you take time to relate to those who pray for you, the better they will be able to intercede. Intercessors need fuel for their prayers, and what prompts them to pray are your prayer requests. Even though I am aware of this, at times my schedule makes it very difficult to do this, so I will ask them to get on a conference call with me so I can share my heart, as it is often hard to talk face-to-face with my prayer partners.

Another point that both Maxwell and Wagner make clear is the importance of gratitude. Philippians 1:3–4 expresses it well: "I thank my God upon every remembrance of you, always in every prayer of mine making request for you all with joy."

People need to be thanked often for their prayer sacrifice. They work hard at this.

Some Cautions

You need to be aware that there are potential dangers in relationships with personal prayer partners. Here are five:

1. *False emotional dependency.* The partners might become emotionally wrapped up in you, or you in them, in a way that is not healthy. Their prayers should not preclude or usurp your own hearing from God on a regular basis as a leader. Neither should having personal prayer partners excuse you from growing in your own prayer life.
2. *Control by intercession and prophecy.* You may become too dependent on your prayer partners, and listen only to them. Remember to maintain ministerial accountability to those over you to keep balance.
3. *Spiritual adultery.* This is a relationship with a prayer partner of the opposite sex in which strong ties of affection are formed. If you are married and spend long hours speaking intimately with a member (or members) of the opposite sex, you are headed for trouble. Spiritual adultery has taken place when more of your thoughts and energies are spent on that person than on your own spouse. Be careful about intimate sharing. Intimate conversations can lead to emotional entanglement.

   This is why some leaders have only prayer partners of the same sex. I would suggest that you be led by the Lord in this. At any rate, do not meet with a member of the opposite sex for prayer without someone else present. Most of the contact with prayer partners of the opposite sex should be by letter or telephone.

A good safeguard is to ask yourself this question: "Why am I calling this person? Is this something God wants me to do or am I drawn on a personal level?" Some ministers feel they can never be deceived in this area. I personally feel that if you think you cannot be deceived, you already are!

4. *Unwise choices*. This is particularly difficult for local pastors. Many have told me that telling the wrong thing to the wrong person has made them the subject of gossip. Be careful about your choices.

5. *Changes*. Be aware that people can change over a period of time and so can their commitment to pray for you. We ask our prayer partners on a yearly basis whether or not they still feel a commitment to intercede for us.

How Much Intercession Do You Need?

There are times when we need to add to our prayer partner list. Here are several indicators that you do not have enough prayer coverage and need to mobilize more intercessors:

1. You and/or your family are getting hit with physical or mental anguish on a regular basis.

2. Your intercessors indicate that they are being attacked on a regular basis and are losing quite a bit of sleep keeping you covered in prayer. Since they are the "heat absorbers" for the fiery darts coming against you, this indicates that the warfare has stepped up and you need to add more strength to the prayer coverage through more intercessors.

3. The situations in your life change when you are under attack but only after long, laborious battles. You need more intercession to pierce the darkness coming against you.

One pastor in Argentina asked that his people pray for him each time they ate a meal with their families. Imagine the power of this even if only one-third remembered to pray for him each day! That is powerful intercessory prayer coverage!

Many people neglect to get personal prayer partners because it doesn't occur to them that they are needed. They think having people pray for them is only for those who are more important or more spiritual than they are. I want to say that such an idea is pure myth! We all need people who pray for us, whether we are called to be a homemaker or the president of a nation.

Tips on How to Be an Effective Prayer Partner

Much of this chapter has been directed toward the Christian leader. Now I would like to address the prayer partners themselves. What are the rewards of being a prayer partner? I am a prayer partner myself for several minister friends. The apostle Paul wrote a wonderful passage about a person whom I believe was one of his prayer partners. "Epaphras, who is one of you, a bondservant of Christ, greets you, always laboring fervently for you in prayers, that you may stand perfect and complete in all the will of God" (Colossians 4:12).

The word *laboring* in Greek is the word *agonizomai*, which means to contend for victory in the public games. It came to mean to wrestle as if in a contest, straining every nerve to the uttermost toward the goal.[3] Epaphras was, among other things, one who wrestled in prayer.

Although I am aware that many of you are not even considering your rewards as a prayer partner, the Lord is faithful in remembering your sacrifice. When the Lord first called me to intercede, I made a list of ministries needing intercession, and I promised to pray for them every day. At that time these verses became very dear to me:

Do not lay up for yourselves treasures on earth, where moth and rust destroy and where thieves break in and steal; but lay up for yourselves treasures in heaven, where neither moth nor rust destroys and where thieves do not break in and steal.

Matthew 6:19–20

Along with this came the Lord's promise: *Cindy, if you will lay down your life in intercession for others now, you will be laying up interces-*

sion for yourself in My heavenly bank. When you are in ministry, many will intercede for you as your prayer partners. This has happened. At that time the partners did not know I was praying for them on a daily basis, but every day when my children took their naps I would spend two or three hours in prayer for those whom the Lord had impressed on me as needing intercession. These are now treasures of service laid up in heavenly places.

If you are an intercessor and have prayed faithfully for a Christian leader's family, you may have a situation come up in your family when you can say, "Lord, there are a lot of my prayers heaped up in heavenly places on behalf of other people's families. Now will You raise up people to pray for my family, too?" He will be faithful to touch other prayer warriors' hearts on your behalf.

Another advantage of being a prayer partner is that you become a prayer missionary. The mandate to "go into all the world" becomes a reality as you pray for the Christian leader who travels there.

How do you become a prayer partner who is a blessing and not a burden?

1. Come as a servant to the leaders. Realize that they are not there to meet your needs and the prayer needs of your family. Although they pray for their partners, do not take advantage of them. They will appreciate that quality in you since most people usually want only to take from them. Rarely are they on the receiving end.

2. When you talk to them on the phone, state what the Lord has given you quickly and concisely. They are often extremely busy people and may feel obligated to talk even though it will cause them to be pressed for time the rest of the day. A good idea is to ask if they are busy or if it would be better to call at a different time.

3. Don't be offended if they don't speak to you in person. They may or may not be able to do so at that moment. This does not mean they don't care.

4. Be careful not to overload emotionally the person for whom you are praying. If you have a heavy warning from God for them, be sensitive as to whether or not they can handle hearing the warning without being overwhelmed.

5. If you have a dream or vision, ask the Lord for the interpretation. It is your job to interpret, not theirs. If you are not sure that something you are receiving is from the Lord, take more time to pray.

6. It may take time to build trust in the validity of your ministry of intercession. Be faithful in your praying and the relationship will come.

7. Do not presume upon your relationship with Christian leaders. They will treasure you both as an intercessor and as a person if you don't tell personal details or flaunt the fact that you are their prayer partner. This is a confidential trust.

8. Remember to pray for the families of the leaders. This is critical because they come under strong attack from the enemy as well.

9. The Lord may give you a focus of prayer. In other words, you may be a "specialist" in certain areas. I have found that some of my partners pray pretty much exclusively for my children. They tell me, "I pray very little for you as a minister." Others will pray for my husband more than they pray for me. Some will pray for me to be free from any moral temptation.

10. Give the leaders feedback on a regular basis on what the Lord is telling you. Either call or write at least every few months. I cannot overstress the need for intercessors to communicate in some manner to those they pray for. Since prayer is a two-way street, I like to hear from those who pray for me as to what God is saying to them.

11. There are two times when ministers for whom you intercede are especially needy: the night before they minister and the time directly after.

    The night before they minister is often a time when family members get harassed and many distractions come to divide the mind of the leader from preparing for the time of ministry. Things break down; strife tries to enter; children come under oppression. Just like Jesus in the Garden, the leader for whom you pray would welcome prayer during the Gethsemane time.

    The time when the minister has finished the assignment is also particularly vulnerable. For pastors this is usually the Monday after a Sunday of spiritual breakthrough. Many have told me how depression will try to hit. This is often the time when people express criticism of the pastor. Leaders are vulnerable to criticism right after they have ministered extensively and exhaustively. Satan knows this. Notice that the angels came and ministered to Jesus after His time in the wilderness.

For some reason it seems that most traveling ministers experience warfare for nearly two weeks after they come home from a prolonged trip. Sometimes it is a physical attack, sometimes financial. It often occurs when they are exhausted and are most in need of a time of refreshing. Prayer partners should not stop praying for the leaders until the Lord gives them a release that all is well on the home front. This will stop or lessen the backlash from the enemy.

12. As a prayer partner, pray for protection for your own family as you intercede. I suggest that you read Psalm 91 out loud daily. The more visible the leader you are praying for, the more that you will also need a prayer shield as you stand in the gap.

My friend Beth Alves, whose ministry is Increase International, has written some fine books on developing prayer strategies for intercessors. She has suggested the following guide for intercession for Christian leaders:[4]

Sunday:	Favor with God
Monday:	Favor with man
Tuesday:	Pure vision
Wednesday:	Spirit, soul, body
Thursday:	Warfare and protection
Friday:	Priorities
Saturday:	Family

---

1. John Maxwell, *The Pastor's Prayer Partners* (Bonita, Calif.: Injoy Ministries), section on Praying for My Leader.

2. C. Peter Wagner, *How to Have a Prayer Ministry* (Pasadena, Calif.: Charles E. Fuller Institute, 1990), section on Intercession for Christian Leaders.

3. Zodhiates Spiros, *The Hebrew-Greek Key Study Bible* (Chattanooga, Tenn.: AMG Publishers, 1984), ref. no. 75:1685.

4. For more information on developing prayer ministries, please contact Beth Alves.

13

Intercessory Praise

A mighty fortress is our God
A bulwark never failing;
Our helper He, amid the flood
Of mortal ills prevailing.
For still our ancient foe
Doth seek to work us woe;
His craft and pow'r are great,
And armed with cruel hate,
On earth is not his equal.

Martin Luther (1483–1546)

It was the end of a powerful meeting for women. The seminar was about to come to a close when a woman came forward and requested prayer. Tears streamed down her face as she told of a serious problem with depression and hospitalization. She was seemingly on the verge of a nervous breakdown.

The ministers gathered around her and started to pray. They prayed and prayed, and there was no breakthrough. The woman still felt horrible oppression on her mind. All of a sudden, the head of the organization sent for a worshiper to come forward. This worshiper began to lead the group in intercessory praise or praise warfare, as some call it. I went to the piano, and we began a type of warfare that is becoming quite frequent in prayer groups today—warring against the works of Satan by worshiping the Lord. This is certainly not a new means of intercession, as we have much biblical precedent, but is one that is largely overlooked in many circles of prayer.

The women in the seminar stood to their feet. They sang; they clapped; they shouted; until suddenly the woman for whom they were praying began to weep and relate that the oppression had completely left her mind. It was as though a cloud had lifted, and for the first time in years her thoughts were clear. How we rejoiced together at the goodness of God on her behalf!

In reflecting on this testimony many questions arise. What does prayer have to do with praise? What does praise have to do with spiritual warfare? Lastly, since this is such a powerful tool, how can I incorporate it into my intercessory group as a leader?

Prayer and Praise

To answer the question of what prayer has to do with praise, let's look at a foundation passage concerning prayer in God's Word. Isaiah 56:7 says: "Even them I will bring to My holy mountain, and make them joyful in My house of prayer. . . . For My house shall be called a house of prayer for all nations."

What does this have to do with intercessory praise? To help answer this question, let me tell you about a seminar we held on this subject in Washington D.C. in 1986.

The name of the seminar was "A Marriage of Prayer and Praise." The purpose was to bring together worshipers and intercessors for corporate praise warfare for the nation. We felt that many people considered themselves to be worshipers, and others, intercessors. The worshipers did not consider themselves intercessors, and the intercessors did not consider themselves worshipers. As Mike and I prayed we felt that if the two groups came together, they would become praisers ("praysers") and that many around the United States would catch the vision of intercessory praise in their prayer groups and worship teams. In turn they would use this as an intercessory tool for America.

One of the speakers for the meeting was a missionary worshiper named Jim Gilbert, who has written many worship songs. Jim explained that God had revealed to him that he needed to learn more about intercession. "I used to think that intercession was going to the closet and having a stomachache," he said with a laugh. As a worshiper, he felt that many of the intercessors he knew had no joy. They were always so depressed he was not sure he wanted to become involved with intercession. But then he discovered intercessory praise and found that Isaiah 56:7—"My house shall be called a house of prayer"—actually means intercessory song.

This was the key. I went home excited to study that verse further and found that the words *of prayer* in Isaiah 56:7, *tephillah*, denote a prayer that is set to music and sung in formal worship. The word *tephillah* occurs 77 times in the Old Testament.

You could safely interpret that verse this way: "My house shall be called a house of prayer and praise." Music cannot be separated from prayer in most of the Old Testament.

The New Testament passage in which Jesus cleansed the Temple and quoted that verse also connotes the idea of worship. The idea is that God will make us joyful in the house of prayer. Many intercessors go around with long faces. If we don't maintain joy in intercession, the enemy will take our strength from us. Nehemiah 8:10 says: "For the joy of the LORD is your strength."

Satan loves to break down intercessors through grief and sorrow over all of the problems they pray about. They become wounded burden-bearers, and many develop health problems. I once heard a true story of a woman who went into travail for a problem. Her husband kept asking her to stop and rest and eat. She refused, not realizing that her travail was really grief and compulsion. She was being driven to pray by Satan instead of being led to pray by God. Her health so suffered from her sustained imposition of grief that she could not regain it, and actually died. Even in the midst of battle we must maintain our joy, or else we can give the devil a lot of glory.

It is wonderful to see how prayer and praise are being intricately woven together as the Lord has raised up such ministries as the International House of Prayer in Kansas City with just such an emphasis.

Mike Bickel was given an amplification of this message of *tephillah* from Revelation 5:8:

Now when He had taken the scroll, the four living creatures and the twenty-four elders fell down before the Lamb, each having a *harp*, and golden *bowls* full of incense, which are the prayers of the saints (emphasis mine).

There are now many 24-hour houses of prayer that minister before the Lord in what has become known as "harp and bowl intercession," where worship, song and prayers are mixed. They also sing new songs unto the Lord that are given to them spontaneously.

Praise and Warfare

Since prayer and praise are linked together in the Word of God, what do they have to do with spiritual warfare? Psalm 149 speaks of praise in spiritual warfare:

Praise the Lord! Sing to the Lord a new song, and His praise in the assembly of saints. . . . Let them praise His name with the dance; let them sing praises to Him with the timbrel and harp. . . . Let the high praises of God be in their mouth, and a two-edged sword in their hand, to execute vengeance on the nations, and punishments on the peoples; to bind their kings with chains, and their nobles with fetters of iron; to execute on them the written judgment—this honor have all His saints. Praise the Lord!

verses 1, 3, 6–9

In the above passage, praising God executes vengeance upon the heathen. It binds kings with chains and nobles with fetters of iron, and executes judgment. Pretty powerful intercession! I earnestly believe that the worship of God in the Church is a type of spiritual warfare, but the believers have not fully understood what was happening as they sang and thanked God. We will describe this further in the section related to receptivity to the Gospel.

One of the most outstanding stories of praise binding the work of the enemy comes out of Shiloh Christian Fellowship in Oakland, California. Dr. Violet Kiteley was the pastor at the time.

Shiloh Christian Fellowship had always been known as a worshiping church, and the members believed earnestly in the power of worship to bind the enemy. They did not realize how much the word had gotten around about their worship until one day when they received an invitation from the Oakland Police Department. Would they be willing to go to Pleitner Avenue and see what could be done for the area? Pleitner Avenue at the time was infested with drug lords, pimps and prostitutes; it was a rough, dangerous part of Oakland.

After they got over their surprise at the invitation, they said they would be glad to go. As they prayed they devised a plan. Working with the police they marked off an area of the street to have a block party. They planned to give away clothes, cook hot dogs, worship God according to Psalm 149 and then preach an evangelistic message. The church went back for three Saturdays in a row. The results were incredible. In fact, the police told the media about the parties and reported the results in the newspaper. According to the police reports, 70 percent of the drug lords moved out of the Pleitner Avenue area after the parties.

I asked Dr. Kiteley if they were praising God in order to come against powers and principalities over the area intentionally according to Psalm 149. She answered quickly, "Of course we were. We were not out there just to have a good time and sing!"

Shiloh Church has now been working with the police for five years. The police tell them where the troubled areas of Oakland are and where they expect the most homicides; the church goes in and defeats the enemy through intercessory praise. According to Dr. Kiteley these block parties have grown all across America as a result of her son's teaching and describing the move of God through worship on Pleitner Avenue.

In addition to binding the enemy, praise allows us to stand in the gap for others so they may be delivered. This is what occurred at the seminar mentioned earlier in which the cloud of oppression was lifted from the woman's mind. We have a biblical model of this when young David sang for King Saul:

> And so it was, whenever the spirit from God was upon Saul, that David would take a harp and play it with his hand. Then Saul would become refreshed and well, and the distressing spirit would depart from him.
>
> 1 Samuel 16:23

Many years ago Mike and I were awakened by a call from a frantic mother. It took us a minute to collect our thoughts to understand what she was saying because it was two A.M.! "Please come immediately," she said. "Our daughter is in a horrible condition. She has been trying to kill us with a butcher knife!" We asked if she had called the pastor. She said, "I have tried everyone; there is no one but you." Mike and I dressed hurriedly, found someone to keep our small children and then drove thirty miles to the house.

When we walked in the door we were greeted by a horrifying sight. A fourteen-year-old girl was pinned to the floor by her father. She was making growling noises. He looked up at us with pleading eyes and said, "I have been holding her down for three hours, but she is so strong that I am worn out." While he was speaking she wiggled a hand free and without opening her eyes clawed at her father's throat. Mike motioned to me and we stood together for a moment. Then, without communicating to one another, both of us began to worship God. We stood and worshiped around them for about two hours. Finally, at the end of that time, the girl was restored to her right mind, sat up and talked to us while we found out what had led to her condition.

This is only one way that we minister deliverance, but it is an effective way and the way we were led to follow that hot summer night. Just as David's music had driven the evil spirit from Saul, the spirits in the young girl were driven out through intercessory praise.

Why is Satan so affected when we praise God? First of all, he was once in heaven and knows the power of worship. In fact, some believe that he was once the worship leader of heaven. Ezekiel 28:13 says: "The workmanship of your timbrels and pipes was prepared for you on the day you were created."

The book *The Rebirth of Music* explains it this way:

Lucifer has tambourines and pipes built into his body and had the ability to play these pipes or tambourines extremely well. It is definitely clear that Lucifer excelled in music and that it was part of him. The Bible refers to pipes, plural, meaning there were more than one.

Lucifer also had tabrets, or tambourines, as part of his makeup, which would give him rhythm, or a beat, to the music that he played. In fact, Lucifer's makeup represented all the instruments that we know today. Isaiah 14:11 says: "Thy pomp is brought down to the grave, and the noise of thy viols." Viols are a six-stringed musical instrument which represents all stringed instruments. So the total spectrum of instruments that we play today except for electronic instruments were built into Lucifer's body. He could play them all.

Another name for Lucifer is "the Anointed Cherub." Lucifer was given a definite anointing for serving or ministering in music.[1]

Second, he knows that when we use the power of God's worship against him in intercessory praise it neutralizes his power.

Third, and most important, he hates it because he knows that when we use Psalm 149 as a weapon in worship that his ruling hierarchy is bound and fettered through intercessory praise.

The Word of God says this in Psalm 22:3: "But You are holy, enthroned in the praises of Israel." When we praise God, He inhabits or enters our praises, and His power overwhelms the power of the enemy. He is a mighty God, and Satan cannot match His strength. Light will dispel the darkness through God's entering into our praise.

This aspect of worshiping God enabled Paul and Silas to be set free from the enemy and dispel his power. Acts 16:25 says: "But at midnight Paul and Silas were praying and singing hymns to God, and the prisoners were listening to them."

Did you ever wonder what motivated Paul and Silas to enter into such high praise? Could it be that they were sitting in the dungeon wondering what was to become of them when Silas said something like this: "Brother Paul, how can we get out of this predicament?"

Paul might have thought a moment and said, "This is not the first time that an Israelite has faced the hindrance of walls—remember Jericho?"

"We can't march around this prison with our legs in chains."

"That's true," Paul returned, "but we can give a shout, and perhaps the walls of this prison will fall down—or at least the door will open."

"You're right. We should praise the Lord," agreed Silas. "It worked for Jehoshaphat when he exhorted the people to praise the Lord and sing their way to victory."

I don't know if the men felt foolish or not when they began, but they must have praised in loud voices because the Bible says that the other prisoners heard them. And as they praised the prison started to tremble! There was a great earthquake, and the doors to the prison house sprang open.

One time while I was in Argentina teaching about spiritual warfare I had an opportunity to practice what I preach on this subject! The team members on the trip were together on an elevator when suddenly it stopped between floors. At first we laughed because we thought it was funny, until we realized the cold, hard facts. We really were stuck in the elevator!

As we waited, wondering what to do, an inspiration came from within me: This was a great time to apply God's Word! If praise got Paul and Silas out of prison, surely it would get us out of the elevator. With this thought in mind a great excitement rose up inside me, and one praise after another came out of my mouth. In a very few moments the elevator started functioning again. Simply coincidence? Perhaps. I think that a good object lesson about the delivering power of prayer would be a more likely explanation. Psalm 8:2 says: "Out of the mouth of babes and infants You have ordained strength [or, as Jesus quoted this verse in Matthew 21:16, "perfected praise"], because of Your enemies, that You may silence the enemy and the avenger."

Not only does praise warfare or intercessory praise still the avenger, but it also brings a receptivity to the Gospel. Notice that the jailer and all his family were saved after Paul and Silas praised God in jail.

Intercessory praise is an effectual weapon to keep the strong man from blinding the eyes of those who need to receive the Gospel of Jesus Christ (see 2 Corinthians 4:4). Terry Law tells of just such an incident in his book *The Power of Praise and Worship*.

He was ministering in Russia with his singing group, Living Sound, in 1972. The group was booked to sing in a nightclub full of some two hundred members of the Youth Communist Party. He had been strictly forbidden to say anything relating to the Gospel. Law agreed and stood in the back while his group began the concert. Halfway through, the singers began to worship God with their hands raised in praise. Several of them were crying as they stood in the presence of the Lord.

God moved mightily as a result of their worship, and at the end of the concert they stayed until 3:30 A.M. leading many to a personal relationship with Jesus Christ.

Law knew that he had witnessed one of the most significant events of his life. He says it like this:

> I discovered that if we would worship God before our audiences, no matter how hostile they were, through the praise and worship we would literally bind the powers and forces that oppressed them. The people then became susceptible to the Gospel and to the anointing of the Holy Spirit that was upon us through our praise and worship.[2]

Many of the great hymns of the Church carry an anointing to release captives from Satan's grasp. One of the most beloved hymn writers of all time was Fanny Crosby. Although she was blind in the physical sense, her hymns opened, and are still opening, countless numbers of eyes to the need for the Savior. In his book about her life, Bernard Ruffin tells many stories of conversions as a result of Fanny Crosby's hymns. Fanny Crosby's own testimony about why her hymns produced such a profound effect on the lost goes like this:

> Fanny explained it in terms of the action of the Holy Spirit. Whenever she wrote a hymn, she prayed that God would use it to lead many souls to him. She prayed that she might be the means of saving a million men through her hymns. And so, whenever she heard of numerous conversions occurring, apparently as a result of the singing of her hymns, she attributed it in part to supernatural means. She said that inasmuch as the hymns were consecrated to the purpose of winning souls, God chose to work miracles through them.[3]

The words of the hymns written by Fanny Crosby and Charles Wesley and Martin Luther and others still carry a powerful anointing today. They touched my life recently when I was struggling with a problem. In looking for hymns to include in this chapter I opened a hymnal and began to read the words of such songs as "God Will Take Care of You," and it was not very long before my heart was comforted and tears were rolling down my cheeks as the heaviness lifted from me.

Worship is intercessory. It doesn't matter whether it is a current praise song or a song from the 1500s; it has power to break Satan's strongholds from hearts and minds.

The Bible gives many ways to incorporate intercessory praise into our prayer groups and our personal prayer times. Let's look into some of the weapons we use in praise warfare, and then we will show how to incorporate these into our actual prayer meetings.

There are seven Hebrew words for praise, and they can all be used at different times in our prayer meetings.

1. *Halal*. To be boastful, excited; tremendous explosion of enthusiasm in the act of praising (the word *hallelujah* is from the word *halal*). The Talmud and the Midrash call attention to the fact that it is connected with the overthrow of the wicked (see Psalm 117:1).
2. *Yadah*. To thank, to give public acknowledgment to, to extend the hand, to worship with raised hands (see 2 Chronicles 20:19–21).
3. *Barak*. To bless, to bow, to kneel in adoration (see Psalm 103:1–2).
4. *Zamar*. To touch the string, to make music to God. This is a musical verb for praise.
5. *Shabach*. To speak well of in a high and befitting way. It means to address in a loud tone, to shout, to command triumph (see Psalm 117:1).
6. *Tephillah*. Intercession for someone, supplication, a hymn (see Isaiah 56:7).
7. *Towdah*. Thanksgiving; also involves the extension of the hand in thanksgiving; to give the sacrifice of praise (see Psalm 50:23).

There are several other weapons of praise including the following.

Walking and Marching

> Every place that the sole of your foot will tread upon I have given you, as I said to Moses.
>
> Joshua 1:3

The march that Joshua and his troops made around Jericho was a type of intercession. It is also an example of persistence in intercession. How many of us have stopped our praying when only one more time around Jericho would have brought a breakthrough in our circumstances?

This type of marching produces deliverance today just as it did for the Israelites. A man named Rick went to a prayer meeting that Joy

Towe was holding in Dallas, Texas. Joy was a forerunner in the area of praise warfare, and ministers on the frontlines in this type of intercession. Rick was a television producer with a big problem. He had a job lined up and no television equipment. He couldn't even rent any.

Joy put Rick in the middle of the circle, and they marched around him after seeking the Lord in prayer. In Rick's words, "We pursued aggressively with warfare—we were militant!"

After Rick left the meeting he ran into someone from a TV production company who was looking for a manager. They had the equipment he needed as well as offices. He ended up making money for them as well as meeting his own need.

Another verse that relates to marching is Psalm 48:12: "Walk about Zion, and go all around her."

Treading

> Through God we will do valiantly, for it is He who shall tread down our enemies.
>
> Psalm 108:13

> "Behold, I give you the authority to trample [tread] on serpents and scorpions, and over all the power of the enemy, and nothing shall by any means hurt you."
>
> Luke 10:19

Treading is very much like marching—only more aggressive. Whereas marching sets boundaries in prayer, treading includes actually stopping the power of the enemy. In Joy Towe's prayer meeting they were evidently treading as well as marching. Psalm 44:5 says: "Through You we will push down our enemies; through Your name we will trample those who rise up against us."

Singing

> You shall have a song as in the night when a holy festival is kept, and gladness of heart as when one goes with a flute, to come into the mountain of the LORD, to the Mighty One of Israel. The LORD will cause His

glorious voice to be heard, and show the descent of His arm, with the indignation of His anger and the flame of a devouring fire, with scattering, tempest, and hailstones.

Isaiah 30:29–30

Our son Daniel was born with a club foot; it would not flex. The doctor said that he could not bend it forward and, therefore, would not be able to walk well. One night as I held Daniel a chorus came to my heart:

> The devil had me bound, but Jesus set me free.
> Well, the devil had me bound, but Jesus set me free.
> The devil had me bound, but Jesus set me free;
> Singing glory, hallelujah, Jesus set me free!

I sang this over and over for an hour and then put Daniel to bed. The next morning while changing his diaper I noticed that his foot was flexible. His little shoe went on easily. Something happened to his foot when I sang over Daniel—the power of the enemy was broken, and God touched his foot.

Clapping

> Oh, clap your hands, all you peoples! Shout to God with the voice of triumph!

Psalm 47:1

The word *clap* in this passage is *teqae*: clang, smite, strike.[4]

Ezekiel 6:11 says: "Thus says the Lord GOD: 'Pound your fists and stamp your feet.'"

Clapping in the Bible is associated not only with praise but also with warfare. Clapping is one means of breaking yokes.

Shouting

> Shout against her [Babylon] all around; she has given her hand.

Jeremiah 50:15

Then the men of Judah gave a shout; and as the men of Judah shouted, it happened that God struck Jeroboam and all Israel before Abijah and Judah.

2 Chronicles 13:15

Once when we were in the midst of a Glory Fire conference in Harlem, New York, we felt led of the Lord to open wide the doors of the church and spill out onto the streets of Harlem with exuberant worship. One elderly African American intercessor started singing an old song of the church, sung in the early days of Harlem.

The sound of that battle cry for souls reached into the streets as we marched up and down—singing without instruments, clapping and shouting. Harlem is a city of music, and we weren't on the top of the list for excellence that day as musicians. However, what we lacked in finesse we made up for in enthusiasm.

People from Spanish Harlem danced with those from Black Harlem, with a few of us white people thrown in for contrast. We sang over the city and cried out for God to revitalize the area.

I am happy to report that is precisely what has happened in that city today. God can save a city by many or even by a few—brown, black and white—making a joyful noise over a city the Lord wanted to heal.

We had a track report of seeing God change cities by the time we got to Harlem, you see. We knew that the power of God could change a city. In fact, in June 1990 a team from Harvest Evangelism was in the city of Resistencia on a spiritual warfare assignment. As we studied the city it became apparent that the strong man of San La Muerte, or the spirit of death, wanted worship through music. The pictures of him painted in the town square depicted him playing musical instruments. One verse that came to us as we prepared to pray over that city was Psalm 32:7: "You shall surround me with songs of deliverance."

When we sought the Lord for a strategy to take the city, we felt strongly that we should use praise warfare since the spirits over the city used music in their worship. God's light would overcome the darkness through worship. We used many of the weapons of warfare described in this chapter—we sang, we clapped, we marched and we shouted. The shouting came at the end of the five hours of prayer. After we gave a great shout of victory, we felt a tremendous breakthrough of joy. Although we could not see anything changed with our natural eyes, we knew in our spirits that the root had been cut that allowed the worship of San La Muerte in the city of Resistencia.

> And the seventh time it happened, when the priests blew the trumpets, that Joshua said to the people; "Shout, for the LORD has given you the city!"
>
> Joshua 6:16

What would have happened if the people had not shouted? Perhaps the walls would not have fallen down and victory would not have been won.

Laughter

The weapon of laughter is extremely powerful and even necessary as an intercessory manifestation. As intercessors we often hear so many serious problems and needs during a day that they can wear us down. There are basically two uses of laughter in intercessory praise: (1) personal protection and emotional health; (2) direct warfare against Satan and his forces. Although these were discussed earlier, I would like to expand on them here.

1. Personal protection and emotional health.

Intercessors have shared with me how they are sometimes overwhelmed and overburdened with the prayer requests they receive. Laughter is an important safeguard against heaviness in intercession.

It may sound strange, but I believe the Lord has gifted me with the ability to laugh in the midst of severe crises so that the situation will not devastate me. There are times my husband and I will read the jokes out of *Reader's Digest*, or I will go to the card shop and look at funny cards simply because Proverbs 15:13 says that "a merry heart makes a cheerful countenance, but by sorrow of the heart the spirit is broken."

What does laughter have to do with intercessory praise? It breaks the power of the enemy to depress and oppress you in the midst of battle. Depression dilutes your spiritual strength. Secular studies have shown how laughter works like medicine. Deep laughter oxygenates the blood and causes positive physical changes.

2. Direct warfare against Satan and his forces.

Laughter in warfare mocks the enemy. Psalm 37:12–13 says: "The wicked plots against the just, and gnashes at him with his teeth. The Lord laughs at him, for He sees that his day is coming."

A little illustration of this comes from writing this book. When I first wrote this book in 1990, I didn't have a computer, but had to use others' machines. I just had my old self-correcting typewriter. It was so frustrating, let me tell you, not to be able to cut and paste through a computer program!

I was having many difficulties with equipment as I tried to write. One harassing thing after the other happened to our office machines. My typewriter broke down about six times. Two computers went crazy, and two fax machines wouldn't function. Things were finally going well as I sat down to type—and the typewriter jammed. Nothing I did made it any better until laughter started pouring out of me. I laughed so hard I had to put my head down. When the laughter finally ran its course, the typewriter operated perfectly. Coincidence? Maybe, but I'll tell you one thing: The typewriter did great after that and I certainly felt a whole lot better!

Joy

Laughter and joy are often interrelated in intercession. As mentioned earlier, joy is an important part of our intercession because it is our strength for battle. Psalm 149:2 says: "Let Israel rejoice in their Maker; let the children of Zion be joyful in their King."

According to Joy Towe in her book *Praise Is*, the word *joyful* here has the following meaning in Hebrew:

> The Hebrew word for *joyful* in this passage is *guwl* meaning to spin around (under the influence of a very violent emotion). The word *guwl* is also found in Zephaniah 3:17: "The Lord thy God in the midst of thee is mighty; he will save, he will rejoice over thee with joy; he will rest in his love, he will joy over thee with singing."[5]

The translation of "He will (*guwl*) over thee with singing" is that He will spin around under the influence of violent emotion.

Somehow our idea of joy is not the same as that translated in this passage. We are much more familiar with the quiet joy that is with us in our everyday walk with the Lord. The joy that comes in intercession, however, can run the gamut from laughter to violent emotion to quiet peace.

Jesus rejoiced in His spirit over the breakthrough the disciples had over the demons. "In that hour Jesus rejoiced in the Spirit" (Luke 10:21). This rejoicing means to jump for joy or exult. Joy breaks heaviness and releases oppression.

Let me give you an example of joy as warfare. In 1989 the Lord impressed upon me the desire to go to the International Aglow Convention in San Antonio, Texas, with a prophetic word. The word was given through the team effort of Beth Alves and myself as we each prophesied before the convention. The last words of the prophecy were about spiritual warfare and a new move to prayer in Aglow, and I said, "Rise up, women of God, it's time for war!" As soon as the words were out of my mouth the sound of rejoicing and joy rang out from the women. It almost sounded like a giant lion's roar as eight thousand women from sixty nations shouted and praised God for the word.

From that joy came the birthing of a movement of prayer that is touching Aglow International worldwide today across 172 nations. Things often happen that we do not recognize as intercession, even though they actually do the work of tearing down strongholds in the heavenlies. Aglow's prayer movement was birthed through prophecy, shouting, rejoicing, clapping and joy.

Joy in intercession can involve jumping, leaping and rejoicing as Zephaniah 3:17 says God does. It is often manifested as a dance. To our Western culture this may seem strange, but it is not at all strange in the Jewish culture, which is full of dancing in which the people spin, leap and rejoice.

An example of this occurred in the prayer room for the Spiritual Warfare Network recently. The intercessors were praying for Mike and me because of a trial we were facing. One of the prayer warriors, Jane, jumped up and began to dance a dance of joy. Jane is quite talented in this area; she has had extensive training in ballet. The other intercessors laughed while they watched the dance because it was so full of joy. Mike and I know that this dance of joy was intercessory, and the power of this form of intercession helped carry us through a rough time with grace.

Practical Application

How can you include intercessory praise in prayer meetings? One of the first things to remember is that the Holy Spirit has many moods and ways by which He manifests Himself. We need to maintain a sensitivity to His desires as to how we intercede.

Another thing to consider is that the Lord works within our culture and often our belief systems. Don't try to force any type of intercession. Let God establish it in your group. What might be appropriate in one church might be greatly out of order in another church.

How do these different types of intercessory praise come together? Here is one possible framework revolving around worship in an intercessory meeting.

It is good to begin with worship because many people come to prayer with heavy hearts.

> "Come to Me, all you who labor and are heavy laden, and I will give you rest. Take My yoke upon you and learn from Me, for I am gentle and lowly in heart, and you will find rest for your souls. For My yoke is easy and My burden is light."
>
> Matthew 11:28–30

As we worship the Lord He will place upon us His yoke or His burdens for prayer rather than our own. Many people are truly unable to intercede for the needs on God's agenda because they are too caught up with their own problems. They end up praying out of their human emotions rather than by the Holy Spirit. Matthew 6:33 exhorts us to "seek first the kingdom of God and His righteousness, and all these things shall be added to you."

It is often good to begin the worship with singing. Some will use hymns and others more contemporary choruses. Either way this is a good opener for your prayer meetings. Psalm 100:4 says: "Enter into His gates with thanksgiving, and into His courts with praise. Be thankful to Him, and bless His name."

Gates in the Old Testament were important places in cities. It was there that the elders sat to decide legal matters. The gates of the Lord are the places where His strategies are developed. As you begin your intercessory meetings with thanksgiving and praise you will come into the revelation of His will.

During this time of worship consider the seven Hebrew words for praise we listed earlier. When God orchestrates our intercession the whole group will move together with the moods of the Holy Spirit. You might have, for instance, a time of *barak* when you adore Him silently. Other times you might lift your hands or clap.

You might then have a time of proclamation: "Violence shall no longer be heard in your land, neither wasting nor destruction within your borders; but you shall call your walls Salvation, and your gates Praise" (Isaiah 60:18). Proclamation means calling out God's attributes—His names, character and nature.

One day in prayer I was mulling over the question of why we tell God how good He is. We praise Him, I knew, because He is worthy of our praise and because He commands us to praise Him. Right in the middle of my thoughts came the words, *Am I selfish?* I sensed this question was from the Lord.

I replied immediately, "No, Lord, You are never selfish. It is impossible for You to be selfish."

Then why do you think that I desire to be praised?

I considered this for a while. Before I gave my answer He went on. *Cindy, I want you to praise Me because when you do, I become what you have praised Me for. When you have a financial need, for instance, and worship Me for being Jehovah-Jireh, I come into your situation and meet your needs. I want you to praise Me for your good, not for Mine.* This was a big revelation and made me respect the Lord for His goodness in an even greater measure.

The bottom line is this: We need to learn to praise specifically just like we pray specifically. If we want God to change nations, then sing to Him about changing nations. If we want to release His comforting presence, then sing that to Him—and that is how His presence will manifest to His people.

How do we practically do that? When seeking the Lord for a time of intercessory worship, ask the Lord not only what to sing but how it should be sung, including the different postures for worship. For instance, a yoke might be broken by our kneeling in humility as we sing, or clapping our hands all together in a repeated pattern.

In addition to preparation, we need to be open to the leading of the Holy Spirit as He particularly anoints a portion of the intercessory worship service in a certain manner. Many powerful moments of intercession are missed in our regular worship services because we proceed with "business as usual" and don't seek the Lord on what the Holy Spirit wants to do through our praise. There should be no "routine" worship services. All worship is prophetic intercession in some manner.

Many times, as a group worships together, a song will come to someone's mind. The leader can determine if it is appropriate. It may be the very thing to bless and comfort someone, to thank the Lord or to break the power of the enemy in the situation about which the group is going to petition.

As you move into the time of intercession, your group may use other methods of intercessory praise. You might all begin clapping, for instance.

This is a smiting, a hard type of clap. It is done with the intention of stopping Satan's devices in the situation about which you are warring. You will know that it is accomplished because everyone will just stop. The Holy Spirit is the divine orchestrator. It is amazing how this happens.

In some cases you might march over a tough case—or actually put your feet down hard or tread. We used this kind of warfare in the prayer room at the North American Renewal Congress in Indianapolis in August 1990. The group was in prayer at one A.M. when one of the leaders of the renewal congress came into the prayer room. When we realized we had a visitor, we stopped praying and inquired what the need was. He explained that the congress was in serious financial jeopardy. They needed a $300,000 miracle by the end of the next day. He had come at a good time because we had prayed so much that nothing seemed impossible to us through God.

One intercessor pulled some money out of his pocket. People who had very little gave sacrificially. One Catholic nun who worked in a leprosarium and lived by faith gave all she had. When the money was piled on the floor, we began to pray with intercessory praise. We *bar-aked*, knelt and adored the Lord, thanking Him for His provision. We declared, "Lord, it will take only one fish to provide this need" (see Matthew 17:27). We said, "Let's go fishing in prayer for that one fish." We wrote Satan a message and taped it to the bottom of our shoes! We let him know that he would not put the renewal congress in debt and cause a blight to come on the name of that organization. Then the intercessors trod upon the enemy. We marched and rejoiced in God for His provision. At last we had a tremendous breakthrough and the joy of the Lord filled our hearts. We knew that the answer was on its way.

The next evening the final session closed and people were starting to leave. The offering taken that night totaled $150,000—a great amount but $150,000 short. Still, the evening was not over yet. Some of us were standing around the platform when a small, unassuming woman came up to Dr. Vinson Synan. She said, "Excuse me, but I would like to know how much the deficit is." Dr. Synan told her that it was $150,000. She then said, "I would like to pick up the deficit. I will have my foundation send you a check next week." We all greatly rejoiced over God's provision.

And He will continue to provide for us—for healing, assurance, financial needs and protection. As we learn more of His own desires for us, and come before Him in an attitude of intercessory praise, we will see breakthroughs we might never have imagined before. Powerful tools are at our disposal. We need only learn from Him how to use them.

---

1. LaMar Boschman, *The Rebirth of Music* (Bedford, Tex.: Revival Press, 1980), 11–12.

2. Terry Law, *The Power of Praise and Worship* (Tulsa, Okla.: Victory House, Inc., 1985), 31.

3. Bernard Ruffin, *Fanny Crosby* (United Church Press, 1976), 151–52.

4. James Strong, *Strong's Exhaustive Concordance of the Bible* (Nashville, Tenn.: Thomas Nelson Publishers), Hebrew and Chaldee Dictionary, ref. no. 8682.

5. Joy Towe, *Praise Is* (Irving, Tex.: Triumphant Praise, 1979), 41.

14

Corporate Intercession

Corporate intercession. Praying in large numbers. This gives an added force to intercession that brings great moves of God. It means greater assurance of His divine presence in evangelization and revival. In his book *The Struggle of Prayer* Donald Bloesch describes this scene of agreeing with others in prayer for evangelization:

> Intercessory prayer was said to be the key to the remarkable success of the China Inland Mission, at least in its early years. At a conference held in China in 1886, the few members of the mission agreed that the pressing need was for no fewer than 100 new missionaries. As they discussed this almost impossible challenge, one of them asked, "Is there anything too hard for God?" The whole company then turned to earnest and passionate intercession. As they continued in prayer, the conviction seized them that their prayers would be answered affirmatively. The meeting ended in thanksgiving and praise for the hundred missionaries whom God promised to send. That very year there was a marked increase in the number of those who volunteered for service with the China Inland Mission, and before the year ended, 100 new missionaries were sent out.[1]

The question "Is there anything too hard for God?" is one that rings out in corporate intercession. Indeed we have God's promise that if two or three agree as if they are touching anything, it will be done by our Father in heaven (see Matthew 18:19). Add to this the assurance from Leviticus 26:8 that "five of you shall chase a hundred, and a hundred of you shall put ten thousand to flight," and a boldness comes up within your heart and mind to ask without doubting.

We are seeing a clarion call to corporate prayer the world over, a crying out to God over the gross sin and wickedness in the nations. Blinders are coming off the eyes of believers who grieve that the world is lost, and they are joining in corporate prayer on behalf of the nations. Second Chronicles 7:14 is the thread running through these prayer meetings:

> If My people who are called by My name will humble themselves, and pray and seek My face, and turn from their wicked ways, then I will hear from heaven, and will forgive their sin and heal their land.

Across denominational lines masses of Christians are coming together to pray for their cities and nations. Certain characteristics are common to these times of corporate intercession:

- Humbling themselves deeply before God
- Repenting for individual and corporate sin
- Asking God to heal their cities and nations
- Engaging in spiritual warfare against the principalities over their geographic regions

Do these groups get results? Consider this example.

Dee Jepsen felt that the Lord was directing her to establish a 24-hour "prayer and praise tent" on the mall in Washington D.C. for a seven-day period after the 1988 Washington for Jesus rally. During this time praise and prayer were continually lifted up to God on behalf of the nation and the capital city. One of the most measurable results was that there were no murders during those seven days in a city dubbed the murder capital of the world! The Lord has promised that He will heal our land if we pray.

This isn't the only time we have had extended times of prayer and seen it affect the geographic region. For instance, several years ago we sponsored, along with Christ For The Nations Bible Institute, what we called 40 Days of Prayer.

The catalyst for this season of prayer was a prophecy given to us through Sam Brassfield. It said that God was going to "re-dig" the wells of revival in Dallas, Texas, and release a healing movement that would affect hundreds of churches in the area and would also touch the world.

We were aware that historically there had been a great revival in Dallas called The Voice of Healing that had been facilitated by Gordon Lindsay, the founder of CFNI. In fact, Christ for the Nations began during that time, in order to teach students who had received this revivalist anointing.[2] Healing evangelists such as Oral Roberts, William Braham, and others had been a part of this move of God. Thousands were healed around the world.

We knew that prophecy is conditional upon obedience and so we called for prayer, to cry out for God to release His movement upon our generation.

In the end, hundreds were healed and saved as a result of our 40 Days of Prayer, and churches in the area did experience the miraculous—as well as many other churches around the world—and it continues today.

However, the true reason I mention this now is because of what happened to the city in which the prayer room was located. Oakcliff has been a troubled area, with violence and drug problems. One night during the 24/7 prayer watch, an intercessor went to a local coffee shop and overheard a conversation between two policemen that went something like this: "How's it going?" The other officer replied, "Slow, really slow. There just isn't anything happening around here."

That is great, great news! Evidently the powers of darkness were bound for a season by the amount of intercession that went on during that forty days. How much more could happen if we filled our cities with intercessory prayer every day?

The effect of corporate intercession in revival and church growth is marked. This can be seen in churches like the Yoido Full Gospel Central Church in Seoul, South Korea, pastored by Paul Yonggi Cho. In his book *Prayer: Key to Revival* he states:

> It is because of prayer that the Full Gospel Central Church has been growing so phenomenally. The people in our church pray without ceasing. Every

weekend at Prayer Mountain about 10,000 people gather to intercede in prayer for souls to be brought into the Kingdom of God, for our church, and for themselves. Prayer is the motivating power to lead this big ship of the Full Gospel Central Church.[3]

The exciting news out of Korea is that this is not the only "prayer mountain" where people pray 24 hours a day. Wouldn't it be wonderful if that were the case in the United States? Over the last few years, we have been improving. There are now some retreat centers in the U.S. that are called prayer mountains, and other centers are currently in the process of being developed.

It isn't difficult to ascertain that God is calling His people to corporate prayer, both in the framework of the local church and in city-wide prayer meetings such as Pray New York, which has prayer-walked every local zip code for the past few years. Many people may wonder why there hasn't been another major terrorist attack in that city. I believe it is due to the power of concerted prayer. In the midst of these powerful examples of corporate prayer, there are some practical issues that need to be addressed.

In order for corporate prayer to be facilitated effectively, there must be structure and order—a prayer leader is needed to bring this about. Someone has to be the point person, to ensure that prayer is not considered a simple byproduct of city transformation movements or churches.

This chapter offers some guidelines and practical applications of how to choose a prayer leader, how to write a prayer leader's packet and how to communicate clearly between the pastor or organizational leader and the prayer leader. This information will show you how to set up parameters and build safeguards that will help prevent many problems.

Choosing a Prayer Leader

The first thing is knowing which prayer leader to choose. How does a church or organization go about knowing if they have the right leader? It goes without saying that the person should have a deep walk with the Lord and be called to the ministry of intercession. Here are some other questions to consider:

1. Is he or she discreet?
2. How reliable and faithful has he or she proven to be toward the ministry and its ongoing meetings?
3. Does he or she have a servant's heart? What are his or her aspirations in ministry? Does he or she want to lead an intercessory group or build a position or ministry?
4. Does he or she exhibit any need to control? Some prayer groups are emotionally dysfunctional. They develop excessive dependence on the opinions of the prayer leader. Sometimes the prayer leader is forced into this by false prophecies or threats that the group must behave the way the leader stipulates or God will not be pleased with them. In other cases the leader treats prayer as a compulsion and causes the people to feel guilty if they don't pray. They do not realize that it is the Holy Spirit's job to convict people to pray.
5. Is he or she teachable? Some display a haughty spirit, although this is not true of most intercessors.
6. Is he or she emotionally whole? The home of the prayer leader needs to be in order. This does not mean that someone cannot lead if his or her spouse is not born again. Watch for signs of bitterness or anger, especially in conversations about other churches or ministries. Old hurts may bleed into a person's leadership style and affect the way he or she relates to the pastor or ministry leader.
7. Does he or she set aside time daily for prayer and Bible study?
8. Is he or she able to bring correction in a loving, kind way? Does he or she display signs of autocratic, harsh leadership?
9. Does he or she tithe? I believe this is an important aspect, although some groups may consider it to be optional. There are times when a spouse will not let the prayer leader tithe monetarily; they consider his or her time to be the tithe.
10. Does the person have the ability to be a leader whom people want to follow?

Prayer Leader's Packet

A prayer leader must have clear understanding and support for the vision of the church or organization. Habakkuk 2:2 says: "Write the vision and make it plain on tablets, that he may run who reads it."

Many times a pastor will assign a prayer leader who has no sense of the style of prayer that will meet the needs of the church, and no goals for developing the prayer life of the church. Worse yet, the pastor may assume that the person placed in charge of leading intercession will lead just the way the pastor does. This is not always the case. The prayer leader does not need to copy a leadership style, but it is important that he or she agree with the minister in doctrine and ultimate goals.

The following is something like a job description. It should be developed by church or ministry leadership to make up the prayer leader's packet:

1. Statement of church doctrine and creed.
2. Commitment form. This is a loyalty oath to the pastor or ministry leadership as well as the doctrine of the church or organization.
3. Authority statement. This should spell out the prayer leader's boundaries of authority. Is the prayer leader being asked to develop a complete prayer ministry or be in charge of just one group? Is the prayer leader supposed to teach the group? Invite guest speakers? How many times a week should they meet? How long should each prayer meeting be?
4. Schedule of meeting times, especially times of consultation with the pastor or ministry leadership.
5. Feedback from the prayer leader. Some organizations may require written feedback of prayer meetings or ask that a prayer journal be kept. Others approach it on a less formal basis. (See the following section on communication.)
6. The prayer leader's written testimony and philosophy of prayer. This document should include things such as personal mentors and books that the prayer leader has found helpful in developing a leadership style.

The most comprehensive book I know on how to develop prayer in a local church was written by my good friend Cheryl Sacks of Phoenix, Arizona. Cheryl and her husband, Hal, work with Bridgebuilders Ministries and have successfully networked prayer across denominational lines for many years.

Her book *The Prayer Saturated Church* includes many tips on getting individuals to pray and helping churches become houses of prayer. It even includes instructions on how to develop a budget and other practical tips.

When choosing a prayer leader, it is wise to put your requirements and expectations in writing. If the prayer leader strays from the agreement you have made together, you can simply pull it out of your files and bring necessary correction. It also protects the prayer leader from misunderstandings.

Communication

Let me stress the importance of clear communication between the ministry leader and the prayer leader. It is important to go over this in detail since this can be a source of great frustration—particularly for the intercessor. There is an old school of thought among ministry leaders that intercessors are just to pray and let God tell them the needs of the church or ministry without any communication from the leadership. This may be because the ministers fear what the prayer leader may have heard in prayer. Or they might fear being vulnerable to someone who may or may not be trustworthy. This is why the prayer leader must be someone the ministry head can trust.

I have known instances in which the ministry leader and prayer leader try to communicate by subtle words or body language that they expect the other will understand. Indirect communication rarely works. It can cause a dysfunctional relationship.

Many times at the end of a meeting, an intercessor will come up to me weeping and say, "Cindy, I am hearing a warning for my church and my pastor. What should I do?" Intercessors need someone they can talk to about what they are hearing in prayer in order to maintain balance. They should be free to share their concerns for the church in a nonthreatening environment without fear of reprisal. On the other hand, the intercessor should not approach the ministry leadership with a finger-pointing "God is saying . . ." What he or she is hearing may need to be adjusted in light of inside information he or she may not know.

Regular communication is important with openness and prayer time for both sides. Although it may be difficult to fit this time into busy schedules, it will save endless amounts of frustration and hurt feelings. Many intercessors would never have become Absaloms if they had had better communication with leadership.

One day a wise woman said to me, "Commitment comes out of relationship." The principle of this proverb has been practiced by some of the greatest leaders. Look at this description of Alexander the Great:

> Alexander led one of the charges against the enemy on the plains of Issus, where he was outnumbered as much as six to one. He was wounded on every limb of his body, and his Companions [his cavalry] gained courage from his personal valor.
>
> After the battle, Alexander visited his wounded warriors, Arrian [a Greek chronicler] tells us, "looking at their wounds, asking them how they got them, encouraging each to tell about his deeds and even brag of them." Alexander gave special funeral honors to the twenty-five fallen Companions, granted tax remissions to their families, and had their likenesses cast in bronze.
>
> Leadership is not a position, but a relationship. As the story of Alexander illustrates, the relationship that inspires followers to great sacrifice is an intimate, caring connection. He was famous for his prebattle consultations with his officers.[4]

There is no doubt that the ministry of intercession requires great sacrifice. Yet many times intercessors who spend hours in prayer and fasting for the leadership do not feel as though they are part of the ministry team. Romans 13:7 says: "Render therefore to all their due . . . honor to whom honor."

Mike and I recently held a dinner in honor of our local prayer partners. We have a prayer room at the international headquarters where they pray on a regular basis. I am also using conference calls more regularly to keep in touch with our own Reformation Prayer Network leaders.

Many leaders of organizations and churches work very hard at honoring their prayer partners. Urbana '90, a missions conference at which I coordinated their 24-hour intercessory team, treated their intercessors like royalty. They thanked us repeatedly from the platform and let it be known that they felt the power of intercession. This, in turn, touched the students of the conference (some 20,000 strong). They reached out often to thank us for our prayer because of the patterning from the platform. We don't mind laying down our lives when such gratitude is expressed, and this is the case with many churches and ministries.

If the ministry leader will take time to affirm the intercessors personally, it will pay off! We see in the epistles that Paul told his disciples constantly that he was praying for them, and showed great love in his salutations.

Peter Wagner has a unique way to thank his personal prayer partners. He keeps a picture of us in his Bible. Each morning in his private devotions, he looks at our faces and prays for each of us personally. What a special way to give back prayer for those who intercede for you!

Guidelines for Intercessory Prayer Groups

Here are some practical guidelines directed to the prayer group that will help you leaders keep order in your meetings. I recommend that you use these or a variation that fits your situation when you form your group. Give copies to members of the prayer group and be sure they understand each point.

1. Follow the leader.

Recognize that the person leading the time of intercession is the one who has the spiritual authority to do so. Do not try to become the leader yourself even if you feel that you know more about it.

2. When you cannot follow the leader . . .

If you feel strongly that the prayer leader is missing God's direction, you still must not try to lead yourself. Instead, pray on your own that the leader will have the mind of the Lord. Bind the enemy from bringing confusion and claim the accomplishment of God's will through the time of prayer.

3. Pray with the flow of the meeting.

The Holy Spirit will begin to move with certain emphases and moods such as rejoicing, stillness or weeping. It is out of order for anyone to express different emotions—to be weeping and travailing, for instance, when the rest of the group is rejoicing. If you feel that God is genuinely leading you into a different flow, excuse yourself quietly and find another place to pray in that manner.

4. Do not break from prayer in order to have a deliverance session.

Keep in mind the purpose of your gathering together: It is to pray and stand in the gap. Satan will sometimes try to divert the purposes of God by manifesting through someone in the meeting. If someone does start to disrupt the group, have a designated person take him or her out for ministry in another place so the prayer can continue. If further prayer is needed for the person, it is best to make an appointment for some time other than the appointed prayer time. This will help you keep on track with your purposes for being there.

5. Pray in a positive fashion.

This can be accomplished through praying the Word of God. Many prayer groups are not much more than a gossip session with everyone's eyes closed. Do not air other people's dirty laundry. Disclose only what is necessary.

6. Do not use prayer time to prophesy over one another.

If you feel that you are receiving a word of a personal nature for someone in the group, share it with him or her after the meeting. If it would be edifying to the group to tell it openly, check with your leader first and have the word judged. Of course, there may be times when the Lord will have the leader minister to the intercessors in the group as they also need uplifting from time to time, but this is not the main purpose of an intercessory prayer group.

7. Be sensitive to the needs of the group as a whole.

This can be done in various ways. Do not monopolize the group by praying lengthy prayers. Make your individual prayers concise and to the point. Do not try to pray on a different topic because you have a need. Listen to what the other members are praying and agree with them. Listen to the volume that the group is praying with. If they are praying quietly, don't pray at the top of your lungs and clap your hands.

Your verbal clues should come from the prayer leader. If the leader begins to increase in volume or if the whole group prays more loudly, then you are in order. Be aware of who is attending the prayer group that particular day. Will anything that you say be offensive to them? For instance, are you putting down or being critical of another denomination's beliefs? This causes division and breaks unity in prayer.

8. Prefer the needs of others over your own needs.

Intercession means standing in the gap for others' needs as well as your own. Be willing to give of yourself for them. Prefer them in love.

9. Guard your heart with all diligence.

Be careful to check your heart motives in your prayers. Are you praying out of a critical spirit or a desire for personal vengeance? Are you praying out of a root of bitterness or rejection? Know why you pray the prayers you pray.

10. Do not talk about the leader behind his or her back.

If you have a problem with the leader, choose an appropriate time and place, other than the prayer time itself, to discuss it with the leader. You can cause strife and division and become like Absalom if you are not careful.

I often listen to the conversations of people who would like to join us in prayer at the ministry. If they share too openly the inner circle problems of the ministry they have previously worked or prayed for, I am wary of including them in our prayer group. I have found that anyone who shares others' problems too easily will probably treat us the same way.

Guidelines for Leaders

There are numerous ways to lead corporate intercession, all of which take a great amount of sensitivity. Here are nuggets concerning leadership I have gleaned through the years that seem to be helpful.

Preparation

1. Ask the Lord for His focus for the time of intercession.
2. Seek the Lord's will as to how He wants the focus implemented. This might include:

   - Petition prayers (petitioning God for the needs)
   - Proclamation prayers (proclaiming the attributes of the Lord concerning the needs)
   - Intercessory praise
   - Prophetic intercession
   - Scripture praying (ask God to give each of the intercessors a portion of Scripture or designate passages yourself and ask everyone to base their prayers on those passages)

3. Spend time before the Lord personally and make sure you are walking in forgiveness toward those in your prayer group and your church. Ask the Lord to show you any hidden bitterness.
4. Talk to your pastor or ministry leader and ask for any prayer requests or direction.

During Prayer

What are the responsibilities of the leader during corporate prayer meetings? Many are implemented naturally by those with good leadership abilities. Here are two suggestions for carrying these responsibilities through.

First, make sure each prayer request is "prayed through" until there is a release from the Lord. When you have peace that the matter is resolved you might ask the intercessors if they have anything else to pray or if they have been given a verse from the Lord about it.

Second, keep the momentum of the group moving. There are a number of keys to this:

1. Discourage one person from being a "prayer hog" and taking all the prayer time. Look at these perspectives of two prayer giants:

> Thomas Aquinas held that frequency, not length, is the important issue in prayer. [He felt that] frequent, short prayers are of more worth than a few lengthy prayers. Dwight L. Moody advocated short public prayers, though he acknowledged the need for constant prayer in the privacy of one's heart. "A man who prays much in private," he said, "will make short prayers in public." Moody regarded lengthy public prayers as something akin to religious pretension.[5]

   Another reason for shorter prayers is that those who are young often don't have the patience to wait for someone who prays lengthy prayers—their attention wanders. Or they may be so intimidated by someone's lengthy prayer that they will not pray at all. A good leader draws everyone into the time of prayer.

2. Instruct your intercessors to listen for God's direction in prayer with one ear, and to the prayers others are praying with the other ear. Being sensitive to both will keep individuals from diverting the general flow of the Spirit's direction. This is a key gleaned from Joy Dawson when she led a prayer watch for us at Urbana '90.

3. Notice if some intercessors have a hearing loss. If so, they need to sit near the prayer leader so they can hear their instructions and to look up if they start to pray to make sure that no one else is praying. Of course, it is always good to pray that they be healed as well!

   Hearing loss of one of our prayer warriors was a problem for us in one of our 24-hour prayer watches some time back. We had one missionary who never stayed with the focus of what the rest of the group was praying. He always prayed for "his" nation regardless of the prayer requests. We finally discerned that he had a hearing loss, and he was counseled about the problem he was causing. After it was brought to his attention, he learned to join with the group.

   It is also important to ask those with soft voices not to pray with their heads down, because those with hearing loss struggle to hear what is being prayed and often feel resentful and left out. You might ask openly if anyone has a hearing loss, so that allowances can be made.

4. Keep the prayer focused. The prayers should stay on one track and not change until the leader switches them. If someone has what I call an SOS, an emergency request, he or she should tell you and ask if it is the time to pray for the need. If you as the leader feel it is not the proper time, the person can pray for it silently.

   As a leader you may need to remind the group of the prayer focus. I have found that there are some people who will refuse to keep on the prayer target they have been given and will always pray instead for what they feel is important to them. This might be a certain nation, situation or family member.

5. Bring correction if needed. Try to avoid correction in the group setting because it might humiliate the person. Meet him or her afterward. There are those who will blatantly refuse to follow your leadership. If you confront them and they will not listen, consult with your pastor or the person in authority over you.

   Remember to pray first and see if the person will be able to hear the Lord's correction directly from Him before you offer correction, unless it is something destructive to the group. This will make your job easier.

6. Assess the spiritual maturity of your group. Give verbal clues to those who are in the group as to the special needs of those present. You might say, "We are glad to have so-and-so visiting us today. This is the first time she has ever been to a group such as ours." They will understand to be careful and not scare or overwhelm the new person. Instruct your intercessors in private to listen for your verbal clues.

   Some churches have intercessory groups on two levels. One level might welcome those who are new to prayer and who need instruction and discipleship. The other might welcome more experienced intercessors for whom manifestations of intercessions such as weeping and travail flow more frequently. I have seen new believers run out of groups in fear when the leader did not properly discern the maturity of those present and someone began to travail. If travail should come and if it is clearly from God, take time to explain what has happened. It might be helpful to have a handout sheet explaining about weeping, travail, laughter, etc.

Whether you enter an intercessory group as a leader or member of the team, I think you will be excited to see the power of corporate prayer at work. It might take a little time to get the team running smoothly, but with patience and a heart for prayer, your group will make a sizable impact for the Kingdom.

---

1. Donald G. Bloesch, *The Struggle of Prayer* (Colorado Springs, Colo.: Helmer & Howard, 1988), 89.

2. Note: CFNI has archives of pictures and documents from the original Voice of Healing movement. Around 250 healing evangelists were involved in the network.

3. Paul Yonggi Cho, *Prayer: Key to Revival* (Waco, Tex.: Word Books, 1984).

4. Lawrence M. Miller, *Barbarians to Bureaucrats* (New York, N.Y.: Ballantine Books, 1989), 44–45.

5. Bloesch, 61.

15

Prayer Watches and Walks

Watchman, what of the night?
Isaiah 21:11

A number of prayer watches—intense, concentrated prayer for a specified time or purpose—have surfaced in the history of prayer and revival. Rees Howells led many during World War II. The Moravians held one lasting a hundred years in ancient Saxony (Germany). During this greatest of prayer watches, intercession was made each hour by 24 men and 24 women.

In his book *Prayer and Revival*, Douglas Thorson describes another interesting watch that took place in the 1600s by the "praying Indians." Approximately three thousand Christians living in fourteen villages were trained by John Eliot. "Eliot taught them to solemnly set apart whole days," writes Thorson, "either in giving thanks and praise or fasting and praying with great fervor of mind and a very laborious piety."[1]

A prayer watch may take a variety of lengths and forms. Some churches have "prayer lock-ins" in which a group stays in the church building in prayer all night long. In other churches people come on a 24-hour rotational basis.

The value of corporate intercession in prayer watches is that God is able to use all different gift-mixes and heart cries to express the needs of His heart. It is always interesting to me to listen to people pray in a prayer watch. They pray from their own personal interests and callings. I have a friend who is greatly involved in government. She always sees a need in terms of raising up good governmental leaders and prays toward that end. Pastors pray from the focus of the ongoing life of the church. Evangelists pray with an eye on the lost.

Corporate intercession offers a fulfillment of the mandate in 1 Thessalonians 5:17 to "pray without ceasing."[2] No one person can pray 24 hours a day, but a team can! Imagine the power and authority of a team of intercessors praying as the Lord prompts them around the clock. What a powerful prayer of agreement of unceasing intercession!

I mentioned earlier the 24-hour prayer watch during the Lausanne II Congress on World Evangelization in Manila. I was privileged to be a part of that team, and it was a life-changing experience for me. Peter Wagner, who instigated the watch, called it a "spiritual nuclear plant." The team came from diverse backgrounds as far as denominations and ministry philosophies went, but we were one in prayer. We found that although we had different beliefs, once we started to pray there was really very little difference. In fact, our differences seemed to be largely a matter of semantics. By the end of the ten days God had forged deep bonds among us.

In a moment I will give practical aspects of setting up a prayer watch, but I would like first of all to give you a glimpse of one of the results of the prayer watches at the Lausanne congress.

One of our first assignments was to pray a team of seventy Russian believers into the congress. Their government gave them permission to come, but the Philippine officials would not grant their visas. The Russians were stuck in airports waiting for the visas to be issued.

In the prayer room we labored over the request. Finally an intercessor named Paul shared his belief that the Philippine government was not granting the visas because of fear and bitterness toward the Soviet Union. They did not want any Russian people on their soil! As soon as he said it, we looked around and nodded our heads. That was it! Communists had caused a lot of hardship in the Philippines;

Satan was stirring up their grief to keep out the Russian pastors and leaders.

As Paul spoke the Lord revealed a strategy to break Satan's plan to keep the Russians out of the congress. One of our intercessors was Russian. She could ask God and the Philippine people to forgive the Communists for their sins and repent for what Communism had done. Then one of our Philippine intercessors would stand in for the Filipinos to extend forgiveness. The air was electric as this occurred, and there was much weeping as they prayed and hugged each other. Then the whole group took authority over the spirit of fear attacking the Philippine officials and declared that the Lord would open an effectual door for the Gospel for the Russians.

We received word the next day that their visas had been granted. How we rejoiced when they finally came into the prayer room to share with us the goodness of God in answering our prayers! After the congress, that Russian group took sixty *Jesus* films and projectors back to their country. These films are having a great impact for the Gospel today.

What if we had not held that 24-hour prayer watch? We prayed for three days that the Russians would be allowed to come. If we had not prayed, perhaps they would never have obtained the necessary visas. Prayer watches are a vital way to see God's will done on earth as it is in heaven.

One time I was praying and seeking the Lord for a deeper revelation on the necessity of 24-hour prayer, and I heard the Holy Spirit speak this loudly in my heart: *The devil uses the cover of the night to do his worst deeds. I created the night and called it good and I want My night back!*

Wouldn't it be wonderful if your neighborhood had the reputation of being the safest in your city night and day? Why is it that some sections of our cities have more evil in them than others? God loves the people who live there just as much. I am convinced that planting prayer rooms in these areas is a major key to their spiritual and physical reformation.

After a word about time segments and team members, I would like to outline some practical aspects of setting up a 24-hour prayer watch. These come as a result of participating in many 24-hour prayer watches since 1989—and various other types of prayer watches before that time.

Time Segments and Team Members

In my first four prayer watches, time segments were assigned to the intercessors. I have seen the 24-hour watch segmented into two-hour, three-hour and four-hour slots. Two hours seems too short. You are just bonding together and praying intensely when your time is up. Four hours seems too long; it is often a strain to finish the watch. Three hours seems to be the best. Three hours is even a biblical model, as the Jewish people prayed every three hours—at nine A.M., noon and three P.M. They taught that Abraham instituted the first watch, Isaac the second and Jacob the last. The ninth hour (three P.M.) was the time when Christ died on the cross and the veil of the Temple was torn from top to bottom (see Matthew 27:45–51).

The size of the team may vary. Peter Wagner gave me these interesting comments concerning team members:

> Each shift should have eight or more intercessors. In order for it to flow smoothly you should have from 32 to 50 on your team. This allows for those who might need to drop out for some reason. Each intercessor would pray two three-hour segments per 24 hours.

For one of our prayer watches we had only 24 intercessors and, although it was great for group dynamics, many of the team took three watches a day and went home physically exhausted. Remember, these intercessors stay up night and day praying intensely. Some of them are not able to sleep well when they come off their shifts. I was so excited about what was happening in prayer at Lausanne II that I foolishly stayed up 24 hours in a row and became sick as a result. A very wise woman once told me, "Cindy, when you break physical laws that God has set up for His universe, your physical body breaks down. Sometimes the most spiritual thing you can do is rest."

Along with segmenting the time and planning the size of the team, you will also need an idea of the various leadership responsibilities and general guidelines for a successful prayer watch. Here are some suggestions.

Leadership

Good leadership is essential. Leadership for a prayer watch generally consists of a team coordinator, a team administrator, a liaison and prayer captains. Let's look at each individually.

Team Coordinator

This is the person in charge of setting up the watch. It is his or her responsibility to:

- Choose the prayer teams.
- Assign prayer captains for each shift.
- Choose resource material.
- Provide the overall framework for shifts.
- Be available for counsel if problems arise.
- Bring emergency needs to the attention of the shifts.
- Cover shifts or assign others to cover shifts when the prayer captain has to drop out.
- If the watch is for a conference, the leader should provide regular prayer updates for the conference *before* it meets.

Team Administrator

This is the person who helps the coordinator with the practical aspects of setting up a prayer watch. It is his or her responsibility to:

- Send out letters of invitation.
- Provide resource materials as requested by the team coordinator.
- Distribute sign-up forms for the prayer shifts (two three-hour shifts per day). An email list is important for those who have this as an available option.
- Make travel arrangements for the group.
- Choose team captains. Call them prior to the watches. Sometimes it is good to choose a "second in command" in case they have an emergency.

- Arrange for provisions in the prayer room, such as water and juice. (Dehydration is a real threat during long hours of prayer. As we speak our bodies lose moisture. This is also the case when we pray for long hours at a time.)

If the prayer watch is part of a conference:

- Arrange a liaison between the conference leadership and the prayer team.
- Make a prayer and praise report for conference operations and leadership.

Liaison

This person is the link between the conference and the prayer room. It may or may not be the same person as the team administrator. His or her job is to:

- Take reports from the intercessors to the leadership of the conference.
- Take reports from the leaders of the conference—concerning prayer needs and answers to prayer—to the intercessors.

Prayer Captain

A prayer captain leads the prayer time during any one shift. Here are guidelines for selection and the duties of the prayer captains:

- Choosing a prayer captain is similar to choosing a prayer leader as described earlier on pages 187–88. The team coordinator should use those guidelines as a basis.
- The team coordinator should hold a training session for the prayer captains once they have been selected in order to let them know how the shifts should be run, what focus they should have, etc.
- Prayer captains may assign others to assist them during their time of leading. If they are not able to lead during their assigned times, however, they need to switch with another captain.

- Prayer captains need to have what I call divine elasticity and flexibility! This is especially important because sometimes people are irresponsible and do not show up for their watches. I suggest the captain call the members of his or her watch prior to their prayer shift.

Practical Guidelines

Physical Aspects

Here are some logistical concerns that need to be considered:

- If the prayer watch takes place during a conference, the intercessors and their prayer room should be in the same hotel as the speakers. This makes it easier for speakers to receive prayer before their ministry time, if they so desire.
- A telephone number should be available for those who want to call in prayer requests. It is good to appoint someone to answer the phone, such as the team liaison, so that the prayer time is not interrupted. If possible, try not to have the phone in the room with the intercessors because it is very distracting.
- Have a white board or chalkboard set up on which to write prayer requests and announcements.
- Display a map of the world.
- Have several copies of *Operation World* by Patrick Johnstone available.
- Have a laptop computer available in order to do a Web search for spiritual mapping information or Scriptures.

Prayer Watch Focuses

It is important that the prayer time have a focus and, as I mentioned earlier, the prayer captains must be familiar with it. Here are some suggestions:

- Begin each shift with a time of praise and worship. It is wonderful if you have an actual worship leader assigned for each session.

- You might want to include a brief time of teaching from Scripture. If you do, limit the time to fifteen minutes at most. The purpose of the meeting is to pray, not to teach. Any teaching should address the focus of the prayer watch.
- Introduce any team members who are new and let them give one or two sentences about themselves.
- You might pray "around the world on your knees" using *Operation World* as a resource.
- Intersperse worship throughout the shifts.

Team Building

The sense of unity among the intercessors is a key to any successful prayer watch. Here are some suggestions to help build unity in your team:

- It is good to have a time of orientation in order to establish parameters for the group as a whole. Orientation should include who is and who is not allowed into the prayer room.
- Any schedules and special team meeting times should be made available. When praying for a conference the entire prayer team should meet together for the first shift in order to establish prayer objectives. Everyone should also attend the final shift to rejoice about what God has done through prayer.
- Allow a little time during orientation for the team members to share information about themselves and what God has said to them concerning the conference.
- Serve Communion (if possible).
- Hold a dinner toward the end of the watch with an affirmation session. Affirmation sessions are those times when team members stand and describe the qualities that they have appreciated in other team members during their times of intercession together.
- Communal meals, if possible, are very good for team building. It is also good to have meals with the speakers and people for whom they pray as it helps them get to know one another.

Other Thoughts on Prayer Watches

If the watch is for a conference, the first day or so the watch usually centers around the physical logistics of the meetings. It is good to send an intercessor to pray over the registration. We saw remarkable results at Urbana '90 when twenty thousand students were registered with amazing smoothness. Now that is a miracle! All conferences seem to have "birth pangs" the first day or so, when all kinds of problems need to be worked out. We find that we also need to pray against any sickness or medical emergencies for the participants.

There are times when you will need to pray for the weather. This is a good topic to pray about before the meetings take place. We have had two major battles with the elements during prayer watches. One was with a typhoon headed straight for us in Manila. The other was a snowstorm predicted at Urbana. The typhoon was greatly weakened and that snowstorm never came.

Let me tell you about the snow prayer. It was part of a prayer watch shift that received an urgent request one night to pray for the weather. Five to nine inches of snow were predicted for the next day. If that much snow fell the students would not have been able to get to the meetings and many flights would have been canceled. I was leading that night and felt impressed that we should seek the Lord for His prayers for the situation.

As we waited, quietly asking the Lord for direction, one of the intercessors, Sandy Grady, saw a picture. She said that it was a weather map, and it clearly showed warm air pushing all the snow just above Urbana, Illinois, where the conference was being held. With this direction from the Lord I asked her to pray. Sandy prayed and we agreed for warm air to push the snow above Urbana. The snow never fell the next day—just rain. It was not too surprising to watch the weather forecast on the news that evening and see a picture like the one Sandy had been given.

In all of the prayer watches connected with conventions, the speakers have been greatly blessed by coming into the room for prayer—especially those with particularly sensitive topics to cover. Many of the speakers in Lausanne received prophetic prayer for the first time in their lives and were touched by the intimate details that only God knew to have caused them anxiety. The word spread about the blessings in the prayer room, and we were kept busy as people came in, one after another, for the refreshing that comes from intercessory prayer.

One underutilized but important form of prayer watch is actually done for and during a church service. I have been in meetings in Argentina where the intercessors would go behind the curtains that were just behind the platform, lay small towels in front of them and put their foreheads down as they knelt throughout the service.

Another pastor I know has an "upper room prayer" where intercession takes place just one floor above where he is preaching.

At the end of these services, many are saved and healed. One preacher told me, "I can always tell when the intercessors are praying or not. When they pray the altars are full of people getting their hearts right with God and those being saved. When they aren't praying, the results are negligible. It isn't my preaching—it's the power of God manifested behind my preaching, which comes from the intercessors' battling the spiritual darkness that comes against the people I'm preaching to."

Reentry

This section might be called "How to come off the mountain without falling." This concerns the time after a prayer watch experience. There are some things that will help you as you leave the prayer watch:

- Realize that you are probably not the same person you were before the experience. God has molded you, stretched you and possibly given you a new ministry direction.
- Do not expect everyone to understand what you have been through. Most will not. Ask the Lord what you are to share. Matthew 7:6 says: "Do not . . . cast your pearls before swine, lest they trample them under their feet, and turn and tear you in pieces." I am certainly not calling anyone a pig, but the principle applies. Some of the things that have happened to you are holy, and you will be able to talk about them with only a few. Many times there is no way to explain what has transpired. You may need time to process it yourself.

- Do not let your emotions spiral downward on you. You have probably been in a very intimate, loving environment. You might have to go back into a difficult and not-so-loving situation. Be aware that your emotions may rebound. Stay in the Word and bring every thought captive to it.

- Mike experienced quite an emotional swing after one trip to Argentina. He went to the crusades where hundreds were born again, many miracles took place and great deliverance occurred. After his first day back at work he was dragging around with a sad face. When I asked him what was wrong he said with a sigh, "What a day. Nobody got saved, nobody got delivered, nobody got healed!" Fortunately he knew what was happening and was able to recover quickly.

- Watch for Satan's backlash. Ask intercessors to pray for you for the two-week period after you return. Some people get attacked so hard and fast that they hardly know what hit them. Use the preventative medicine of prayer. Be sure to live a life of praise during this time and dwell on the good things God has done.

This brings up a key point: Many intercessors do not realize that they need prayer partners themselves—and even more so when they are in deep spiritual battle in prayer. Also, as I've mentioned before, the more visible or well-known the person or persons they are praying for, the stronger the personal battle will be for their intercessors. Don't forgot your own prayer shield when you go into prayer.

Prayer Walks

Prayer walks are a form of corporate intercession that take the intercessors directly to the battlefield, usually a home or neighborhood. John Dawson speaks of battling for your neighborhood through prayer walks in his book *Taking Our Cities for God*. John moved into an ethnic neighborhood in Los Angeles full of gang violence and drugs. He says:

Several years ago my staff and I went on a prayer walk around our neighborhood. We stood in front of every house, rebuked Satan's work in Jesus' name and prayed for a revelation of Jesus in the life of each family. We are still praying. There is a long way to go; but social, economic, and spiritual transformation is evident. There were times when demonic oppression almost crushed my soul. I received a death threat. My tires were slashed. I was often depressed at the sight of boarded-up houses, unemployed youth, and disintegrating families, but I was determined not to run away.

Today there are at least nine Christian families in the block where I live, and there is a definite sense of the Lord's peace. The neighborhood is no longer disintegrating. People are renovating their houses, and a sense of community is being established around the Christian families.[3]

Prayer walks are being implemented across many nations. Graham Kendricks has had up to 150,000 people involved in marches in England. Some churches such as the Dwelling Place in Hemet, California, have entered the Christmas parades in their cities to witness and pass out tracts. Joshua 1:3 says, "Every place that the sole of your foot will tread upon I have given you." In prayer walks you work to "take the land" for the Gospel or establish the borders of your city. As you walk you are taking back land from the enemy.

Prayer walks are not limited to walking the land physically; you can also walk the land in prayer by declaring that certain geographic regions are put under the Lordship of Jesus Christ. This was done by a group of pastors and leaders from the San Nicolas/Rosario area in Argentina who had gathered at Harvest Evangelism's Training Center in Villa Constitución:

Spiritual warfare was the subject. The realization that close to 109 towns within 100 miles of the Training Center had no Christian witness prompted the gathering. Preliminary studies had singled out the town of Arroyo Seco as what appeared to be the "seat of Satan" for that region. Years before, a well-known warlock by the name of Mr. Meregildo operated out of that town. He was so famous and his cures so dramatic that people from overseas would trek to Arroyo Seco. Before dying he passed on his powers to twelve disciples. Three times a church was established in Arroyo Seco, and three times it closed down in the face of severe spiritual opposition.

After several days of Bible study and prayer the pastors and leaders came together in one accord and placed the entire area under spiritual authority. A few of them traveled to Arroyo Seco. Positioning themselves across the street from the headquarters of Mr. Meregildo's followers they served an eviction notice on the forces of evil. They announced to them that they were defeated and that Jesus Christ would attract many to Himself now that the church was united and pledged to proclaim Him.

Less than three years later 82 of the towns had evangelical churches in them. An unverified report indicates that as of today all of them have a church or a Christian witness.[4]

I will write more extensively on spiritual warfare in the next chapter. For now, let's focus on some practical guidelines for a neighborhood prayer walk. They can be used or modified for either individual or group intercession.

Before you begin your prayer walk, it is important to dress yourself spiritually for the battle just as you would dress appropriately for other occasions. Stop and pray before you head out the door and clothe yourself with the armor of God. Pray for protection for yourself, your home and your family according to Psalm 91. Claim that you have the mind of the Lord as you walk. You need spiritual exercise each day just as your body needs physical exercise. These walks will actually do both: cause you to stretch yourself in the spirit and buffet your body in the natural.

This is meant as a jumping-off point and not a rigid pattern. Trust the Holy Spirit to guide you as you walk and pray. Start with a prayer like this:

Father, I thank You that my neighborhood has been claimed for Jesus Christ. Today I raise the banner of the Lord, His standard, over my neighborhood and claim it for the Kingdom of God. Like Joshua, every place that the sole of my foot treads upon is put under the authority of God's Kingdom. I now place the blood of the Lamb over this neighborhood even as the children of Israel placed the blood of the Passover lambs on the doorposts and lintels of their houses.

Lord Jesus, please forgive the sins of my neighborhood. You say in Your Word that "if [we] forgive the sins of any, they are forgiven them; if [we] retain the sins of any they are retained" (John 20:23). So I now ask You to forgive the sins of my neighborhood. [At this time if there is any known sin such as strife, murder, greed, love of mammon, false religions, drugs, etc., ask God specifically to forgive them.] Lord, would You heal the people in my neighborhood of the rejection, pain and hurts that these things produce? Forgive them, Lord, for not following You, for any selfishness, racial prejudice, etc. [After remitting the sins boldly proclaim the Lordship of Jesus Christ over your neighborhood.]

If you know of specific areas of demonic activity, do not try to attack these alone but ask others to go with you to pray. Make sure there is no known sin in your life when you go to pray. Ask God to show you the specific sins that are giving the demons the right to establish strongholds. If it is a stronghold like witchcraft you may want to fast first; the same for New Age. Sometimes these require soaking prayers and speaking the Word as Jesus did in the wilderness. If there is an establishment, such as a place that sells witchcraft articles, please do not forget to pray that the blindness will fall away from the eyes of those who own the shop and those who come into the shop. Bind the spirit of witchcraft from operating in and through them and claim them for the Kingdom of God. *Remember that we are fighting against principalities and powers and not against the people who own these establishments.*

Do not measure results by what you see or hear. Every prayer that you pray is effective and is like a seed planted in the ground. Continue to water it in prayer and it will surely produce fruit. Keep on claiming the promise that no weapon formed against your neighborhood will prosper. Establish borders around the houses and your house by the blood of the Lamb and declare to Satan that it is off-limits.

Be sure to ask God for His purpose or redemptive plan for your neighborhood. If there is a lot of wealth, speak boldly that the wealth of sinners has been laid up for the righteous and command Satan to stop blinding their eyes and, of course, to stop any hindrance from their being born again. Some neighborhoods are dying and a spirit of death seems to pervade. Plant Scriptures that will bring life, such as Psalm 1, over the neighborhood. Break the power of death and declare that the resurrection life of Jesus Christ is coming into your neighborhood.

Ask God for Bible verses to pray over the houses. Stretch yourself to believe Him for a different verse for each house. Ask the Lord which blocks you are responsible for in prayer. If elderly people live there, they are likely lonely. Pray that God will give them peace and bless them with His presence and love—and try to visit them yourself. If your land is in rebellion, forbid the rebellion from operating in your neighborhood. Bind the enemy from operating through drugs or pornography or prostitution and pray that every hidden and secret thing will be revealed. If the people are isolated, ask God to give them love for one another. Most of all, pray for the salvation of the people in each and every household.

God may call you to participate in a prayer watch or a prayer walk. Remember that He has planted you, like Adam, in your neighborhood and in your nation to tend it, water it and care for it. Under the Word of God, they will prosper and bloom.

---

1. Douglas Thorson, *Prayer and Revival* (Seattle, Wash.: Intercessors for America, 1989), 7.

2. Dick Eastman gives this definition of praying without ceasing for the individual: "The expression *without ceasing* is from the Greek *adialeiptos*, a word commonly used in ancient Greece to describe someone with a hacking cough. The person certainly couldn't plan his coughs throughout the day but coughs whenever necessary. The need occasioned the response." Dick Eastman, *Love On Its Knees* (Tarrytown, N.Y.: Chosen Books, 1989), 65.

3. John Dawson, *Taking Our Cities for God* (Lake Mary, Fla.: Creation House, 1989), 28–29.

4. Edgardo Silvoso, *Spiritual Warfare in Argentina and the "Plan Resistencia."* Paper taken from the Spiritual Warfare Tract of the Lausanne II Congress (San Jose, Calif.: Harvest Evangelism, July 1989), 4.

16

Possessing the Gates of the Enemy

The church holds the balance of power in world affairs. . . . Even now, in this present throbbing moment, by means of her prayer power and the extent to which she uses it, the praying church is actually deciding the course of human events.[1]

Paul Billheimer

July 1990 brought a crashing of walls between nations, a time of unprecedented answers to prayers. The Gospel of Christ was being taught in nations in an open manner that amazed even the strongest prayer warriors. Riding on the crest of world events, seven women, including myself, from the Strategic Prayer Council of Aglow International went into the U.S.S.R. to meet with Soviet women, intercede on their behalf and touch the lives of those who had had little, if any, personal ministry.

On one of our last days in Moscow, Barbara Byerly, Mary Lance Sisk and I were passing out our few remaining Russian tracts before returning home to the United States. At times it was mind-boggling to realize that we were actually praying and handing out the Gospel in the Soviet Union. We had been witnessing across the street from Red Square. Barbara and Mary Lance crossed over to Red Square.

When I joined them after a short while they said, "Cindy, no one will take our tracts." This shocked me as everywhere else we had been, people took them eagerly from our hands. Not one was ever thrown to the ground. Thinking this strange, I decided to try giving out the ones I had. To my amazement no one would take them. In fact, they ignored me, staring straight ahead as though they had not heard or seen me. Stopping in my tracks, a prayer rose within me: "Lord, what is the matter?" Immediately 2 Corinthians 4:4 came to me: "Whose minds the god of this age has blinded, who do not believe, lest the light of the gospel of the glory of Christ, who is the image of God, should shine on them."

Could this be what was happening in Red Square? Could it be that we had entered the territory of a spirit ruling over Red Square itself, and it was blinding the eyes of the people? With this thought I hurriedly asked Mary Lance and Barbara to agree with me that Satan would not blind the eyes of those in Red Square to the glorious light of the Gospel. Our little prayer group stormed heaven right out in the open and believed that God would move and open a door for the Gospel. We prayed and commanded the blindness to fall from the eyes of those who would be given a tract. After praying we split up, and within moments all the tracts were gone from our hands. The group I approached took them and asked for more! After our prayer Satan could no longer blind their eyes. We had taken possession of territory Satan wanted to control.

In reflecting on this story many questions arise. Are we supposed to take an offensive stance against the enemy? Should we not just wait for him to come find us? Does the New Testament have anything to say about warring against principalities and powers? What are territorial spirits anyway? Did Jesus ever war against high-level spiritual wickedness? Do we have much biblical fabric to make a case for the growing movement worldwide of spiritual warfare and tearing down evil strongholds of the enemy? If so, who should participate, and how do we go about doing it in a safe, balanced manner?

These and other questions are ones I have struggled with over the years as the Lord has called me to be a leader in strategic spiritual warfare over nations. The questions are legitimate and need to be addressed. Even though I have been teaching on this subject and leading groups in prayer over their nations for a number of years now, I do not begin to presume that I have found out all there is to know about spiritual warfare.

One thing I do know, however, is that spiritual warfare is a volatile subject. It is not a topic the enemy likes to see discussed, but it is one people are eager to study. As people are praying over their cities, villages, towns, provinces and nations, many are doing a great work for the Lord while others are getting into an enormous amount of trouble. I pray that this chapter will help those who feel a deep call from God to pray for their cities and nations. Psalm 2:8 is a rallying cry for those who are hearing this call: "Ask of Me, and I will give You the nations for Your inheritance, and the ends of the earth for Your possession."

We are in a holy war for the souls of men and women. We are wrestling in heavenly places against an enemy who is ruthless in his desire to steal, kill and destroy. He is a master strategist who wants to pervert God's design for the nations. He has undermined the rule of the Kingdom of light and established his thrones and dominions. And one of his greatest weapons is passivity on the part of believers. While we have been busy in the churches he has been carefully instituting his rule in the nations of the world.

As more and more believers wake up to the fact that we must reach the unreached in the world today, this great praying army is using terms that are quite militant in tone. Turn-of-the-century pastor S. D. Gordon spoke of this military language:

> The greatest agency put into man's hands is prayer. And to define prayer one must use the language of war. Peace language is not equal to the situation. The earth is in a state of war and is being hotly besieged. Thus one must use war talk to grasp the facts with which prayer is concerned.
>
> Prayer from God's side is communication between Himself and His allies in enemy country. True prayer moves in a circle. It begins with the heart of God and sweeps down into the human heart, so intersecting the circle of earth, which is the battlefield of prayer, and then goes back again to its starting point, having accomplished its purpose on the downward swing.[2]

This chapter is targeted at encouraging those "militant" troops to learn about tearing down strongholds over nations for the advancement of the Gospel. There are many different aspects of the subject of spiritual warfare, and many good books have been written about some of these. I have felt led to focus on high-level warfare, which occurs on the battlefield in the heavenlies and contributes to capturing a city or nation for Christ.

This spiritual battle is described in 2 Corinthians 10:3–4: "For though we walk in the flesh, we do not war according to the flesh. For the weapons of our warfare are not carnal but mighty in God for pulling down strongholds."

When we possess the land over our cities, we gain control of their political, physical and spiritual arenas. This is because rulership of these areas is really based in the heavenlies and not in earthly places. As we pierce the darkness over our cities, more and more of God's light and glory will pour into them. Ephesians 3:10 says: "To the intent that now the manifold wisdom of God might be made known by the church to the principalities and powers in the heavenly places."

We, the Church, are to make known God's manifold wisdom to the principalities and powers ruling over our cities!

What are these principalities and powers? The Bible gives only glimpses of what they are and how they operate. It has been said that this is to prevent our becoming fascinated with high-level wicked spirits. I have to agree that there is a real danger of fascination to the point of being consumed by them in our thought lives. I will be giving you safeguards later in this chapter, but let me add that we should not become too interested—nor should we be fearful. Nothing should stop us from taking the Kingdom of God violently for our heavenly King (see Matthew 11:12).

There are and will be differences in teaching on this subject of high-level spiritual conflict. This is the time to look at the fruit of what is accomplished rather than become judgmental because someone else's approach is not exactly like ours. Mark 9:38 says: "Teacher, we saw someone who does not follow us casting out demons in Your name, and we forbade him because he does not follow us." The enemy loves to polarize Christians around dissension about methodology.

The Unseen Hierarchy

The Bible talks about two kingdoms in conflict with each other. One is the Kingdom of God and the other is Satan's evil kingdom, the kingdom of darkness. In God's Kingdom His angels are messengers sent to those who will inherit salvation (see Hebrews 1:14) to establish God's purposes as Ruler of the universe. Satan's emissaries, fallen angels, are sent to establish his kingdom of darkness. How do these evil beings intend to accomplish this, and what legal right do they have to do so?

Satan's representatives position themselves at his command over geographic regions. They rule illegally and have a direct effect on the people living in their assigned areas. Most people, unaware of Satan's devices, fall prey in some measure to the influence of these territorial spirits. The evil spirits use various means to take dominion over the population of their regions, such as moral decay and addictions. Territorial spirits work to "brainwash" citizens from having the mind of Christ and thus neutralize the power of the Kingdom of God.

Many people do not realize how much their lives are affected by the spiritual strongholds of their particular regions. For instance, if there is a strong principality such as the spirit of religion, there will be a great hindrance to seeing the supernatural power of God in manifestation.

Years ago I was ministering in Australia and began to find myself feeling oppressed and rejected as a woman. There was really no apparent reason for these strong feelings; yet I would wake in the night gripped by these types of emotions. Finally I realized that this was not normal. I asked the Lord to show me what the problem was and felt His leading to look into the history of Australia. The next day, as I studied Australian history, I was surprised to find out about the mistreatment of the first women who settled in the land during its history as a penal colony.

During the conference soon after that, my friend John Dawson, who is now the president of Youth with a Mission, stood up to teach and said, "I feel from the Lord that we need to have gender reconciliation here because of the historic breeches between the genders." He then led in prayers of identificational repentance between men and women.

I was amazed at what transpired! Women wept and wept, and poured out their hearts describing feelings very similar to what I had been wrestling with. From that time, those prayers and many others like them across the nation have led to great strides in healing this powerful nation down under.

In retrospect, what did I learn on a personal level? There are times when the emotions I am feeling are being influenced by the territorial spirits of the region I have traveled to for ministry. Often when I realize this and rebuke them from affecting me in any manner, the oppression I am feeling totally lifts. I often believe that they are overplaying their hand, as I then know what to study to see the nation healed.

One of the major strategies of Satan's kingdom is to assign ruling spirits to influence governmental leaders. Once the leaders are conquered, the evil spirits work to get them to enact laws that prohibit any further advance of the Kingdom of God.

What is the biblical evidence of the influence of these high-level territorial spirits? In order to understand the patterns of these beings, it helps to understand something called the law of double reference. According to Finis Jennings Dake's *Annotated Reference Bible*: "This law occurs when a visible creature is addressed, but certain statements also refer to an invisible person who is using the visible creature as a tool."[3]

Two passages in the Bible refer to a human ruler as well as Satan. These are found in Ezekiel 28:11–19 and Isaiah 14:3–27. They begin by addressing physical rulers, the first being the prince of Tyre and the second the king of Babylon. In the middle of the chapters both begin to address a being with attributes far beyond that of a human ruler. For instance, Ezekiel 28:14–15 says:

> You were the anointed cherub who covers; I established you; you were on the holy mountain of God; you walked back and forth in the midst of fiery stones. You were perfect in your ways from the day you were created.

Other rulers in the Bible were affected by the territorial evil spirits over their kingdoms. Nebuchadnezzar was affected by the prince of Persia to the extent that he made a golden image of himself and commanded all to bow down and worship him as god. The prince of Persia also used Nebuchadnezzar as a pawn to force demonic worship. God broke the power of the territorial spirits when He displayed His glory in the fiery furnace as the fourth man in the fire. The light of His glory dispelled Satan's darkness.

This same prince of Persia tried to kill Daniel. This time he tricked Darius by the ploy he had used on Nebuchadnezzar and stirred up the governors of the kingdom: the administrators, counselors and advisors. Things looked pretty bleak for Daniel. It appeared that the prince of

Persia had done his homework well. But God rescued Daniel from the lions' den, and once again the power of the prince of Persia was broken for a season.

Do territorial spirits affect nations today? Absolutely! Consider the lust Saddam Hussein had to take all the land once governed by Nebuchadnezzar! The prince of Persia wanted to get his territory back.

There are other *empire* spirits today that are trying to regroup and take back ancient territory such as that conquered and ruled by the Ottomans. Islam sees its mission to be conquering the whole world in the name of Allah. Satan wants to fill the earth with terror and terrorists and we must close the breeches that give him any legal right to advance his kingdom.

There are numerous other places in the Bible telling how wicked territorial spirits tried to destroy the children of God. Remember Esther? And look at the times in the New Testament when new territories were opened up to the Gospel. In Acts 19 the territorial spirits of Diana stirred up the silversmiths. Acts 19:27 says: "So not only is this trade of ours in danger of falling into disrepute, but also the temple of the great goddess Diana may be despised and her magnificence destroyed, whom all Asia and the world worship."

Ephesians 6:12 teaches about the hierarchy of these ruling spirits: "For our struggle is not against flesh and blood, but against the rulers, against the authorities, against the powers of this dark world and against the spiritual forces of evil in the heavenly realms" (NIV).

In his book *The Believer's Guide to Spiritual Warfare,* Tom White calls this passage a depiction of hell's corporate headquarters. He has this to say about the hierarchy:

> Paul brought light to the topic by depicting the powers as organized in a hierarchy of rulers/principalities (*archai*), authorities (*exousia*), powers (*dunamis*), and spiritual forces of evil (*kosmokratoras*). It is reasonable to assume the authority structure here is arranged in descending order. Daniel 10:13 and 20 unveil the identity of the *archai* as high-level satanic princes set over nations and regions of the earth. The word *exousia* carries a connotation of both supernatural and natural government. In the Apostle's understanding, there were supernatural forces that "stood behind" human structures. Paul no doubt is voicing the Jewish apocalyptic notion of cosmic beings who were given authority by God to arbitrate human

affairs. Presumably, the *dunamis* operate within countries and cultures to influence certain aspects of life. The *kosmokratoras* are the many types of evil spirits that commonly afflict people, e.g., spirits of deception, divination, lust, rebellion, fear and infirmity. These, generally, are the evil powers confronted and cast out in most deliverance sessions. Even among them there is ranking, the weaker spirits subservient to stronger ones.[4]

One of the names being used for this hierarchy of evil spirits is "territorial spirits." While this is not a biblical name, it is descriptive of the Ephesians 6:12 list of ruling spirits.

I believe this is a season where many, even seasoned intercessors, are being led by God to revisit the arena of spiritual warfare and how to pray to dispel territorial spirits over their cities and regions. We have, for a myriad of reasons, lost ground on many spiritual battlefields. Part of the reason is that some of us simply stopped praying in the ways we used to.

What exactly is meant by the term *territorial spirit*? A territorial spirit is one that rules over a certain geographic region. There is, for instance, apparently a "prince of Persia." Daniel 10:13 says: "But the prince of the kingdom of Persia withstood me twenty-one days; and behold, Michael, one of the chief princes, came to help me, for I had been left alone there with the kings of Persia."

Evil spirits do not have sole dominion over territories. It seems that God's angels are on assignment over the nations as well. The Septuagint version of the Old Testament translates Deuteronomy 32:8 as follows: "When the Most High gave to the nations their inheritance, when he separated the children of men, He set the bounds of the peoples according to the number of the angels of God."

F. F. Bruce, who suggests that the Septuagint reading represents the original text, says:

> This reading implies that the administration of the various nations has been parceled out among a corresponding number of angelic powers. . . . In a number of places some at least of the angelic governors are portrayed as hostile principalities and powers—the "world rulers" of this darkness of Ephesians 6:12.[5]

A good resource for a more comprehensive study of the subject of territorial spirits is C. Peter Wagner's essay in the book he and F. Douglas

Pennoyer edited entitled *Wrestling with Dark Angels*. In addition, Peter Wagner has written *Praying with Power*, which is another excellent source for gaining a comprehensive grasp of this subject.

Some of you may be saying, "Well, I believe that Satan's hierarchy exists, but it is not biblical to be on the offensive in dealing with them." You may speak of the armor of God in Ephesians 6 and point out that it is mostly defensive in nature. Is there any New Testament pattern for warring against principalities and powers?

The answer is yes. One of the best examples comes from the Matthew 4 passage about the temptation of Christ. The first ministry act that Jesus performed after His baptism was a power encounter with Satan himself in the wilderness. Jesus was not a weakling and, in my opinion, He was not at all afraid of meeting His opponent. He did not hide in a cave and hope that the devil would never bother Him. In other words, He did not act only on the defensive.

As Jesus was led into the wilderness by the Holy Spirit, He warred against the spirit who claimed dominion over the earth. We will discuss the various strategies He used in spiritual warfare shortly. First, let's see Satan's battle plan.

Satan usually overplays his hand and reveals his strategies to us. In the wilderness he showed his three main areas of warfare. Jesus shot down these attempts by the power of the Word.

1. The Physical
"If you are the Son of God, command that these stones become bread."
But He answered and said, "It is written, 'Man shall not live by bread alone, but by every word that proceeds from the mouth of God.'" (verses 3–4)

2. The Spiritual
"If You are the Son of God, throw Yourself down. For it is written: 'He shall give His angels charge over you,' and, 'In their hands they shall bear you up, lest you dash your foot against a stone.'"
Jesus said to him, "It is written again, 'You shall not tempt the LORD your God.'" (verses 6–7)

3. The Political
Again, the devil took Him up on an exceedingly high mountain, and showed Him all the kingdoms of the world and their glory. And he

said to Him, "All these things I will give You if You will fall down and worship me."

Then Jesus said to him, "Away with you, Satan! For it is written, 'You shall worship the LORD your God, and Him only you shall serve.'" (verses 8–10)

It is interesting to note that once Jesus spoiled Satan's plan in the wilderness His ministry grew quickly. The disciples followed Him; people were saved, delivered and healed. For a season the enemy's power was bound. I believe that Jesus used spiritual warfare techniques in the wilderness to give us a pattern for tearing down strongholds.

There are five keys to the battle strategy Jesus used in the wilderness. The first is often overlooked in Christ's preparation for battle: He humbled Himself before God by submitting to baptism. James 4:6–7 says: "But He gives more grace. Therefore He says: 'God resists the proud, but gives grace to the humble.' Therefore submit to God. Resist the devil and he will flee from you."

How different the birthing of Christ's ministry than many today! He humbled Himself, the opposite of a prideful announcement that He was the Messiah.

John Dawson speaks of humility as a battle plan for taking a city in *Taking Our Cities for God*. He was in Cordoba, Argentina, with a team from Youth with a Mission to witness during the finals of the world soccer playoffs. The team was not having any breakthroughs until they discerned a spirit of pride over the city. The Lord led them to kneel and pray in the midst of that proud, beautiful city. John tells it like this: "I remember vividly how Christ strengthened me when I set aside my dignity and knelt in the street. The intimidation of the enemy was broken along with our pride."[6]

The Lord gave his team a great harvest that day. The spirit of pride was broken from the people with the weapon of humility.

The second key to Christ's strategy was fasting. Matthew 4:2 says, "And when He had fasted forty days and forty nights." Fasting is a vital element in treading down strongholds over cities. In his book *Revivals of Religion*, Charles Finney quotes Jonathan Edwards on this subject:

If we are not to expect that the devil should go out of a particular person, that is, under a bodily possession, without extraordinary prayer, or prayer and fasting, how much less should we expect to have him cast out of the land and the world without it?[7]

The third key is one of the most critical. The unshakable accuracy of the Word of God was written on the tablets of Christ's heart. Many become deceived with half-truths when they go into spiritual warfare. In order to war effectively we must be intimately acquainted with God's Word and be able to wield it as a sharp sword against the enemy of our souls.

The fourth key is perseverance. That battle was not won in one day. Jesus had spent forty days praying and fasting. We sometimes become discouraged if we have to persevere for one or two days. Some of you have battled so long for your cities that you feel like giving up. *Don't give up!* One day the enemy will lose his grip on your city, and revival will come. Do not become weary in well-doing. Most of all do not let the strength of the battle dissuade you from fighting the good fight of faith.

The final key is one that people are sometimes criticized for using. It is actually addressing territorial spirits and commanding them to leave the regions. We sometimes overlook the few, but powerful, words that Christ used in the wilderness. Ending the battle, He said with great authority, "Away with you, Satan!" (Matthew 4:10). The Bible says that he left Jesus and the angels came and ministered to Him.

An interesting thought: Jesus battled without anyone to intercede for Him. There was not one born-again Christian on earth, and yet He won the victory through the keys given in Matthew 3 and 4: humility, His knowledge of the Word, fasting, perseverance and command of authority.

Entering Warfare

As I travel and teach on spiritual warfare I have found that there are many theorists but not many practitioners. Many who are teaching about warfare have never actually engaged in it and have many questions. One of the most common questions is, "How do I discern the strongholds of the enemy?"

Before I endeavor to answer this question I must address the dangers of such warfare and give some safeguards. In writing this chapter I felt as though I should put a label on the front: *Danger, Handle with Prayer!* Spiritual warfare is not for the immature.

Personally I would not have chosen to become a spiritual warfare specialist. The calling on my life is that of a prophet-intercessor, which brings with it an authority to tear down strongholds over nations. This is not to say that any believer cannot be trained in spiritual warfare, but that it must be done with care.

Safeguard Number One

There are two safeguards to be considered when participating in seasons of spiritual warfare over your city. First, this high-level battle should be done only on a corporate basis by those who know what they are doing. One should *never* enter into the battle lightly. Never underestimate the enemy. You need to have a healthy respect for his capabilities and not, as I said earlier, a fascination with his abilities and power.

In *Wrestling with Dark Angels* Peter Wagner tells of two Presbyterian ministers in Ghana who underestimated the enemy.

> One of them, contrary to the warnings of the people in the area, ordered a tree which had been enshrined by Satanic priests to be cut down. On the day that the last branch of the tree was lopped off, the pastor collapsed and died. The second minister commanded that a fetish shrine be demolished. When it was, he suffered a stroke.

Wagner goes on to say:

> As the Fuller Seminary community heard Timothy Warner say recently, "Welcome to war!" The purpose of power evangelism is to glorify God through demonstration of divine power. But if the power of the enemy is underestimated, the opposite can occur.[8]

There are some, like Omar Cabrera of Argentina, whom God has called to sequester themselves in a hotel room, fast, pray and war against the territorial spirits over the areas where evangelistic campaigns will be held. This is not the norm. Cabrera is especially anointed by God to do so just as God called Gideon to tear down the altars of Baal under a special anointing.

We must always wisely discern the scope of the battle and whether or not we have enough intercession to fulfill our mission, plus protect us from the onslaught of the evil one. There are some battles that simply are not yours to fight. If you try to enter into that war you will be wounded. However, there are some people who don't spend enough time developing their spiritual warfare intercession strategy, even though there are fighting in the right war.

Safeguard Number Two

Second, stay under spiritual authority and use godly wisdom. The Huguenots of France received a powerful filling of the Holy Spirit in their lives, but they unwisely went into the Catholic churches and tore down the statues of the saints. This so infuriated the Catholic king that he had them massacred.

There are many prayer groups that God is genuinely leading to tear down strongholds over their areas, and I do not want to scare you away from doing so. As long as you are careful, you will be fine. Here are some points to consider:

1. Are you and your team prepared? Are you walking in forgiveness and do you have a clean heart?
2. Have you done the spiritual mapping and considered the scope of the battle?
3. Do you need additional intercessors? More fasting?

Some ministries center around the call of spiritual warfare and send out the SWAT (Spiritual Weapons And Tactics) teams mentioned earlier. One of these is Sister Gwen Shaw with the End-Time Handmaidens. Sister Shaw recently sent a team out to pray against an earthquake that had been predicted along the New Madrid (Arkansas) Fault.

The New Madrid Fault extends 120 miles, crosses five state lines and cuts across the Mississippi River three times and the Ohio River twice.

Dr. Iben Browning predicted that an earthquake would hit there on December 3, 1990. He had predicted the Mexico City earthquake in 1985 and the one in San Francisco within a day of its occurrence in

1989, as well as the Colombian volcano and the eruption of Mount St. Helens, each within one week.[9]

Many took his prediction seriously, among them the End-Time Handmaidens. A team of five top intercessors went to five areas to pray over the land and the fault, and against the earthquake. The warfare was quite heavy, according to Sister Shaw.

The day of December 3 came and went and no earthquake struck. The newscasters were amazed and said that Browning must have missed his prediction. It is likely we will never know how many disasters have been averted through fervent spiritual warfare.

How does one discern the strongholds over a geographic area? How did Sister Shaw's intercessors know what to pray to avert the earthquake? This is a subject on which I teach eight hours a day for several days before teams are taken into cities. What follows is simply a thumbnail sketch of the ways to discern strongholds.

Discernment Point Number One

The first thing to remember when finding the spiritual strongholds of a city is to be led by the Holy Spirit. God has a plan for each city. You cannot simply duplicate what has been done somewhere else. The strategy God has for your city can be obtained only through fasting and prayer. You must also determine the legal entrances that have allowed Satan to establish the strongholds in the first place. These could be called the gates of the city.

As I mentioned earlier, gates were strategic to the welfare of cities in biblical times. The city gates were symbols of authority. It was here that the elders met to discuss the welfare of the city and governmental issues. Satan works hard to gain entrance to cities. The gates that open to him do so because of the sin of people in the cities. Once he can legally enter the city through sin or a "gate of hell," he moves in and out freely.

The city does not have to be lost forever. Matthew 16:18 gives us a precious promise concerning this: "On this rock I will build My church, and the gates of Hades shall not prevail against it." When we found our cities on God's laws or reclaim them according to those laws, then the gates of hell cannot prevail.

There are other beautiful promises in Scripture concerning gates. One of these is Isaiah 28:6: "And . . . strength to those who turn back the battle at the gate." God will be our strength as we battle the enemy at the gates of our city. Another one is found in Genesis 22:17: "And your descendants shall possess the gate of their enemies." As we are faithful to the Lord, He will raise up our descendants, or "our seed" as some translations say, to possess the gate of the enemy.

Discernment Point Number Two

In order to close Satan's gate into the city, we must discover the sins of the city. Then we must repent of these sins to stop his kingdom from ruling. Sin must be repented of corporately because the sin is corporate. This is not always an easy concept for Americans to grasp. You might ask, "But it isn't *my* sin. Aren't those people responsible for what they have done before God?" Of course they are. But God judges cities as a whole. Look at the judgment of God that fell on Babylon and other wicked cities. Cities do not have eternal souls so they must receive their judgment in the here and now.

We as intercessors stand in the gap for our cities and cry, "In judgment remember mercy. We deserve judgment, but please spare us." Each person in the city will stand before God for his or her individual sin, but we can still repent for a city or nation and ask God to forgive it as a whole.

Remember that Daniel stood in the gap for the sins of his nation even though he was righteous: "We have sinned and committed iniquity, we have done wickedly and rebelled, even by departing from Your precepts and Your judgments" (Daniel 9:5). Nehemiah also repented of the sins of his people: "We have acted very corruptly against You, and have not kept the commandments, the statutes, nor the ordinances which You commanded Your servant Moses" (Nehemiah 1:7).

Actually, humankind has territorial dominion. Adam was told to tend the Garden of Eden even though a whole world existed. The disciples were given specific directions of strategy for possession of the Kingdom. You and I are, in a sense, "territorial spirits" because it is God who chooses when we will be born and, if we are following Him, where we will live. He has destined us to be in certain places geographically to possess the gates of the enemy in the land.

How do you discover the sins against God in your city? Begin by looking at the three areas where Satan establishes his rulership—physical, spiritual and political. You may well uncover ungodliness in each area. Do research in the library with books written about the city or the nation. Talk to local historians and those who have lived in the community for many years. I am convinced that God has set aside people for the task of researching the city's history whether or not they realize it. Here is a list of questions we use when we research cities for Generals International:

1. Why was the city established? Is there any indication of corruption in government?
2. Who were the first people who lived in the area and what happened to them?
3. What does the city say about itself? Any slogans or mottos?
4. What were the principles upon which the city was established? Were those who organized the government godly or corrupt?
5. Who introduced Christianity into your area? Is there any evidence of religious deception?
6. Has the city, or its people, ever suffered any type of physical disaster? Any evidence of traumas that would affect the whole community?
7. Is there any evidence of greed in the economic system?

You can also find evidence of demonic influence by studying the music, culture, architecture and art. Many times visible things are clues to the invisible realm:

For since the creation of the world His invisible attributes are clearly seen, being understood by the things that are made, even His eternal power and Godhead, so that they are without excuse, because, although they knew God, they did not glorify Him as God, nor were thankful, but became futile in their thoughts, and their foolish hearts were darkened. Professing to be wise, they became fools, and changed the glory of the incorruptible God into an image made like corruptible man—and birds and four-footed animals and creeping things.

Romans 1:20–23

We have discovered ruling spirits over several cities from folk art. In Resistencia we found three panels painted with the symbols of the spirit of death. Sometimes the paintings are sensual and may indicate a spirit of lust or sensuality. Not surprisingly those cities often have a high rate of sexual crimes.

In America it is not hard to discern the ruling spirits over some of our large cities through the architecture. When you drive into the downtown district the tallest buildings will invariably be the banks. At one time the tallest structure in a town or village would have been the church. In fact, steeples were put on churches so they would be the highest points in the city.

A few years ago I was teaching in San Antonio, Texas, on spiritual warfare. Right in the middle of the message I realized suddenly why there was such a spirit of murder and violence over the city. Not a mile from the conference hotel was the Alamo, the cradle of Texas liberty. Much blood was shed between the Mexicans and the Texans at the Alamo. This gave legal entrance to the spirit of murder and spirit of violence.

Tearing the Strongholds Down

Once you discover the spirits over a city, how do you tear down the stronghold of the enemy? Again, please let me reiterate the fact that this chapter is only a snapshot of an involved process.

The Personal Level

The first place to battle is on a personal level. It is important to close up all the holes in our own armor that might let the enemy come in and hit us. We can stand and quote the verse all day that "a curse without cause shall not alight" (Proverbs 26:2), but we do not always realize that strongholds in our own lives make us susceptible to the enemy.

In the early '90s we met with a dialogue group to discuss this kind of intercessory prayer. The members of the round table included many who have since written major books on prayer and intercession as well as other topics.

The group was called the Spiritual Warfare Network. Ed Silvoso, who went on to write such classics as *That None Should Perish* and *Anointed for Business*, made a statement that was life changing for me. He said, "I have found that in every place where the Scriptures speak about spiritual warfare it is always in conjunction with teaching about relationships."

After that meeting I did a study on the passages we all know on warfare. What I found was eye-opening! We have been trying to claim Ephesians 6:10, for instance—"Finally, my brethren, be strong in the Lord"—without doing the things that precede the *finally*. Most of Ephesians deals with relationships—in the home, in marriage and in the Church. If the enemy has a foothold in any of these areas it must be dealt with before we can ever wrestle against principalities and powers.

Another stronghold on a personal level is that of self. Any right that we try to hold on to will be played upon by the enemy of our souls in time of battle. Some of the rights we have to give up in order to tear down strongholds are:

- the right to be offended;
- the right to our time;
- the right to do what we want with our possessions;
- the right to self-pity;
- the right to self-justification;
- the right to be understood; and
- the right to criticize.

Dealing with these issues will "shut the door and keep out the devil."

These strongholds are not all going to be overcome overnight, but just because you are in the process does not mean you cannot go to war. The Holy Spirit will convict you of any issues in your life with which He is not pleased.

Some of these things may seem rather tough. When you sign up for God's prayer army, however, it is rather like going to boot camp. They cut your hair to the length they want, give you shots, tell you when to get up and where to go. God knows how to make good soldiers out of us.

The Mental Level

Another stronghold that has to be demolished in order to take a city for God is in the minds of believers. Satan too often convinces Christians that the city cannot be won for Christ. Satan has worked for years to set limits on what you believe regarding your city. He has implied that some will be won for Christ, but that citywide revival is impossible. He insinuates over and over again that some people are simply too hard to win to Christ and that we should not bother with believing for their salvation. Remember the definition of strongholds from Ed Silvoso: "A stronghold is a mindset impregnated with hopelessness that causes the believer to accept as unchangeable something that he/she knows is contrary to the will of God."

I have personally found the battle that comes against my mind to persuade me to give up is one of the hardest battles to overcome. Mike and I have a saying between us: "If you are going in to possess the land and there are no giants, you are only tourists." You are not in the right territory.

Seeking Unity

As I have also learned from Ed Silvoso, strongholds against unity must be broken down in the minds of the leaders of the city and then the believers in order to captured. The pastors must first believe that God can tear down the ideological strongholds among Christians—between denominations and groups of believers. They must see that they are all one Body and that their city will never be won with just part of the Body working. Every joint and member must supply effort to win a city for Christ. Just as it took all the tribes of Israel to conquer the Promised Land of Canaan, it takes all the parts of the Body of Christ to inherit our promised land in a city.

How can this unity be accomplished? Many times God will anoint a leader to be the Joshua for the city. This Joshua will have unusual favor with God to gather pastors and leaders together. Other leaders appointed by God will join in a covenant relationship of prayer for unity.

Humility has a particularly devastating effect on the power of religious disunity. As pastors and leaders in an area bless each other instead of putting up more walls, as they realize they are often paranoid and protective of "their" sheep, God's unity will come and ideological strongholds will be broken. Sometimes these strongholds are broken when a church takes up an offering for another church. Wouldn't it surprise you if a pastor from a neighboring church offered to help with a day of yard work around your church?

The Crisis and Warfare

Another way that ideological strongholds are broken down is through crisis. A crisis tears apart haughtiness and brings people back to basic beliefs—the Lordship of Jesus Christ and the need for all to know Him as Lord.

When people are hurting they are hungry for God's power. Walls have often tumbled down because Christians have asked God for miracles during a crisis.

Opposition

Another powerful weapon in spiritual warfare is that of moving in the opposite spirit. I first learned about this weapon from John Dawson. If you are seeking to overcome a spirit of greed, give. If you are breaking down a religious spirit of isolation and haughtiness, humble yourself and be a blessing.

Repentance

This is the singular most effective weapon to change an area because it takes away the legal right of Satan to "own" the territory. This is the weapon we find in 2 Chronicles 7:14:

> If My people who are called by My name will humble themselves, and pray and seek My face, and turn from their wicked ways, then I will hear from heaven, and will forgive their sin and heal their land.

This Scripture has been the subject of numerous books on prayer, but it can never be reiterated enough! In our many times of prayer with leaders around the world, repentance is the weapon we use more frequently than any other.

Pioneer Intercession

Before I transition to the next stage, let me mention the periodic need of pioneering in intercession. At times there may not be pastors and/or believing leaders of different sectors of society in the nation to pray against the strongholds. This is where pioneer intercession needs to take place.

Pioneer intercession was done by prayer teams through the 10/40 window during the '90s, and is still taking place in many nations that are almost totally unreached for Christ. This is where prayer walking and breaking of spiritual strongholds must be done by the Body of Christ at large in order to see souls released from the spiritual darkness of the area.

Then there comes a day when local, indigenous leaders rise up and take their place in intercession, and the intercessors from other nations change roles to strengthen rather than lead the prayers.

A Frontal Assault

The last aspect of spiritual warfare to be addressed in this chapter is warring against the territorial spirits over cities and nations with a frontal assault. The other types we have discussed are effective but more indirect in nature.

I want to go a little more in depth in this section and show you how major prayer generals in different sectors of society lead prayer teams to tear down the territorial strongholds over their cities. I am not saying this is the only way or the best way, but it is highly effective. Remember that you must follow the Holy Spirit and that each situation is different. Perhaps this brief overview will help you develop a model for your city.

1. There needs to be a high level of unity among the leadership of the region in a particular sector of society. (I will explain more about this in the last chapter.) This means that a majority of the

leadership in the area are in agreement about the need for spiritual warfare and will participate in tearing down the strongholds. Without this we can only work on tearing down local, personal and ideological strongholds. I have come to understand that at times one reaches a level of *cohesion* that creates a strong sense of unity, rather than needing every single person in agreement, and allows this level of spiritual warfare to take place.

2. It must be God's time, the *kairos* (strategic time), to move in and assault the principalities. This can be done only after their grip has been weakened through unity in the churches, repentance prayer for the sins of the city and also tearing down personal strongholds. Also, large moves that minister personal deliverance from demons weaken the power of the territorial spirits.

   This occurred when Jesus sent His advance prayer teams into every city and place where He would go. When they returned rejoicing, saying, "Lord, even the demons are subject to us in Your name," Jesus said, "I saw Satan fall like lightning from heaven" (Luke 10:17–18). I believe that Jesus was speaking of the power of the territorial spirits being broken through the disciples' casting out demons as well as through powerful evangelism and healings.

3. The leadership in the local area should agree to fast and pray for lengths of time specified to them by the Lord through intercession among themselves.

4. The leadership should agree to bring their people to a seminar about spiritual warfare so that they can have their minds renewed in this area and receive instruction. In Argentina, Harvest Evangelism led by Ed Silvoso brought the leaders together in different cities. The longer we taught them, the easier the cities were to deliver. (Eight hours of teaching per day, four days in a row was the longest I taught in Argentina.)

5. The local leadership should be willing to participate in the actual prayer for the city. One missionary said it like this: "When the Israelites went into Canaan, it was the priests who went first and stood in the Jordan so the rest of the people could pass over."

6. Research on the history of the city should be completed. (See questions mentioned earlier.)

7. This research should be passed out to a core group of pastors of local churches and/or leaders of various sectors of society.

8. The leaders should be asking the Lord for the names of the strongholds over the area.

9. If our ministry is helping to coordinate the event, copies of the research should be sent to our office to pray and study over for strategy for the area.

10. Meetings with the local leadership should take place before the larger groups meet, if possible.

11. Pastors and/or leaders should make a scouting trip of local strongholds in the city.

After preparation has been made, the seminars teach the people about the scriptural validity of what we are going to do. At the end of the seminars we ask the people to pray and ask God if they are to come with us to pray for the city. The rest are asked to intercede while we go. These recruits include the pastors and leaders who make up our SWAT team for the assault. It is best to do this if possible when physically rested, but there are times when one is on a "forced march" because of time and you simply have to press forward. Here are the qualifications we suggest for the SWAT team. The individual should:

1. come to pray by a leading of the Lord;
2. be mature in the Spirit;
3. be free from known sin;
4. be unafraid; and
5. be under submission to a local church.

Who does the actual praying when the territorial spirits are addressed? This can be done by those who have legal authority through right of anointing or right of birth. It can be accomplished through others if this is not possible, but it has proven infinitely more effective if it is done through local leadership. This is one reason God has planted them in their city. I earnestly believe God wants each generation to learn to war because they will have their own giants to face. No stronghold can be permanently torn down until Jesus comes and once and for all throws

Satan into the bottomless pit. Each generation will break his power and bind him "for a season" from their land. Judges 3:1–2 says:

> Now these are the nations which the LORD left, that He might test Israel by them, that is, all who had not known any of the wars in Canaan (this was only so that the generations of the children of Israel might be taught to know war, at least those who had not formerly known it).

Now the background work is done. How do you go about praying against territorial spirits?

Remember first to pray protection over each person there and all of their family members, loved ones, churches and intercessors praying on their behalf. We often read Psalm 91 out loud and other such Scriptures pertaining to protection. Many times we stop to put on the armor of God from Ephesians 6. Oftentimes we kneel and humble ourselves under the hand of almighty God as we begin to realize we have no power or authority but from Him.

Then we begin remitting sin. It seems especially helpful to have a representative of the area you are praying about do the remitting. Has the government, for instance, passed any laws that are not godly? If so, have a lawmaker repent of this sin on the city's behalf.

Once sin has been repented of, I usually ask the local pastors or leaders of various areas, marketplace, etc., who have strong anointings and authority to lead in the actual prayer against the territorial spirits and command their power to be broken. This must not be done until the sins have been remitted or the power of the strongholds will not be broken. This is an area where one must rely carefully on the leading of the Holy Spirit. The leadership has a great responsibility for those they have taken into battle with them. To attempt to rail against the territorial spirits when it is not the time can be disastrous. God puts tremendous peace and faith into the hearts of the pastors and leaders when it is time to pray against the spirits.

The final portion of this type of spiritual warfare is a time of "planting God's Word" into the city in two ways.

First is to fill the vacuum made when the wicked spirits depart by planting the Word of God in its place. When we prayed against San La Muerte (spirit of death), for instance, we proclaimed together, "Jesus is life!" In one of His parables Jesus said:

"Then he says, 'I will return to my house from which I came.' And when he comes, he finds it empty, swept, and put in order. Then he goes and takes with him seven other spirits more wicked than himself, and they enter and dwell there; and the last state of that man is worse than the first. So shall it also be with this wicked generation."

Matthew 12:44–45

Then, second, speak restoration of the city to its original calling.

Each city has been established by God for His purpose, even if it looks as if the enemy has taken it over. It is important to seek the Lord for the reason that the city was established.

The city of Resistencia was originally founded as a "buffer" to keep the sister city of Corrientes across the river safe from enemy attack. Its redemptive gift was quite different from this. We found as we prayed that the gift of the city was the arts. God wanted these used in various ways for His Kingdom. The gift of music is used in intercessory praise to "resist the devil" and so the name of Resistencia, or Resistance, is quite appropriate. We "released" those gifts to do their good work.

This is the way we have been led to pray over cities in Generals International. Sometimes I feel as though I am hearing the proverbial story of the blind men trying to describe the elephant when I am talking to leaders about spiritual warfare. In the story, you remember, one person touches the elephant's tail and says the elephant is very much like a piece of rope. Another touches his side and says he's more like a wall. And so on.

Thus, since God causes certain leaders to be specialists in tearing down different kinds of strongholds, they each feel that his or her area is all-important. Some will work on the level of personal strongholds and teach, "We must be holy." Others declare, "When everyone is in unity, then all the strongholds will be broken down." Still others state, "No, if you do not directly address the principalities and powers over a city, nothing will happen." Each of these is proclaiming a part, but each alone will not have a lasting effect. It is my belief that all are needed in some measure to capture a city for Christ.

May God bless you as you possess the gates of the enemy. And may He use your intercessor's heart to further His Kingdom. I pray that the principles in this book will be a guide and encouragement to you as you fulfill this calling. It is a privilege to pray what is on the heart of God!

The final chapter of this book brings us into a whole new arena of intercession that we had only glimmers of light about during the era of the '90s. In order for nations to remain open to the Gospel in every area of society, these strategies are essential, and are able to see a nation reformed and transformed by the power of the Holy Spirit through militant intercession.

---

1. Paul Billheimer, *The Technique of Spiritual Warfare* (Santa Ana, Calif.: TBN Press, 1982), 58.

2. S. D. Gordon, *Quiet Talks on Prayer* (Pyramid Publications, 1967), 27.

3. Finis Jennings Dake, *Dake's Annotated Reference Bible*, 7th ed. (Lawrenceville, Ga.: Dake Bible Sales, Inc., 1977), 42.

4. Thomas White, *The Believer's Guide to Spiritual Warfare* (Ann Arbor, Mich.: Servant Publications, 1990), 34.

5. F. F. Bruce, *The Epistle to the Hebrews* (Grand Rapids, Mich.: Eerdmans Publishing Co., 1964), 33.

6. John Dawson, *Taking Our Cities for God* (Lake Mary, Fla.: Creation House, 1989), 19.

7. Charles G. Finney, *Revivals of Religion* (Virginia Beach, Va.: CBN University Press), 27.

8. C. Peter Wagner and F. Douglas Pennoyer, eds.; *Wrestling with Dark Angels* (Ventura, Calif.: Regal Publishing, 1990), 87.

9. Dee Lynn, *Freedom Alert Prayer Network Newsletter* (Minneapolis, Minn.: November 20, 1990); Gwen Shaw, *Angel Letter*, November-December 1990 edition.

17

Reforming Nations
through Militant Intercession

While on a ministry trip to Berlin, Germany, Mike and I were led by the Lord to visit the city of Wittenberg. You probably remember it from your study of history. Its name invokes pictures of a man named Martin Luther and a church door.

One might call this hallowed entry to the massive stone church in Saxony the "door of reformation." For in 1517, a man who saw the need for action posted 95 theses. It is thought provoking to realize that one man's words could change the world and still touch our lives in the 21st century.

Mike and I drove to Wittenberg on a bright, clear morning with a group of friends on Reformation Day, October 31, 2007—the day all of Germany commemorates Luther's actions and the resultant world-shaking events that produced what we now call the Lutheran Church.

As we piled out of the car, I felt a deep excitement that we were about to pray in a manner that would release a whole new move of God in the earth. This seems like a bold statement, and I do not mean to imply that we were the only ones sensing that a page of history was about to be turned—as you will soon read.

My last visit to this city was life changing for me on a personal level, and I wrote about it in the opening chapter of my book *The*

Reformation Manifesto. At that time the cathedral was shut up and no one was around in the city. Today was different: Wittenberg was packed with festivities and people.

Our reason behind the trip was a prophetic word one of our group had received from the Lord. Reiner Huss, a young German with an emerging prophetic gift, had written me to say, "Cindy, we need to go to Wittenberg on this trip. It will be 490 years after the last reformation. I received this while reading Daniel 9:24. Seventy times seven equals 490 years. God wants to start a new reformation and we need to go pray for that to happen!"

I must admit that Mike and I really didn't quite understand what he meant by the 490 years since the last reformation, nor the Daniel 9:24 connection to a new move of God. Yet, the part about beginning a new reformation resonated strongly in our hearts, and so off we had gone to Wittenberg. It was a holy adventure.

We walked on the ancient streets, caught up in the spirit of the day. A group of school children were singing fun songs led by none other than "Martin Luther" in the costume of the day! Twenty thousand people were running around the city in celebration.

Even though we weren't Lutheran, we knew we were touching a piece of history through our footsteps. At last we came to the door. The original one had burned, and the current door is bronze, with the 95 theses inscribed on its surface.

Our group stood in front of the door and prayed what God had put in our hearts: "O Lord, start a new reformation that will change our nations! Reform the nations, Father God!"

After that moment we walked away, with a strong sense from the Lord that He was going to answer our prayers. But God wasn't finished yet—as we would soon find out.

Mike somehow became separated from the rest of us when we toured the church and saw where Luther was buried. All of a sudden he came up to me with a big grin on his face and said, "There is someone I want you to meet! Follow me—and let's find the rest of the group and bring them, too."

Somehow we all assembled back at the door to hear Mike's story. He had been walking through the crowd when a man said to him, "Mike, what are you doing here?" The man was an Argentine who lived in New

York City. We were astounded to find out that God had spoken to him from Daniel 9:24 in 1998 that he was to go to Wittenberg, Germany, to pray at noon for a new reformation to begin, at precisely the same time Luther had tacked his 95 theses to the door. This was significant because Latin America had never experienced the kind of reformation that had affected all of Europe.

The Argentine, named Hugo, prayed and wept in Spanish and English. Tears coursed down his face, which lit up like an angel as he cried out to the Lord for his people. We stood in prayer as a holy hush came upon us all.

As we walked away from the door, a German-American woman who had come with us quietly said, "God spoke the same thing to me twelve years ago. He spoke to me out of Daniel 9 and said that a new reformation would begin today."

Oh my! Heaven was opening up before us and I know the angels must have been singing! And still we were to find later in the day that God wasn't finished confirming His word.

That night I stood to preach in a beautiful old church in Berlin. It was the same place Hitler used for commissioning his troops to die in his name. When I shared with the group what had transpired in Wittenberg that day and its significance, a leader stood up from the Jerusalem House of Prayer and declared, "God told me the very same thing!"

Four confirmations of God speaking to people that a new reformation was beginning! Being an intercessor, I always contextualize these kinds of prophetic events in light of my calling to the nations. I realized that God was giving me a challenge to bring prayer into the 21st century in a way that would reform nations. We needed new prayers for a new day.

New Prayers for a New Day

What does that mean? New prayers for a new day? How do we take the wealth of our understanding from past prayer movements and build on them to see how God wants us to intercede in our generation?

Sometimes the answer doesn't come all at once; rather, it is revealed through a series of events. That is exactly what happened with me. This event in Wittenberg and Berlin, mixed with a meeting of the Reformation Prayer Council, gave me the content for this chapter. The answer is militant intercession that reforms nations.

This whole book focuses on training for militant intercession. There are other excellent books that focus on other areas such as contemplative prayer, and they are good. God is calling a new generation of generals of intercession, however, who will change nations with an understanding that sometimes prayer is from Matthew 11:12: "And from the days of John the Baptist until now the kingdom of heaven suffers violence, and the violent take it by force."

Lest I scare you by using that strong Bible verse, let me tell you I am speaking of spiritual violence and not the kind that terrorist organizations are using. Militant intercession breaks down strongholds in heaven that release heaven to earth. It is also done onsite and makes a statement on earth. This type of prayer sees that God's Kingdom does indeed come, and His will shall be done on earth as it is in heaven (see Matthew 6:10).

Another way to describe this militant kind of praying might be "dominion intercession" because it establishes God's rule into an area, taking it back from the illegal usurper, Satan. In fact, another word for *kingdom* is "dominion."

Prayer Activism

The United States Reformation Prayer Network leaders convened in New York City just before the first World Day of Prayer for Economies, held on October 29, 2008. Wall Street was shaking, as well as businesses around the globe.

As we sat in a roundtable meeting, we asked ourselves some hard questions. One of the strongest that resonated with the whole group was this: "Why haven't we seen more nations changed by the power of God?"

The next question was quick to follow and seemed to erupt from the whole group in frustration: "We have prayed and prayed, yet our nation is still in a horrible moral condition! What is wrong?"

I went to the board and wrote two words: *prayer activism*. After those two words I wrote: *prayer acts*. We all knew that we needed new prayers and we needed to get more militant in those intercessions.

Why is this necessary? As I mentioned in the previous chapter, Satan has blinded the eyes of those who should believe. Many times in our intercession we try to deal with the seen realm rather than the unseen realm.

Why is this necessary? Many of us have fallen back into Greek thinking that causes us to believe we only have to deal with the *seen* realm in our intercession, rather than believing we have authority and dominion in the *unseen* realm as well. In fact, people are even afraid to go to war according to Ephesians 6:12, which says:

> For we do not wrestle against flesh and blood, but against principalities, against powers, against the rulers of the darkness of this age, against spiritual hosts of wickedness in the heavenly places.

That verse gives a very clear X-ray of spiritual reality! More things are real and affect us on the earth than we can see! The Word of God tells us that in the beginning God created the heavens and the earth. There are evil rulers that do not want the Lord's will to be done on earth as it is in heaven, and they will not let go of the places they are ruling without someone on earth binding the strongman and pulling him down. If this is to happen we must first understand where the strongman has entered and who he is!

Over the past ten years I have found more and more people who used to be active in the prayer movement but are now afraid to pray in a militant fashion—or worse yet, have simply declared détente! From what I've seen as I have traveled to different countries, I actually believe that in some instances we have lost ground, with some nations becoming more violent and increasingly hostile to the Gospel.

This is one of the many reasons that I believe this new edition of *Possessing the Gates of the Enemy* is timely! It is time to pray not only in the light given us in previous moves of God—but to press into God for the "new wine" prayers for whole nations to experience a reformation!

I believe part of the reason we see nations transformed but then fall back into decay is that the different sectors of society were not reformed. Many people might have been saved, but they did not understand how to change the way their nations were run—or they stayed in their church buildings without attempting to bring lasting reformation to their nation.

Militant Prayer for the 7M Mandate

If we are going to reform nations, we need to understand how to pray militant prayers capable of binding the strongman over different sectors of society. We have been interceding in a more general way in our societies rather than seeing there are strongholds built into parts of our culture and nations that hinder God's will.

I mentioned Matthew 6:10 from the Lord's Prayer earlier as, for the past few years, there has been a clarion call from leaders calling for focus on the Kingdom. Add to this the fact that we are called to make disciples of all nations (see Matthew 28:19–20).

Rather than looking at our nations from the viewpoint that if we pray and revival comes to people's lives then the people will change their nations, we need to understand that, in each sector of society, there are strongmen such as humanism and corruption. In some nations corruption is actually a principality.

Here are some sectors of society that need to be spiritual mapped and the strongman pulled down for a nation to see true change:

1. Religion
2. Family
3. Education
4. Government
5. Business
6. Arts / Entertainment
7. Media

The same principles that pertain to the spiritual mapping of areas of sin such as abortion need to be applied in each of these areas of society. My friend Lance Wallnau calls these areas the seven mountains, or the 7M Mandate.

In the past few years we have focused quite a bit on the religion mountain in areas such as spiritual unity, but not many have developed prayer for the other six mountains in a systematic way. There are hit-and-miss prayers going on for these mountains, but most of us stay in our religion mountains without discovering the spiritual strongholds of these other areas. In order to see God's Kingdom come into our nations, we first need to reform our nations through intercession.

Here is the point: Our intercession has been done mainly for areas in the religion mountain, rather than expanding our intercession to include all six other mountains.

The truth is that there is a strongman over each of these areas. In fact, many times there isn't just one but several in different, specialized sections. For instance, the religion mountain could have a strongman of religion, or legalism. The family mountain could have divorce. The education one—humanism, business—mammon, government—corruption, arts/entertainment—sexual perversion and greed, and media—mental control.

You cannot know for sure what the strongholds are in the area you are looking into until a study is done. As my friend George Otis Jr. says, there is a reason that darkness lingers where it does. It has been given a welcome mat by the actions of the people who live in the area.

Just as darkness lingers in certain geographic regions, it also lingers in certain sectors of society. I often find that there has been an adoption and an adaptation of the strongholds from the sectors of society of other nations that create this welcome mat.

For instance, in the United States, the unholiness of movies made in Hollywood has polluted and affected the film industry all across the world. Therefore our sin in this area is greater, and we need to repent and study the film industry to find out where the roots of perversion are.

C. Peter Wagner has an excellent chapter on spiritual mapping in his classic book *Praying with Power*. In it, he quotes our friend Harold Caballeros's observation that the devil, due to his unlimited pride, frequently leaves a trail behind.[1] It is important to understand that those who first introduced government, businesses of different sorts, or educational practices often have patterns that are demonically inspired even though the people may not know it. People, such as the Free Masons, build cities according to a certain pattern—this is the trail. While the founders may not realize the demonic inspiration, it still affects the city.

In looking at education, for instance, one of the framers of modern American educational philosophy was John Dewey. Some of you may remember him from shelving books in a library according to the

Dewey decimal system. While he made this excellent contribution that many have benefited from, Dewey was also one of the writers of the 1933 Humanist Manifesto. Here are a few of the fifteen points of the manifesto:

> First: Religious humanists regard the universe as self-existing and not created.
>
> Fifth: Humanism asserts that the nature of the universe depicted by modern science makes unacceptable any supernatural or cosmic guarantees of human values.
>
> Ninth: In the place of the old attitudes involved in worship and prayer, the humanist finds his religious emotions expressed in a heightened sense of personal life and in a cooperative effort to promote social well-being.
>
> Tenth: It follows that there will be no uniquely religious emotions and attitudes of the kind hitherto associated with belief in the supernatural.[2]

Not only has this been worked into the core beliefs of the educational systems of the United States and other nations, but there are strongholds that must be torn down to break the power of this Humanist Manifesto. This has resulted in blind eyes and hearts for those who have been taught to believe in humanism: They cannot see the truth of God's Word that He is the Creator. Therefore, the trail left by Dewey is humanism.

It is interesting to hear the stories of people who have prayer walked the schools of their cities to break the spirit of humanism. Some have done prophetic prayer acts, such as praying to negate the Humanist Manifesto point by point through decrees.

One prayer group in the eastern part of the United States banded together and as pastors and intercessors visited every school in their large city. After their prayer time the test scores of the city's students went up dramatically. Could there be a correlation? I think so.

Because humanism has such a huge hold on the school systems of most nations, we will need persistent, persevering prayer to bring about a massive change. We need to fast and pray to pull down the strongholds that have been built by more than a generation of a teaching philosophy that says there is no God. These strongholds have also been strengthened through the teaching of evolution and the writings of Charles Darwin. Humanism mixed with Darwinism is a potent deception.

The top levels of the National Educators Association of America also flouts God's laws in His face through giving funds to advance homosexual agendas. Another way they indoctrinate children is by placing books with this kind of orientation in their libraries, and encouraging teachers to read them to their students.

I recently heard of a case in the eastern part of the United States where parents who objected to their child being read the book *The King Marries the King* took the case to court and lost! There are numbers of books along this theme being introduced in our public school systems.

While teaching in Germany, I was told about "gender mainstreaming" in Europe. In a nutshell, this is boys and girls being told that they will not know what sex they are until they grow up and decide. Toys such as trucks for boys and dolls for girls are not permitted in some of the daycares because they give the children "gender orientation." Are you shocked? We must mount up a prayer storm to protect the generations to come.

We must be militant in our intercession to pull down the strongholds built within our education systems and societies. God is calling for intercessors to pray especially for the schools of their nations because, as it has been said by many, "The teaching of today becomes the way the government is run tomorrow."

Dutch Sheets gives an excellent explanation of "pulling down strongholds" in his book *Intercessory Prayer*. He begins with quoting 2 Corinthians 10:3–5.

> It is true that I am an ordinary, weak human being, but I don't use human plans and methods to win my battles. I use God's mighty weapons, not those made by men, to *knock down the devil's strongholds*. These weapons can *break down every proud argument* against God and every wall that can be built to keep men from finding him. With these weapons I can capture rebels and bring and bring them back to God, and change them into men whose hearts' desire is obedience to Christ.
>
> TLB (italics mine)

The phrase "knock down the devil's strongholds" is "pulling down of strong holds" in the King James Version. Dutch goes on to say this:

"[to] pull down is the word *kathairesis*, which means 'to bring down with violence or demolish' something."[3]

There are many things that happen in our nations that we bemoan, complain about or personally decry, yet we feel helpless to do anything about them. This chapter is designed to help you out of that situation in order to become victorious in your life and that of the country where you live!

Many of you might be familiar with one of my favorite Scriptures: "For David, after he had served God's will and purpose and counsel in his own generation, fell asleep (in death)" (Acts 13:36, AMP).

That is my assignment as a Christian and an intercessor in the earth today. I believe I was born at the time I was, in the year I was, to steward the nations of the earth in intercession. Is this biblical?

Of course, it is the mandate given to us in the book of Genesis:

And God blessed them and said to them, Be fruitful, multiply, and fill the earth, and subdue it (using all its vast resources in the service of God and men); and have dominion over the fish of the sea, the birds of the air, and over every living creature that moves upon the earth.

Genesis 1:28, AMP

In this new move of God, we are learning where we haven't stewarded the earth with intercession. In fact, we have mostly been waiting to leave the earth without a care as to its condition either physically or spiritually. The good news is that societies can be repaired through militant reformation intercession. Remember when I explained in the chapter on Generals of Intercession how the Lord showed me that nations could be healed? His analogy to me was that a nation could be likened to an individual who has sin, broken relationships, and so forth. Sectors of society are healed the same way.

This leads to an important point: God has intercessors whom He wants to assign to each mountain of society.

We have fallen down on our assignment, but God will give us a supernatural ability to accelerate the healing of our nations as we learn to sharpen the way we pray. The good news is that God has redemption for nations as well as for individuals. Dutch Sheets expresses it this way:

"Before we fell from grace in the garden God had already decreed how He would fix our mistakes."[4]

Both Chuck Pierce and Dutch Sheets write about how God will redeem our past as individuals. Chuck writes in his book *Interpreting the Times*, "This is one of the functions of the power of salvation and deliverance: *redeeming the past from the hand of the enemy so it is no longer a weapon against us.*"[5] We must look back in our history and, applying this biblical concept of redemption on a corporate level, realign our future with God's original design.

In order to redeem the past of the seven mountains, we need to study each one systematically to see where the sector went off course from the principles of God—or was never set on the path at all!

I believe that one reason we have not seen the transfer of wealth that many teach about, among other things, to eradicate systemic poverty, is that there are strongmen over areas such as mining, banking and economic systems (see Proverbs 11:22). These strongmen do not want us to fight poverty, build orphanages, find cures for medical disease or establish godly government, among other things. They want to keep enslaving people through prostitution and human trafficking.

After this spiritual mapping of the sectors of society, there needs to be a time of seeking the Lord for a plan and time for militant intercession over the strongholds. Here is one way we have already prayed for a portion of the business sector and the financial structures of the United States:

1. How were our first banks established?
2. Who established our banks?
3. How has the stock market factored into our economy?
4. Does our economy have any ties to others in the world?

I must admit that, as I started researching this issue on a micro-level, it was such a deep subject I almost didn't know where to begin. My first venture into this study came when I was writing *The Reformation Manifesto*. At that time I pondered why, since poverty came through the sin of Adam and Eve (see Genesis 3:17–19), have we let it grow and grow even though we have been given authority over all powers of the evil one? Why haven't we eradicated systemic poverty?

Of course, at the simplest level we haven't seen this eradication as part of our job descriptions as Christians. Perhaps we also haven't understood our role as intercessors to break the strongholds of greed, mammon, etc., that blind men's eyes to the needs of the poor.

These are some of the things we have targeted in prayer for the economy. After doing research on a rudimentary level, we called for a World Day of Prayer for Economies to begin healing our economic systems and bringing them under the rule of God.

Actually, this was the result of the prophetic word God gave me in January 2008 that we were to go to Wall Street to pray on October 29, because the stock market was going to shake. Then God spoke another startling word to me in August 2008 when He said, *There will be no more business as usual*! I now understand that He meant worldwide.

The reason the Lord specifically wanted us to pray in New York City at Wall Street on October 29 was, as I mentioned earlier, because Wall Street crashed on that date in 1929, on what is known as Black Tuesday, providing the final blow that precipitated the Great Depression.

In partnership with Graham Power and the Global Day of Prayer, we called for intercession on that day at stock markets around the world. Prayer teams went to the Temple Mount and Mt. Carmel in Israel; others prayed over the banking system related to Artemis in Ephesus. Stock exchanges all across Asia received prayer as well. Hong Kong, Japan, Singapore and Korea had prayer teams covering their markets. Intercessors went with Sharon Stone to London, England. Prayer went up all the way from South Africa to the ends of the earth.

Here in the United States we prayed for Wall Street on the trading floor. We also went to the Federal Reserve Building to pray. This included going deep underground into the vaults that hold billions of dollars' worth of gold bars.

One powerful prophetic prayer act that we did near the bull statue, the unofficial symbol of Wall Street, was to issue a "decree of divorce" from the god of mammon. This was a legal document, read by John Benefield of Oklahoma, such as those read in court to dissolve a marriage.

We asked the great Judge of the universe to witness us as we declared our ties with mammon broken. One could actually feel the heavens cracking open while we prayed on that bright fall morning in New York City.

What was the result? As of this writing, we are still in the midst of the shaking. We are just beginning our militant intercession, however, and I believe it will shift the wealth in many areas if we continue to pray.

Here are some things I've observed since that prayer time:

1. God is shifting and sifting economic systems.
2. Those who are hearing the voice of God are getting out of debt through believing God will supernaturally intervene in their finances.
3. Property that was "untouchable" because it was so expensive is now becoming available to the Body of Christ.

The fruit that we hope will remain from this kind of shaking is, among other things, a purging of greed, a repositioning of wealth for the Body of Christ and a great harvest of souls.

While speaking at a conference in January 2008, I felt led by the Lord to make some prophetic prayer decrees over the stock markets. At that time I called several different leaders to come to the platform. One of these, Joseph Askins of New York, had shared with me a vision that he had while praying by the statue of the bull on Wall Street. He said that while they prayed over the bull and bear markets, he had a vision of a great lion's head forming on top of them.

At that point I began to prophesy that there would be a new "lion's" market that would arise. (One of the names for Jesus, you recall, is the Lion of Judah.) The prophecy went on to state that the Lord would change the markets from that of the bull and the bear and that *He* would have the lion's share of the market.

We are not finished, of course. Rather, we are just beginning with this prayer assignment. The task is huge, to say the least! But never let the size of the assignment sent from God daunt you. Simply begin. The Holy Spirit will guide you on your journey.

This lead me to another important and critical phase in praying new prayers for a new day: militant prayers with a message. As I mentioned earlier, in the dialogue we had with the United States Reformation Prayer Network, one of the phrases I wrote on the board was *prayer activism*.

Prayer activism is intercession that is itself a visible statement or message both in heaven and earth. Let me explain: Through the decade of the '90s we understood that we needed to intercede with our feet through onsite prayer. During that time we also went outside our church buildings and worshiped God in a visible way. We went outside our four walls to pray. Since that time, while there are exceptions such as The Call and others, we have done building prayer meetings. Most visible meetings are not in sectors of society at all.

Worship in the '90s was not done, for the most part, for a specific intercessory reason. These events, like the March for Jesus rallies, were powerful and brought the Church together in a visible manifestation of unity. They were wonderful and I personally participated in many of them. I passionately believe that Jesus is worthy of our worship for no other reason than He is God.

There is an aspect of intercessory praise that I wrote about in this book, however, that adds another dimension to worshiping on the streets—to bind the strongman. Psalm 149:6–9 tells us that our high praises of God execute vengeance on nations and bind their kings (strongmen) with chains. It concludes with this earthshaking proclamation: "To execute on them the written judgment—this honor have all His saints" (verse 9).

Our worship of God actually has the ability to execute the power of God's authority into the earth, in every sector of society. This means that God's Word has something to say concerning business ethics and education as well as governmental systems. Since humankind has free will, we are called to do battle in the heavens through His Word, to execute judgment on the strongmen that stop God's will from being done in the earth.

Our worship, therefore, should bring heaven's rule to earth! This means that His will *shall* be released supernaturally through our intercessory prayers and praise!

In this new move of intercession, I have seen visions of people introducing worship into their daily routines in their office buildings, schools and medical centers. What a way to break open the day and command the blessing of the Lord!

In addition to worshiping God in this way, I believe that militant intercessory song and prayer will happen again on the streets of our cities, specifically to make a statement. These "statement" prayer and praise gatherings will be reformational in nature, as they will not only release supernatural power but show natural kings and rulers of the earth the need for change.

Remember the songs sung during the civil rights movement in the United States? Some might have thought they were simply to encourage the people who were marching. Perhaps so, but there was something that happened in the *unseen* realm as well as the *seen*. There were invisible strongmen with names like racism and prejudice that blinded and gripped people's minds, and I believe they were brought down through these statement songs.

I'll never forget watching television as a child and hearing the haunting melody of "We Shall Overcome Someday." Could that song have been executing decrees into the heavens against racism? I believe so. Music is a weapon of warfare.

It is time to use the power of worship to break spiritual strongholds. For too long we have stayed in our buildings while worshiping. It is time to worship intentionally, to release sectors of society from the kingdom of darkness to the Kingdom of light.

There is an interesting connection between worship and the marketplace in the Word of God. I wrote earlier that it seems quite plausible that Lucifer was the worship leader of heaven before his fall. There is an interesting portion of Scripture in Ezekiel 28 describing the precious stones that were his covering.

It is possible that Satan became enamored of wealth and began some kind of sinful trade with these precious elements. There is some substantiation for this in Ezekiel 28:16:

> By the abundance of your trading You became filled with violence within, And you sinned: Therefore I cast you as a profane thing out of the mountain of God; And I destroyed you, O covering cherub, from the midst of the fiery stones.

This disclosure of Lucifer's sin is again reiterated in verse 18 of the same chapter. What does this tell us? It is interesting how this passage follows Ezekiel 27, in which the prophet gives one of the most complete listings of the commerce in his day. Could these two passages be linked for a reason? It is entirely possible.

As we look around the world, we know that there are emerald cartels, as well as ones for gold and diamonds. It is interesting to note how many wars have been fought that had the control of wealth at their root. Much bloodshed and violence has happened in the fight for control of gold, diamonds and precious gems.

Many mines that contain precious metals are dedicated to false idols. We need militant intercessors to release the wealth needed to fulfill our God-given role to help those in need as well as to change nations.

Let's fill the commercial districts of our cities with worshipers. I think one of the reasons so many youth are becoming amazing worship leaders is that we are going to need thousands to fill our societies with God's glory through worship.

A group of radical youth, mainly young Asian people, take this mandate to a new level in what they call *prayer strikes*. Jonathan and Sharon Ngai have a group called Strike LA (Los Angeles, California) and they go with their worshipers to places of cultural influence around their city. For instance, they have gone with their team to the Kodak Center (where Hollywood awards its Emmys) as well as the University of California, Los Angeles (UCLA). Can you imagine this on-fire group of youth walking to the large open areas of a university, pulling out their guitars and starting to dance and worship God with abandon? Surely revival will break out in those places in the coming days.

Another very important aspect of militant intercession is one that strongly stirred my heart as I mentioned earlier—prayer activism, also called "statement intercession" or "cause intercession."

Cause Intercession

We see in 1 Samuel 17 that young David is sent to check on his elder brothers who are in a great battle for the nation against a giant—Goliath. When he arrived at the Israelite army camp, this Goliath had taunted the soldiers for forty days and nights and they were scared and intimidated.

It is probable that David was under eighteen years of age, because of the Hebrew word used for "youth" in verse 42. But the real difference between him and the others: He was not afraid.

There are many giants in our cultures today. Each of them seems to have, in many situations, backed the Body of Christ into a corner. In fact, in some nations that corner has become a jail cell for those who preach the Gospel.

Some countries, like the U.S., are seeing the emergence of hate crimes against Christians who speak out against issues such as homosexuality. For example, a group of youth from the Justice House of Prayer (JHOP) in San Francisco had been going down to the Castro District of that city for three years. They would stand on the street corner and worship and pray.

These youth were attacked by people from the homosexual community, who pushed two of the girls down to the pavement, poured hot coffee over one of their heads and harassed them. The police finally came and had to escort them off the streets to protect them.

Was there a huge protest from the news media? No! Why? Because people who live in a country that predominately calls itself a praying nation either believe in the gay agenda or are intimidated by 5 percent of the population.

While I am extremely opposed to hate crimes against the gay community, I am 100 percent in favor of God's Word being honored from Romans 1. It is interesting that the people were shouting at the JHOP youth, "We don't want your God here!" In the U.S. we have a First Amendment right of assembly that the gay community violated when they attacked the JHOP youth.

Where does prayer activism play into this scenario? The JHOP youth would most likely not have thought they were engaging in prayer activism. They cared about the people in the Castro District coming to Christ—as we all should. It is clear, however, that our voice will be squashed and even abused if we do not begin to stand up and pray publicly.

It is time to lift up the banner of Christ and take prayer and worship to the streets in large numbers. When a school refuses to allow students to pray in the name of Jesus, masses of people need to mobilize to sit on the steps of that school and intercede.

I am not talking about angry mobs! There is no hate speech in true intercessory prayer. The difference is that the voice of prayer is heard in heaven and earth through a prayer manifestation. Heaven invades earth in prayer activism.

30 Second Kneel Down

Why is it that people of other faiths are unashamed to kneel face down and pray in public and we are too embarrassed to do the same?

There is one youth organization that has not been afraid to kneel down in front of their schoolmates. In fact, the name of the group is the 30 Second Kneel Down. Each day they kneel down in the hallway of their schools and pray this prayer:

1. God, thanks! God, I bow my knee in humility to You. I know Your loving presence will be with me all day. Thank You for loving me today. I love You, too!
2. God, touch them! God, I touch the teachers, administration and students on my campus today. One touch from You, Father, can change someone's destiny. Touch them through me.
3. God, tell them! God, the message of Jesus' love for my campus must be told. Use me as the messenger. I will tell those around me how much You love them.[6]

In this coming move of God, we are going to see prayer mobilizers who move people—at times large groups—to do prayer acts *en mass*. Technological advances will allow for this kind of mobilization to "hot spots" that need intercessory prayer. Each sector of society needs their own mobilizers to be an intercessory voice.

It is time to make prayer visible both in heaven and earth! Dietrich Bonhoeffer described his belief in what he called the *visible church* as opposed to the church that has nothing to do with what is happening with the government and its actions.[7]

Years ago the Supreme Court of the United States essentially outlawed prayer in school in the case of *Engle vs. Vitale* (1962). The prayer they outlawed was simple but powerful:

"Almighty God, we acknowledge our dependence upon Thee, and we beg Thy blessings upon us, our parents, our teachers and our country."

After the Supreme Court ruled against this prayer, millions of students stopped praying. As my friend David Barton eloquently states, since that time we have gone from the worst problems in the schools being spit wads and chewing gum to being machine guns.

Where was the visible church in front of the Supreme Court in 1962, with a cry unto the God of heaven and a visible manifestation of a people who refused to stop praying? Where were the students who refused to be silent after that time? Did we fail a generation? It is quite possible.

I have often watched activist groups on the television and thought how different and respectful the voice of God's people should be compared to the voice of the anarchist. Yet it is still time to find our voice and let it be heard. The news services of the land should have our voices on the nighttime news as we tell the world we want prayer back in schools. There are groups such as the American Center for Law and Justice, who stand by with legal expertise should we need it in our battle.

Prayer activism is part of a new moral reformation—not the kind that simply touches people on an individual basis, but the kind that releases a cry against spiritual wickedness on a corporate scale.

If we do not give voice in this generation with prayer acts, there will come a day when it will be entirely illegal for us to preach and pray the whole counsel of the Word of God. "Impossible!" you might say. But it is very, very possible, and history backs me up on this statement.

So what do we do now? God is calling an unafraid and not intimidated Body of Christ to visibly pray at all times, in all ways and in every place. It is time to draw a line in the sand, plant our feet on that line and give our lives in militant intercession until we bring heaven to earth in our nations.

1. C. Peter Wagner, *Praying with Power* (Shippensburg, Pa.: Destiny Image, 1997), 108.
2. Cindy Jacobs, *The Reformation Manifesto* (Bloomington, Minn.: Bethany, 2008), 113.
3. Dutch Sheets, *Intercessory Prayer* (Ventura, Calif.: Regal Books, 1996), 168–69.
4. Dutch Sheets, *God's Timing for Your Life* (Ventura, Calif.: Regal Books, 2001), 13.
5. Chuck Pierce, *Interpreting the Times* (Lake Mary, Fla.: Charisma House, 2008), 12.
6. For more information on the 30 Second Kneel Down, visit http://www.30kd.org/what.htm.
7. Jacobs, *Reformation Manifesto*, 200.

Study Guide

Key Scriptures

Isaiah 14:12	2 Corinthians 2:11
Jeremiah 1:10	2 Corinthians 10:4
Ezekiel 28:11–19	Ephesians 1:21
Daniel 10:12–13	Ephesians 3:10
Matthew 11:12	Ephesians 6:11–12
Matthew 16:18	Colossians 2:15
Luke 11:17–22	

Chapter 1: The Call to Intercede

1. Have you ever awakened suddenly in the night with an urge to pray? How did you know what to pray about? Did you ever learn if your prayers made a difference?
2. What does it mean to have an answer to prayer "given in the heavenlies" before it happens in the natural? Do you agree with this concept?
3. Would you consider praying this kind of "rash" prayer: "God, I will do anything You want me to do; go anywhere, anyhow"? If you did pray it, what might God call you to? What might He ask you to sacrifice?
4. Do you think you are one whom God has chosen to be an intercessor? Give reasons for your answer.

5. If "intercession is not so much taught as caught," do you have opportunities to observe and experience God's power at work through the lives of mature intercessors? Name some "prayer giants" you could spend time with and learn from personally.

6. What books have you read that have challenged or spoken to you in the area of intercession?

Chapter 2: Generals of Intercession

1. Why is unity in intercession important for effective prayer? How does this kind of unity differ from doctrinal unity?

2. What particular strategies can your church or denomination offer the Body of Christ in intercession?

3. What do repentance and forgiveness of sins have to do with tearing down Satan's strongholds?

4. Has God ever given you a vision that later ran into roadblocks? Did you begin to doubt what God said? Describe your struggle.

5. Have you ever considered the daily newspaper as a prayer journal? What are some ways it can be used as such?

6. Do you know any out-of-balance intercessors or prayer groups that have turned others off to intercession? How can you help Christian leaders you know to become more open to receiving the intercession they need?

7. Have you, as a temple of the Holy Spirit, ever thought of yourself as "a house of prayer for all nations"? Discuss.

Chapter 3: The Clean Heart Principle

1. When God reveals something to you about another person, what is your first impulse? What does this say about your heart's motives?

2. Do you sometimes feel more awe toward an effective intercessor than toward the God who answers prayers? Have you ever given yourself a pat on the back when your prayers were answered?

3. Are you aware of any ways your prayers are sometimes biased by your own will or desires?

4. Are you aware of ways your prayers are sometimes tainted by the wounding of your heart from past hurts, bitterness or unforgiveness?

5. Are there ways the Lord needs to make your heart clean right now? Ask Him to show you your heart and its motives.

6. Sometimes our intercession averts unknown disaster or quietly covers secret sins. How do you respond to the idea that neither we nor others will know exactly what our prayers have accomplished until we get to heaven?

Chapter 4: The Enforcers

1. If "the law of prayer is the highest law of the universe," what implications does this have for the notion that God does not will evil but allows it to happen because of the fallen state of the world?

2. Do you agree with the concept that God sometimes holds back from working His will until an intercessor prays it into being? Why or why not?

3. How do you feel about the idea that we, the Body of Christ, have responsibility through active intercession to enforce the will of God? What happens if we do not pray?

4. Do you know of times when prayer for a person, city or nation changed the course of history?

5. What if Jesus had not won the victory in Gethsemane by "praying the price" of submission and actively interceding for God's will to be done? Do you think God would have gone ahead with His plan of redemption at Calvary?

6. Name some situations in your own community in which God is not being glorified. How can the local Body of Christ begin to "pray forth" (enforce) God's will in those situations?

7. Would you personally perform any of the intercessory actions mentioned in this chapter: planting a Bible in the ground, fasting, repenting for your generation's sins, lying across an airstrip, praying through the news, praying over names in a telephone book and driving or walking through a neighborhood while interceding for it?

Chapter 5: The Ministry of Intercession

1. In what ways can intercession be thought of as warfare? As defensive or offensive?
2. Where do you currently see yourself in the army of Christ?
3. Describe some possible devices, wiles or strategies of the devil against the Body of Christ. (Consider aspects of military or guerrilla warfare, for example.) For each one, can you think of a counterstrategy the Church can use?
4. Are you a "watchman on the wall" for your family, church, community or nation? What has God shown you to pray about?
5. If you belong to an intercessory group, how can you help keep meetings from turning into spiritual gossip sessions?
6. What if Dutch DuPuis had awakened but not known why? How can an intercessor learn to hear God clearly?
7. What is the relationship between prayer and revival? How can you help prepare for revival in your city or nation?

Chapter 6: The Gift of Intercession

1. Do you love to spend your free time in prayer? If not, do you wish you did?
2. Has God given you a special prayer focus? What is it?
3. What do you think Gordon Lindsay meant by "violent prayer"?
4. How do you react to people who pray differently than you do? Can intercessors with different styles pray together in the same group?
5. What are some spiritual disciplines that can help you to persevere and grow in prayer (whether or not you have the gift of intercession)?
6. Do you find a prayer list helpful or burdensome? If you use one, do you also take time to listen to God to find out if He wants to preempt those requests?
7. How often do you pray Scripture over others? Describe some of the benefits of this kind of prayer.

8. Have you had dreams that seemed to have spiritual significance? How did you interpret them?
9. How do you typically react to a dream about disaster? How does God want us to react?

Chapter 7: Prayer Leaders

1. How can intercessors prevent their compassion for others from leading them into prayer overload and burnout?
2. Think of some prayer leaders you know (including yourself, if you are one). What do you think is each person's gift-mix? Why?
3. Does your church have a recognized prayer leader on staff? What are some ways you can help your church give priority to this ministry?
4. How do you as an intercessor feel about receiving direction and accountability from your local church body? Who counsels and prays for you? Who is close enough to you to offer correction when needed?
5. When was the last time you asked God if He wanted you to make a change in ministry?
6. Have you been through a season of restlessness in ministry? Was it a time of transition and release or a result of wounding and discouragement?

Chapter 8: The Language of Intercession

1. Have you ever been involved in an intercessory group that used language you were not sure you understood? Describe your feelings and reactions.
2. If you occasionally use specialized terms of intercession, can you give a concise, biblical definition for each?
3. How does the prayer of agreement both reduce and emphasize the role and responsibility of an individual intercessor?
4. Why do you think fasting multiplies the effect of prayer?

5. Have you ever been assured that your prayers had been answered before you saw any change in the natural? How did you know you had prayed through?

6. Give some specific examples of strongholds—territorial, ideological and personal—in your nation, city or family.

7. Reread Edgardo Silvoso's definition of a stronghold and think of some "hopeless" situations in your family, city, nation or world. Are they really unchangeable? If you had all the faith in the world, what "impossible" thing would you like to believe God for?

8. How do you respond to the idea that intercession is sometimes a matter of life and death?

9. If someone prays to bind the enemy and no change seems to take place, does this mean the person prayed in error or presumption?

10. Why is it crucial for intercessors to understand the extent of our authority in Christ?

Chapter 9: The Manifestations of Intercession

1. Does God have emotions? How would it affect our personal relationship with Him if He did not?

2. Demanding that God answer our prayers can be dangerous. What are some indicators that we have prayed a legitimate prayer of travail?

3. Have you ever been in a prayer group when someone went into travail? Did that person keep within appropriate boundaries of self-control? How did you and the other intercessors respond?

4. Is it difficult for you to show emotions such as weeping, even in private? Why might this be a hindrance in intercession?

5. If you tend to express your emotions freely, have you found yourself laughing in prayer as often as weeping? Does God weep more than He laughs? Substantiate.

6. What is the difference between laughing at or mocking the enemy in intercession and taunting or baiting him?

7. Is your church's prayer group usually solemn? How can the intercessors come to know more of the joy of the Lord in their prayers?

Chapter 10: Flaky Intercession

1. Did you recognize yourself or other members of your intercessory group in any part of this chapter? Take time now to repent and ask God to show you your heart and His will.

2. How much time do you as an intercessor spend meditating on God's Word? Do you also receive guidance from those the Lord has placed over you? What else will help safeguard the integrity of your prayers?

3. Describe what you would do if you felt the Lord telling you your pastor was in error. What if another intercessor at your church began sharing this message?

4. Do you know intercessors who often seem to receive harsh words of judgment on others? Are there woundings from their own background that need to be healed?

5. Does God ever change His mind? Give biblical evidence to support your answer.

6. If God has shown you certain situations that need judgment, what are specific ways you can intercede for Him to move in mercy instead to change the situation?

7. Intercessors who stand as "prayer shields" for others may discover they have stepped into the line of fire. What should you do if you find yourself getting hit?

8. Do you agree that prayers of manipulation and control are similar to witchcraft? How are they similar?

9. Have you ever worked out an event or solution in your mind and then asked God to do it? How can we recognize and guard against praying outside God's will?

Chapter 11: Prophetic Intercession

1. Does the idea of prophetic intercession make you nervous? How can we tell if certain prayers are from God if we have little knowledge in the natural to guide us?

2. Has the risk of acting in presumption or error kept you from praying bold prayers that sprang up from inside you?

3. How can a prayer journal help us learn whether we are hearing God correctly? What other benefits can a prayer journal give?

4. Do you take seriously the idea that children can move in prophetic intercession? What can we do to train and encourage our children in this?

5. Have you ever felt an unusual sense of urgency about your prayers? Could this have been prophetic intercession? Why or why not?

6. If Margaret Moberly is right, why are all prophets intercessors?

7. Does a word of prophecy always indicate a foregone conclusion? Why did the parents in Hemet, California, "war in intercession" over their daughter after receiving the prophetic word?

8. What do you think about the idea that Jesus' intercession for us, mentioned in Hebrews 7:25, might actually be accomplished through the prayers of His people?

9. With whom can you share insights or knowledge you receive in prayer, to receive help in weighing it? Are you willing to wait for God's timing to speak the things you hear?

Chapter 12: Personal Prayer Partners

1. If you are a prayer leader or have a gift of intercession, do you have others who closely support you in prayer? Do you communicate specific needs to them regularly?

2. If you do not have committed prayer partners, who are some people the Lord would have you ask to take on this responsibility?

3. What are some reasons leaders might be reluctant to have prayer partners?

4. Besides those mentioned, what are some risks involved in a close prayer partner relationship? How can leaders find the right people and minimize the hazards?

5. Describe the dangers for a leader or minister who is not receiving regular intercession.

6. Do you believe that witches and satanists actively fast and pray against Christian leaders? If so, why can their curses sometimes hit the mark?

7. If you are in a position to receive prayer regularly, how do you feel about the fact that God may show your intercessors your weaknesses? How do you feel about giving them access and sharing intimate needs? Are there limits?

8. Do you agree that a leader's intercessors share equally in the responsibility and rewards of the ministry? In what ways might this be true?

9. Does your pastor, your ministry leader or another person you intercede for have formal prayer partners? How can you encourage him or her to enter this kind of relationship?

Chapter 13: Intercessory Praise

1. Have you thought of spiritual warfare typically as a grim undertaking? Why is it important to include praise and joy?

2. Have you thought of praise and singing typically as "feel good" exercises that build up the Body? Why is it important to recognize how much the devil hates our worship of God?

3. What are some of your favorite praise and worship songs? In what ways does each of them involve a form of intercession? Does this suggest anything about the prayer focus God has given you?

4. Think of some neighborhoods in your community that are as troubled as Pleitner Avenue was. Can your church organize a block party there, including intercessor praise warfare?

5. Have you observed or participated in a group that exercised any of these intercessory praise actions: walking, marching, treading, singing, clapping, shouting or laughing? Were the actions appropriate and effective components of the intercession?

6. What forms of intercessory praise might be appropriate in your small group fellowship? In your churchwide meetings?

7. Why might we not see God's answers to our needs until we recognize in praise some attribute of God that can meet those needs?

Chapter 14: Corporate Intercession

1. Is there a practical upper limit on the size of group suitable for corporate intercession? What variations on the suggestions in this chapter might be needed in a large group (too large, for instance, for individual prayers to be heard by everyone)?
2. Describe how corporate intercession can increase the faith level of those praying.
3. Has your congregation ever joined with other churches to pray corporately for your community? What are some benefits of this kind of partnership?
4. Does your church or organization have good accountability and communication between the prayer leader and the ministry leadership? Assess the strengths and weaknesses of that relationship (to your knowledge).
5. Are there people in your intercessory group who have trouble following the leader and the flow of the meeting? What can be done to help them?
6. Why is it important to have a good gift-mix among members of an intercessory group? Name some gifts that could prove useful in the group setting.
7. How often does your prayer group use these different forms of intercession: petition prayers, proclamation prayers, intercessory praise, prophetic intercession and Scripture praying? Do you need greater variety or balance?

Chapter 15: Prayer Watches and Walks

1. Have you ever taken part in a prayer watch or attended a conference covered by one? Why do some people travel to a conference at their own expense to do nothing but intercede for it?
2. If you have taken part in a prayer watch, what was it like for you? Describe your experience and reactions both during and after the watch. Did you have any reentry problems?
3. What other situations or purposes besides conferences might call for a prayer watch?

4. Do you know any churches that maintain 24-hour prayer rooms with continuous intercession? What would it take to start one in your church or community?

5. What are some of the benefits when God's people go out to pray onsite in the community?

6. Describe the different purposes and effects of an "undercover" prayer walk by an individual or small group, in contrast to a large public praise march such as March for Jesus.

7. How often should prayer walks take place? How long might it be before noticeable changes occur in a particular neighborhood?

Chapter 16: Possessing the Gates of the Enemy

1. Do you agree with S. D. Gordon that "to define prayer one must use the language of war"? How do you respond to people uncomfortable with the militant vocabulary of spiritual warfare?

2. What are some carnal weapons we might be tempted to use against strongholds of evil? What effect might using them have?

3. Why did the Lord leave His Church with the responsibility for waging spiritual warfare?

4. If God's angels have territorial assignments just as demonic spirits do, what are the implications for our strategies of intercession and warfare?

5. What are some current or historic sins in your own community that have given Satan legal entrance (a "gate of hell")?

6. Why are human relationships such a prime target for the enemy's attack?

7. How does extensive deliverance of demonized individuals in an area weaken the power of the territorial spirits there?

8. After a territorial stronghold has been torn down, why are the effects usually not permanent? What is the ongoing responsibility of the Body of Christ in that city or region?

9. What do you see as the redemptive gift of your city? How has the devil tried to corrupt or twist this godly purpose?

10. With whom is God leading you to join in prayer for your community, so that the full range of His gifts and strategies can work together to help establish the Kingdom of God in your midst?

Chapter 17: Reforming Nations through Militant Intercession

1. Have you ever thought you could intercede in a manner that would reform your nation?
2. How will you change the way you are praying in order to incorporate an understanding of the 7M mandate into your intercession?
3. Has God called you to spiritually map or to spend time in prayer for reformation for a particular sector of society?
4. Why do we need to pray for certain societal changes to be made?
5. Is there a cause, such as eradication of systemic poverty, that God is calling you to focus upon in prayer?
6. What is prayer activism, and how might it apply to your personal life?
7. Have you ever been in a prayer time that used intercessory worship to bring about social change?
8. Why does "darkness linger," as George Otis Jr. says, over the city or region where you live?
9. How should you or your prayer group change the way you are praying in order to reform different sectors of society, such as education or government?

Suggested Reading List

Alves, Beth. *Becoming a Prayer Warrior.* Ventura, Calif.: Gospel Light, 1998.

Barton, Dave. *America: To Pray or Not to Pray?* Aledo, Tex.: Wallbuilder Press, 1988.

Bernal, Dick. *Storming Hell's Brazen Gates.* San Jose, Calif.: Jubilee Christian Center, 1988.

Bloesch, Donald G. *The Struggle of Prayer.* Colorado Springs: Helmer & Howard, 1988.

Boschman, LaMar. *The Rebirth of Music.* Bedford, Tex.: Revival Press, 1980.

Bounds, E. M. *Power through Prayer.* Grand Rapids: Zondervan, 1987.

Bryant, David. *Concerts of Prayer.* Rev. ed. Ventura, Calif.: Regal Books, 1988.

Cho, Paul Yonggi. *Prayer: Key to Revival.* Waco: Word Books, 1984.

Christenson, Evelyn. *What Happens When Women Pray.* Wheaton: Victor Books, 1975.

Dawson, John. *Taking Our Cities for God.* Lake Mary, Fla.: Creation House, 1989.

Eastman, Dick. *The Hour That Changes the World.* Grand Rapids: Baker, 1978.

———. *Love On Its Knees*. Tarrytown, N.Y.: Chosen Books, 1989.

———. *No Easy Road*. Grand Rapids: Baker, 1978.

Eastman, Dick, and Jack Hayford. *Living and Praying in Jesus' Name*. Wheaton: Tyndale House, 1988.

Greenwald, Gary. *Seductions Exposed*. Santa Ana, Calif.: Eagle's Nest Publications, 1988.

Grubb, Norman. *Rees Howells, Intercessor*, 3d ed. Fort Washington, Pa.: Christian Literature Crusade, 1983.

Harper, Michael. *Spiritual Warfare*. Plainfield, N.J.: Logos International, 1970.

Hayford, Jack W. *Prayer Is Invading the Impossible*. New York: Ballantine Books, 1983.

Kinnaman, Gary. *Overcoming the Dominion of Darkness*. Tarrytown, N.Y.: Chosen Books, 1990.

Law, Terry. *The Power of Praise and Worship*. Tulsa: Victory House, 1985.

Lea, Larry. *Could You Not Tarry One Hour?* Lake Mary, Fla.: Creation House, 1987.

LeSourd, Leonard E. *Touching the Heart of God*. Tarrytown, N.Y.: Chosen Books, 1990.

Matthews, R. Arthur. *Born for Battle*. Robesonia, Pa.: OMF Books, 1978.

Maxwell, John. *The Pastor's Prayer Partners*. Bonita, Calif.: Injoy Ministries, 1989.

Murray, Andrew. *With Christ in the School of Prayer*. Grand Rapids: Zondervan, 1983 (first published in 1885).

Peretti, Frank E. *This Present Darkness*. Westchester, Ill.: Crossway Books, 1986.

Sandford, John and Paula. *The Elijah Task*. Tulsa: Victory House, 1986.

Shaw, Gwen. *God's End-Time Battle-Plan*. Jasper, Ark.: Engeltal Press, 1984.

Sherrer, Quin. *How to Pray for Your Family and Friends*. Ann Arbor, Mich.: Servant Publications, 1990.

Shibley, David. *A Force in the Earth*. Lake Mary, Fla.: Creation House, 1989.

Tippit, Sammy. *The Prayer Factor*. Chicago: Moody Press, 1988.

Towe, Joy. *Praise Is*. Irving, Tex.: Triumphant Praise, 1979.

Wagner, C. Peter. *How to Have a Prayer Ministry*. Pasadena, Calif.: Charles E. Fuller Institute, 1990.

———. "Territorial Spirits." In *Wrestling with Dark Angels*, edited by C. Peter Wagner and F. Douglas Pennoyer. Ventura, Calif.: Regal Books, 1990.

———. *Your Spiritual Gifts Can Help Your Church Grow*. Ventura, Calif.: Regal Books, 1979.

White, Thomas B. *The Believer's Guide to Spiritual Warfare*. Ann Arbor, Mich.: Servant Publications, 1990.

Willhite, B. J. *Why Pray?* Lake Mary, Fla.: Creation House, 1988.

Wimber, John. *Teach Us to Pray*. Anaheim, Calif.: Vineyard Ministries International, 1986.

Subject Index

30 Second Kneel Down, 258

Aaron, 66
abortion, 72–73, 246
Abraham, 15, 145, 202
Absalom, 122, 131, 193
Adam, 47, 77, 251
adultery, 96
  spiritual adultery, 157–58
Alexander the Great, 190
Alves, Beth, 162, 178
America: To Pray or Not to Pray (D. Barton), 20
angels, 117, 219, 222
Anna, 65, 145
Annotated Reference Bible (Dake), 220
Anointed for Business (Silvoso), 232
anointing, 96, 181
Aquinas, Thomas, 132
Askins, Joseph, 253
Azusa Street revival, 80

Ballard, Mark, 45, 46–47
Barton, Cheryl, 19–20
Barton, David, 19–20, 52–53, 94, 258
Believer's Guide to Spiritual Warfare, The
  (T. White), 221–22
Benefield, John, 252
Berlin Wall, 88–89
Bickel, Mike, 165
Billheimer, Paul, 215
binding, 95, 99–100, 105, 106
  negative binding, 100–102
  positive binding, 102–3

Birch, Robert, 103
Bloesch, Donald, 183
Bonhoeffer, Dietrich, 258
Born for Battle (Matthews), 50–51
Bounds, E. M., 27
Braham, William, 185
Brazil, action of enforcers in, 54
Bridgebuilders Ministries, 188
Browning, Iben, 227
Bruce, Alexander, 100
Bruce, F. F., 222
Bush, George W., 142
Byerly, Barbara, 215–16

Caballeros, Harold, 247
Cabrera, Marfa, 115
Cabrera, Omar, 115, 226
Call, The, 72–73, 79, 254
Carey, William, 149–50
Carter, Katherine Pollard, 49
Change the World Ministries, 25, 81
Cho, Paul Yonggi, 185–86
Christ for the Nations Institute, 68, 185
  in Germany, 89
Christianity, 80
Christians, hate crimes against, 257
Church of the Lord Jesus Christ, 78
  pouring of the Holy Spirit on (1960s), 52
  as a praying army, 49, 52
Churchill, Winston, 49
Connell, Don, 114
Copeland, Vinita, 62, 66–67, 73–74
Corrientes (Argentina), 116, 239
Crosby, Fanny, 171

Scripture Index